PELICAN BOOKS

THE PELICAN HISTORY OF MUSIC

VOLUME ONE

EDITED BY ALEC ROBERTSON
AND DENIS STEVENS

*The Pelican
History of Music*

I

ANCIENT FORMS TO
POLYPHONY

*

EDITED BY ALEC ROBERTSON
AND DENIS STEVENS

PENGUIN BOOKS

Penguin Books Ltd, Harmondsworth, Middlesex, England
Penguin Books Inc., 7110 Ambassador Road, Baltimore, Maryland 21207, U.S.A.
Penguin Books Australia Ltd, Ringwood, Victoria, Australia
Penguin Books Canada Ltd, 41 Steelcase Road West, Markham, Ontario, Canada
Penguin Books (N.Z.) Ltd, 182–190 Wairau Road, Auckland 10, New Zealand

—

First published 1960
Reprinted 1962, 1965, 1966, 1969, 1970, 1973, 1974

—

Copyright © Penguin Books Ltd, 1960

—

Made and printed in Great Britain
by Richard Clay (The Chaucer Press) Ltd,
Bungay, Suffolk
Set in Monotype Imprint

CONTENTS

CONTENTS

IV · ARS NOVA *by Gilbert Reaney*

LIST OF PLATES

Preface to Volume One

'THE study of the history of music,' wrote Robert Schumann, 'supplemented by hearing actual performances of the masterpieces of different epochs, will prove the most rapid and effectual cure for conceit and vanity.' It is in many ways unfortunate that the truth of Schumann's words has not yet been perceived by our modern musical educators, at least not in England. Incredible though it may seem, no satisfactory course of instruction in the history of music is available in London, capital city of England and the Commonwealth, in spite of its handful of academies and its imposing university. The result, as far as musicians and music-lovers are concerned, might well be an excess of that 'conceit and vanity' mentioned above; and were it not for the broadening examples of the B.B.C.'s Third Programme (now, alas, truncated) and of the more intelligent among the heads of gramophone record companies, the present situation might be much the worse for wear.

As it is, there is a strong tendency towards an overwhelming adulation of the 'tyro's triptych'. This is a small though well-worked vein of musical history which may be visualized as a group of three panels, one large panel in the centre, and two small ones outside. The large panel represents the years 1800–1900, the outside ones 1750–1800 and 1900–1950 respectively. It seems not to have dawned upon the hardened watchers and listeners that roughly a thousand years of musical history remain unknown to them. Yet if they were connoisseurs of art, architecture, or literature they would not dream of ignoring the masterpieces of the Middle Ages, of the Renaissance, or of the Baroque era. To do so would be to ignore such magnificent manifestations of the artistic impulse as Romanesque and Gothic ecclesiastical architecture, the paintings of van Eyck, Botticelli, and Michelangelo, the poetry of Dante and Chaucer. Only when the music of Pérotin, Machaut, Landini, and Dunstable (to name only four of the greatest) becomes really familiar to concert audiences will it be possible to say that music has reached a plane of appreciation and understanding on a level with some of the sister arts. And only when early music is properly performed, by professional musicians who have devoted at least as much time and study to its intricacies of style and feeling as they have to *Lieder*, opera, and chamber music will the public begin to realize that there is more to a motet, Mass, or *ballade* than mere antiquarianism.

The study of the history of music will play its part, too, in the growing realization of a vast cultural heritage and its artistic importance: its relevance for the music of today and of yesterday. For there is nothing new under the sun in music, and many of the devices of modern serialists pale into insignificance when compared with the more elaborate structures of the Middle Ages, just as the thematic disintegration practised by a latter-day Viennese school is as child's play when contrasted with integrative devices of the fourteenth century. This is where Schumann's reference to 'conceit and vanity' makes its greatest point: only by donning the weeds of intellectual humility will a musician be able fully to comprehend the entire range of the art which he loves without really knowing more than one-tenth of what it has to offer.

This *History of Music*, although written by specialists, has been designed to satisfy the needs of intelligent and open-minded readers who know something about the history of art and literature yet lack the opportunity to link their knowledge with the more detailed aspects of musical art-forms. It cannot be, and is not intended to be, a comprehensive account of composers and their works, but rather an account of music seen against its various backgrounds – social, aesthetic, religious, and historical. The lists of recordings will serve as a guide to those who wish to explore in sound what they have absorbed in print, and the brief bibliographies are offered as a guide to further reading rather than an indication of works consulted in the compilation of individual chapters. The Editors extend their sincere thanks to the authorities of the Bodleian Library and the British Museum for help in providing illustrations, and to Mr Peter Crossley-Holland for allowing some of the instruments in his private collection to be photographed.

ALEC ROBERTSON
DENIS STEVENS

1960

I · NON-WESTERN MUSIC

Peter Crossley-Holland

1. Ancient Mesopotamia

THE once fertile plain between the 'Two Rivers', Tigris and Euphrates, in what is now Iraq, was the home of man's earliest known civilization. Partly owing to the Semitic peoples who had long been there, especially in the north (Akkad), and partly to the non-Semitic Sumerians who came from further east to occupy the south (Sumer), ancient Mesopotamian civilization was already far advanced six thousand years ago. These peoples interpreted the universe as a state, and in each of their cities raised a monumental temple with a stepped tower. Here, with words and music, they worshipped their gods. These early agriculturalists were animists and all nature was alive to them. Ramman their thunder-god destroyed their crops in the tempest and Ea the ruler of the deep flooded their lands. But these gods could be worshipped and propitiated by the appropriate use of the human voice and of musical instruments. The sound of the reed-pipe (*halhallatu*)[1] was compared with Ramman's breath, and the hour-glass drum (*balag*) was written with the sign of Ea's name. Such ideas, coming perhaps from an even earlier prehistoric time, lay right at the heart of their temple services.

THE SUMERIAN TEMPLE RITUAL
(4th and 3rd millennia B.C.)

In each service, during the fourth millennium B.C., a single hymn or psalm was chanted in honour of one or more of the gods. The liturgies were very often lamentations, and numerous words survive to show highly organized and concentrated poetical forms. The forms of their chants were no doubt closely based upon them. By the twenty-first century B.C. or earlier, the techniques of temple chanting included those of response (alternate singing by priests and choir) and antiphon (alternate

1. Some accents have of necessity been omitted in this and other chapters.

13

singing between choir and choir). Each poem had its proper chant (Sumerian *sir*), and in performance such a chant was considered to have a particular *ethos* or quality which fitted it for communion with a chosen deity or caused it to have a definite magical effect.

The word often used for the vocal or choral pieces, *ersemma*, literally means a psalm or hymn set to a reed-pipe (*sem*); and other instruments used included the vertical (i.e. end-blown) flute (*tig*, *tigi*); drum (*balag*); kettledrum (*lilis*), and tambourine (*adapa*). How far the singers and the instrumentalists were separate bodies of persons it is now difficult to know, but it seems clear that the cantillation (*kalutu*) was undertaken by precentors (Sum. *gala*; Akkad. *kalu*) who, rather like the vicars-choral of medieval Europe, lived in colleges attached to the temples. For the rest, there were instrumentalists called *zammeru* who might also sing to their instruments, and musicians called *naru* who, it appears, could be both choristers and instrumentalists.

In the third millennium B.C., with a First Dynasty beginning in the twenty-eighth century, our knowledge of Mesopotamian instruments increases thanks to excavations in the Royal Tombs of Ur (twenty-fifth century) and to other sources. In addition to percussion instruments, we find the lyre (*algar*) and two main kinds of harp: one with a lower sound-chest (*zagsal*) and one with an upper sound-chest (*zaggal*). The former type originated when the warrior's bow was given additional strings. There are no convincing theories as to the tuning of these instruments, and how any of this music may have sounded we do not know. The attempts so far made to transcribe what is believed to be a musical notation of a Sumerian hymn from a later period unfortunately leave us little the wiser.

BABYLONIAN ELABORATION
(19th–13th centuries B.C.)

About the year 1830 B.C., after more than two millennia of predominantly Sumerian culture, the Semitic peoples of the north part of the country (Akkad) reached a high cultural level. The

Babylonians became rulers and their three dynasties lasted in all about 540 years (*c.* 1830–1270). Already the temple service consisting of a single hymn or psalm had been superseded by a complete liturgical service which combined several (from five to twenty-seven) such psalms or hymns, and varied them with instrumental interludes. Many of the poems used have been traced back to Sumerian times. Each song-type had its particular tune and such rubrics as 'A Song to the tune "Thou wilt not cast me down"' seem to be perpetuated in the much later Jewish tradition which in turn survived in the early English psalters. During this millennium the temple appears to have added female singers to male, and processional movements to the general ensemble, the whole conduct of religious music becoming more elaborate than hitherto.

IN ASSYRIAN TIMES
(13th–7th centuries B.C.)

Alongside the music of the temples throughout these long ages there must have been a music reflecting the labours and lives of the people, but the fact that only the temple officials kept records means that most of our information concerns music in the service of religious worship. During the period of the Assyrian rulers (about 1270 to 606), however, secular music becomes more prominent. It was important in the various festivals, and musicians were attached to the royal households. The court minstrel was held in high regard, and musicians performed not only for the royal household at banquets and on other occasions but also gave public performances which the people at large could hear, and played for martial occasions. Such performances no doubt influenced music in its more popular forms.

CHALDAEAN TRADITIONS
(7th–6th centuries B.C.)

The musical life continued throughout the Chaldaean period (626–538 B.C.) and it is to this time that the description of the band of King Nebuchadnezzar (604–562 B.C.), recorded some four centuries later in the Book of Daniel, refers. The famous passage is probably to be interpreted as follows: 'As soon as ye shall hear the sound of the horn (*qarna*), the pipes (*masroqitha*), the lyre (*qatros*), the lower-chested harp (*sabbeka*), the upper-chested harp (*psantrin*), the full consort (*sumfonyah*), and all kinds of instruments, ye shall fall down and worship the image which Nebuchadnezzar the King hath set up.' The mention of the instruments first separately and then together suggests a performance where prominence was given to the solo instruments before the ensemble got under way, as in the *taqsim* or prelude of Arabic classical music to this day.

From early Sumerian times (fourth millennium) the temples had been centres of learning where priests, liturgists, mathematicians, and astrologers worked together. In Chaldaean times, some three thousand years later, the tradition of astrology emerges more clearly, and we know that musical theory was already closely connected with astrology and mathematics. The peoples who studied the motions of the stars, and believed in their effects on men's destinies, held that there was a perfect harmony existing throughout the universe. Since the universe (or macrocosm) and man (or microcosm) were closely inter-related, man could make music whose principles reflected this perfect harmony and thus come into tune with it. Mathematical speculation and symbolism loomed large in these studies, leading to numerous cosmic correspondences demonstrated by the harmonic divisions of a stretched string. Thus the primary divisions of a string-length gave four intervals which can be expressed in mathematical ratios as follows: $1:1$ (unison); $1:2$ (octave); $2:3$ (fifth); and $3:4$ (fourth). These they correlated with the four seasons (spring, summer, winter, autumn). The properties of particular numbers were also important, especially those of the number 4 and the number 7 – the latter being most probably the number of notes in the ancient Chaldaean scale.

Though we know of these things only from the works of various classical writers (Philo Judaeus, Plutarch) who refer to the Chaldaeans, there is some reason to believe that, after a long period of study in the Mesopotamian schools of learning, not to mention those of Egypt, the philosopher Pythagoras (sixth century) brought back the science of harmonics and the principles of the musical scale to Greece. There he and his followers formulated their doctrines relating to the harmony of the spheres, the *ethos* (magical effects of modes), and the efficacy of numbers, which were later handed on to Europe. Thus it may be in Mesopotamia that the origins of our musical scale and much of our theory of music had their beginnings, though there have been many changes during the successive stages of transmission.

THE LAST HALF-MILLENNIUM
(6th–1st centuries B.C.)

From 538, Babylonia became part of the Persian Empire and so continued till the end of the Seleucid Dynasty (312–65 B.C.). During this period more popular and sensuous forms of music appear to have come into fashion. There were singing-girls in the palaces not unlike the *qainat* who became popular in Arabian life. The older musical tradition appears largely to have been lost in the country of its origin.

The musical legacy of man's first known civilization was, however, very wide, and aspects of it will be mentioned in almost every chapter which follows; for something of it passed into Egypt, something into India, and something each into Palestine, Greece, and Islam, and even China may have been touched by it or by a common cultural source.

2. Ancient Egypt

HIGH civilization came to Egypt, as to Mesopotamia, at the dawn of history (fourth millennium B.C.), and musically speaking a number of factors, both indigenous and foreign, went into its making. The Hamitic peoples of the Nile Valley have been agriculturalists since early time and some of their instruments had a utilitarian origin. For instance their clappers (two sticks struck together), which are used today much as in antiquity to chase away the pests from their crops, came to accompany dances designed to ensure the fertility of these same crops, and by their rhythmical beat to ease the work of the labourers in the vineyards.

As early as the fourth millennium Egypt appears to have been open to new influences, and was possibly in contact with Mesopotamia until about 2700 B.C., since the two regions had so many instruments in common. From the meeting of these two streams, the indigenous and the foreign, a new culture grew, and this was already advanced at the beginning of the third millennium when Egypt at length became unified and entered upon the first of her numerous dynasties under the so-called Old Kingdom.

THE OLD AND MIDDLE KINGDOMS
(Early 3rd–mid 2nd millennia)

The dwellers in the Nile Valley were great temple-builders and in the temples solemn ceremonials took place daily; the priests chanted in praise and supplication of their numerous gods. The human voice was regarded as the most powerful instrument for contacting the powers of the invisible world, and a special knowledge of the use of the voice underlay the ceremonial utterances of the hierophants. The words of many of these ceremonies still survive, such as the 'Songs of Isis and Nephthys' which made up a ritual lasting five days. Since the chant was transmitted orally, however, no music has come down to us in notation. But the poems of this ceremony suggest that the

18

music took the form of alternate duets between the two priest-
esses and solos by the priestess representing the goddess Isis,
with a hymn to the god Osiris sung by a male precentor in the
middle of the ceremony.

The chanting was often accompanied by instruments, and
countless representations survive to show the importance of
these in religious worship. A priestess is often shown holding a
strung rattle with a U-shaped wooden frame attached to a
lower prong which served as a handle, with cross-bars holding
circular metal plates. The Latin name by which we know this
instrument, *sistrum*, comes from Greek *seistron* ('thing shaken'),
and when it is shaken the plates make a jingling sound full of
silvery overtones; the Egyptians called it *sehem*, 'power', that
is the divine power of which it was a symbol. Sometimes the
accompaniment to the chanting was provided by clappers, and
sometimes by large tambourines (*ser*).

The most highly regarded of all instruments in ancient
Egypt was the harp (*ben*, cf. Mesop. *ban*). The harp with the
lower sound-chest of the twenty-sixth century B.C., the time of
the famous pyramids at Gizeh, is an even older form than the
twenty-fifth century B.C. Mesopotamian instrument from the
royal tombs of Ur – closer, that is, to its ancestor, the hunter's bow.

Wind instruments included a vertical flute (?*seba*'), whose
type may still persist in the Coptic *sebe*; and a double clarinet
(*ma*', *met*). The latter, an instrument of cane, consisted of two
parallel reed-pipes; these were played in unison, and since the
player breathed through his nose the sound continued without
interruption (cf. present-day Arabic *zamr*).

The Egyptian Pharaohs were priest-kings and their court
music was naturally linked with the tradition of the temples.
The court musicians held privileged positions from early times,
and male musicians sang, played instruments, and danced.
Harp, flute, and reed-pipe are found, as in worship, though in
the secular music they appeared to combine in larger ensembles
in accompanying the voice. Such ensembles most probably
played more or less in unison with the voice, each treating the
melody in its own way; and if, as is possible, the harp played
occasional intervals of octave, fifth, and fourth, it would not

have been for the sake of harmony as we know it, but as a decorative device comparable with the intervals occasionally found in the Arabic music of later times.

Representations of musical scenes manage to convey the impression of a music and dance of some solemnity, in both the religious and the secular sphere. A kindred static quality is found also in the early Egyptian temple architecture, and seems to reflect the peaceful and established way of life in the Nile Valley. Little subject to change over long periods of time, this was in some contrast with conditions on the Mesopotamian plain of the Tigris and Euphrates, where the hazardous weather conditions provided a very different background for Mesopotamian cultural life.

Towards the close of this epoch, and following the invasions from Central Asia of the whole of the Near East, nomadic tribes (Hyksos) entered Egypt, bringing new music and musical instruments with them, including drums and castanets. And already from about 1890 B.C. bands of Semitic nomads (perhaps Hebrews) are pictured as bringing the lyre into Egypt. The result of the nomadic invasion was, however, virtually to destroy the civilization of the Middle Kingdom (c. 1989 to c. 1570 B.C.).

ORIENTAL INFLUENCE AND THE NEW KINGDOM
(16th–11th centuries B.C.)

It was not long after this (c. 1500 B.C.) that the armies of the warlike Pharaohs of the time moved eastward and this had the result of bringing Egypt into direct contact with Mesopotamia. But so far from influencing Mesopotamian culture, Egyptian music was influenced by it. Dancing girls were sent to Egypt by subject monarchs from Syria and other Semitic lands, and these girls, becoming part of the harems, for a time created an entirely new fashion for oriental music of a secular cast. A wide range of human emotions found expression in the songs they sang, and although the music has unfortunately not come down to us, there are reasons for believing it to have been more sensuous than the music known in Egypt up to that time.

Later, the temples adopted female musicians and these

began to figure in the religious ceremonial of the New Kingdom (*c.* 1570 to *c.* 1090 B.C.). Perhaps inspired by oriental
fashion, dancing appears to have been livelier and quicker
than it had been under the Old and Middle Kingdoms. The
oriental influence is, however, most clearly apparent in the
numerous Asiatic instruments which flowed into Egypt over
many centuries.

Important among these was the double oboe with two canes
set at an angle. The right-hand cane played the melody and the
left-hand cane accompanied it with a continuously sounded
lower note. This adoption of a drone as the fundamental note
of the scale used seems to suggest the existence of a model system. Though the old Egyptian flute and double clarinet did
not entirely disappear, they were largely superseded by the
new instrument. The straight trumpet (*sneb*) came to be used
on martial occasions and in processions; the two trumpets, one
of copper and one of silver, recently excavated from the tomb
of the Pharaoh Tut-ankh-amen (*c.* 1400 B.C.), were found to
have a brilliant and distinctive sound.

Angular harps with upper sound-chest first began to appear
in Egypt around this time, and by 1250 B.C. the Egyptian harp
had become a magnificent instrument. Reaching a height of
six feet or more, it had variously ten or twelve strings stretched
across its richly-carved frame. The provenance of the long lute
or pandore is less certain, but this instrument has survived in
a much degenerated form in north-west Africa (Sudanese
gunbri) where it still has two or three strings.

Such instruments continued to reach Egypt throughout the
New Kingdom, and during the subsequent period when the
Nubians were already in the ascendant (1090–664 B.C.) most of
them came to be adopted as Egypt's own.

LOSS OF NATIONAL CHARACTER AND LEGACY
TO GREECE

At about this time the cultures of the various countries of the
Near East were beginning to lose something of their separate
national characters and the whole region was taking on a
more cosmopolitan character. This phase covers more than a

millennium from the time of the Saïtes (from 664 B.C.) to the time when Egypt was occupied successively by the Greeks (from 332 B.C.) and Romans (from 30 B.C.).

In Greek times cymbals were brought into Egypt, but most of the musical influence between the two countries appears to have been in the opposite direction. Though no actual works on the Egyptian theory of music survive, it may be inferred from the Greek writers that much of it entered into the Pythagorean music theory of Greece; for Pythagoras, whose Babylonian studies we noticed in the previous chapter, is believed to have engaged in similar studies in the Egyptian temples (sixth century B.C.). The important mathematician and 'Greek' music theorist Claudius Ptolemy (*fl.* A.D. 127–51) was an Egyptian, though his period corresponds with the end of a distinctively Egyptian culture when much was already shared in common between Egypt, Syria, and Greece. It is clear at least that the Egyptians, like the Mesopotamians, knew the intervals of the octave, fifth, and fourth, though this is not to say that they knew or used harmony in our sense of the word. Their harps may have been tuned in a five-note scale (major third plus semitone type) and their lyres in a different five-note scale (minor third plus tone type); while the symbolism of the number 7 and the pictorial and other references to it in connexion with musical performances make it probable that the Egyptians also knew a seven-note scale.

Though Greece is usually given the credit for it, the so-called 'water organ' (*hydraulis*) was invented by an Egyptian, Ctesibius of Alexandria (*fl.* 246–221 B.C.).

If some of the ancient Egyptian culture passed into Greece through Crete, we also know that some came down in the Coptic Church (such as the little bells from the Egyptian temples used in the Coptic Mass); and some, blending with the Arabic and Islamic civilization of more recent times, found new forms. For the rest, as we have seen, certain types of instrument persist in various parts of North Africa. Moreover, in the popular music and dance of the Nile Valley itself, particularly that connected with the festivals, there may still be some living links with the ancient forms.

3. India

THERE is one easy gateway into India in the north-west and no outlet except for the sea. The successive waves of peoples who have flowed into this sub-continent over some six thousand years, most of them by this route, have each tended to push the previous inhabitants southward. Thus already in the earliest times there began that divergence in the racial and musical tradition of north and south which is so clearly discernible to this day. Moreover the number and variety of the races who have come to stay, each bringing their own music with them, have made India a vast compound of musical lore into which its age-long tradition of classical music has frequently and abundantly dipped. But however numerous and varied the ethnic influences which have gone into its making, and notwithstanding the changes to be traced in its history, this artistic tradition found its decisively Indian character under an influence greater than that of race.

For the beginnings we must look to the most ancient peoples. Some of these, like the Negritos (Asiatic pygmies) – probably India's first inhabitants in Old Stone Age times (fourth millennium B.C.) – are now extinct as such, but have left traces over a wide area of southern and eastern India. A systematic examination of tribal music could provide a basis for the earliest musical stratification of the country. Though India boasts not less than fourteen main languages and a very large number of tribes, the music of few tribes has as yet been seriously studied.

In this same ancient period (third millennium B.C.), India was invaded by peoples believed to have some relationship to the Australian aboriginals. The Veddas of Ceylon, a primitive hunting folk who belong to this type, confine their melodies, it seems, to only two notes.

But the ancient Dravidian peoples knew a higher culture,

and their fertility cult worship, such as that of Sisnadeva, called for a good deal of music and dance. Like their architectural styles and much of their philosophy, their deities and the cult-music associated with them passed into later tradition. Remnants of their musical lore certainly persist among the folk-music of their descendants, the dark peoples speaking Tamil and other Dravidian languages south of the river Godavari. The persistent tradition that each note of the Indian scale represents an animal cry no doubt found its beginnings in their nature worship.

From New Stone Age times various peoples of Mediterranean stock found their way to India. A proto-Egyptian people, believed to have introduced a Megalithic culture, may have brought a number of musical instruments, including the snake-charmer's reed (southern *magudhi*; northern *pungi*) or its prototype, and various kinds of drum.

During the Chalcolithic Age (*c.* 2500 B.C.–*c.* 1500 B.C.) a people related to the Sumerians flourished in the north and formed the so-called Indus Valley civilization. Excavations at Harappa (Punjab) and Mohenjodaro (Sind) show them to have been an artistic people of advanced culture. Among their remains are figurines of dancers and one of a woman drumming; and an ideograph of an arched harp of early Mesopotamian type.

THE AGE OF VEDIC CHANT
(*c.* 1500–*c.* 250 B.C.)

Between about 1500 B.C. (or 2000 B.C. at the earliest) and 1000 B.C. the Aryan-speaking peoples, who before their diffusion lived in western Asia as early as the third or even fourth millennium, reached India. And like Iran and the greater part of Europe, India (excepting in the south) is predominantly Aryan to this day. The earliest sacred knowledge of the Aryans, orally transmitted up to that time, was first written down by *rishis* (sages) between 1500 B.C. and 500 B.C. (or possibly earlier), and the resulting four books called Vedas (*Veda*, lit. 'knowledge'), contain prayers, hymns, and ritual formulas connected with their gods.

The sacrificial ceremonies at which these hymns were employed, designed as they were to uphold the order of the world, laid stress on the efficacy of a correct intonation. The hymns of the *Rigveda* (Veda of Hymns), the oldest of the four books (*c.* 1500 B.C.–*c.* 1200 B.C.), were chanted on three accents connoting definite differences in pitch: *udatta* ('raised' or upper note); *anudatta* ('not raised' or lower note); and *svarita* ('sounded' or middle note). The notes followed the words closely in pitch and in prose rhythm, one note to a syllable. Such chanting is still to be heard in temples in many parts of India and has changed little, it seems, over a period of three thousand years.

A less austere form of chanting, melodically enriched under the influence of Dravidian song, is found in the *Samaveda* (Veda of Chants) whose words, chiefly adaptations from the ninth book of the *Rigveda*, are supplied with musical notation. Here, by contrast, the music is more important than the words – an emphasis which still obtains in vocal music today. Connected with the larger offerings and sacrifices, Saman chant is sung in unison by three priests. Its scale was once a five-note, and later a seven-note scale was used. Normally fewer notes are used in practice, and often enough the patterns of melody move within a tetrachord (compass of a fourth). The scale is essentially vocal in that it was originally conceived as descending, and such a scale is still found in the songs sung in certain valleys in the Himalayas. The chant is also characterized by a chromatic element having no parallel either in Greek music or in the Hindu classical music of later times, though it has something in common with the Hebrew (Sephardic) chant of the prophets.

Today there are sixteen different time-units, but in older Saman chant there are only three: *hrasva* ('short') and *dirgha* ('long') – corresponding to short and long syllables – and *vrddhi* ('augmented'). This last, which deliberately prolongs the end of a phrase, has (like many other features) its counterpart in Christian plainchant. In vocal techniques, too, there are comparisons to be made. The oriental tremulant singing found in Vedic chant as late as the seventeenth century, for instance, was also represented by the *tremula voce* to which in the Middle Ages certain plainchant neumes (*quilisma*, *pressus*) were directed to be sung.

Hinduism (*Sanatana dharma*, 'the Eternal Law'), always the principal religion of India, embodies the traditions of the Vedas. But to what extent the chants now used by orthodox Hindus faithfully represent early forms is difficult to say. Ancient treatises give little information; surviving schools differ in approach. Moreover secrecy enshrouds the utterance of a chant believed to be of supernatural power, though this, no doubt, has worked to keep the tradition intact.

Among the ancients vocal music was all-important. At the same time, the Sanskrit word for music, *Samgita*, has a wider meaning: the art and science of singing with music and dancing. Already in the Vedas and other ancient sources instruments are mentioned, though they were used with restraint in the Vedic ceremonies themselves. The dance element, too, was probably restricted to hieratic hand-movements – partly symbolic and partly no doubt designed to help the musical memory. These movements, however, formed the basis for that later religious and most classical of Indian dance-forms of the south, *Bharata Natyam*. The development of the instrumental and dance elements was certainly stimulated by the aboriginal arts: Siva, for instance, originally a non-Aryan god, later became the Hindu Nataraja, Lord of the Dance.

From earliest times and throughout the ages Hindu music has been intimately associated with religious rites, court ceremonies, and private occasions. In all these performances the religious element is never very far away, and the repertoire of the modern street-singer is chiefly concerned with deities. The sacred and secular were, however, always carefully distinguished: *Marga* (lit. 'the sought') was music 'composed by the gods' which, when sung according to rule, could lead to liberation and break man's circle of lives; *Desi* (lit. 'regional') was music for entertainment.

The great epics compiled later in this epoch, the *Ramayana* (sixth to fifth centuries B.C.) and the *Mahabharata* (400 B.C.–A.D. 400) – which includes the famous *Bhagavad-gita* –

26

frequently refer to music, showing it already well advanced. Scenes from these epics form the substance of the musical dance-dramas, whose tradition lives today especially in the *Kathakali* of Kerala in the south.

The oldest writing specifically devoted to Hindu music, comprising chapters 28 to 33 of the *Natyasastra*, is now dated to about 200 B.C., and codifies practices already well established at that time. The Hindus, whose present art-forms owe so much to this period, take the traditional author of this treatise, the sage Bharata, as the founder of Hindu classical music.

BUDDHIST AND HELLENIC INFLUENCES
(*c.* 250 B.C.–*c.* A.D. 600)

The classical tradition, however, did not flower all at once, and for a time the Vedic tradition became the exclusive preserve of the priests. Meanwhile two factors combined to influence music in India, more especially in the north: the Greek or Scythian culture following the campaign of Alexander of Macedon in 327 B.C., and the sudden rise of Buddhism (founded over two centuries earlier) after the acceptance of that creed in 262 B.C. by the Hindu monarch Asoka. An arched harp comparable with that of the Indus Valley civilization already referred to appears on temple reliefs from the time of the Bharhut (Central India) stupa (180 B.C.) and, though there is no trace of it in India now, it must have been much in use since it still adorns temple reliefs as late as A.D. 800. But the new culture developed especially in the first century of the Christian era. The outstanding wind instrument of ancient India, the cross-flute (Skt. *vanici*), appears on reliefs at this period (e.g. Sanchi, Central India). The Graeco-Buddhist sculpture at Gandhara (region of modern Kandahar, Kashmir) shows a wealth of instruments – strings, wind, and percussion – which must already have been in use. Hand-drums were evidently as popular then as now. Of the instruments actually brought by the new culture only the lute came to stay, and on Indian soil it developed important new forms. The Gandhara culture had professional musicians called *Gandharvas*, and these 'celestial' beings brought the sacred art-forms to more popular notice. They are said to have used a scale based on a non-diatonic principle and called *Gandhara grama* (i.e. *Gandhara* scale), though it is less safe to think of them as having transmitted the Greek double-tetrachord theory to early exponents of the Indian division of sound.

What the specific influence of Buddhism may have been is difficult to determine, since, musically speaking, this epoch has been among the least studied, though fervent hymns composed by Ashtaghosa were a means of spreading the faith. Certain it is, too, that when Buddhism spread beyond India it carried many Indian features deep into the musical styles of the Far East (see Chapters 4, 5, 6, and 7), and in India it no doubt acted as a powerful organizing force.

THE CLASSICAL SYSTEM OF RAGAS AND THE MIDDLE AGES

Early in the seventh century, following a period of gradual religious revival, India again became Hindu. The sculpture of Hindu temples from this century shows new musical instruments, including the gong (*kamsya*) from Aihole, hand-bell (*ghanta*) from Aurangabad, and a two-stringed prototype of the important *vina* (zither) from Mavalipuram. The evidence of the wonderful reliefs found outside India at Borobodur (Java) where migrant Hindus built an enormous temple about A.D. 800, with other data, shows that India now abandoned the arched harp of antiquity in favour of zithers, lutes, and fiddles.

The several instruments were not combined to form orchestras of any size. Orchestral music has never found a place in Indian court and temple, as it has in the Far East. On the contrary, the basis of Indian music is and always has been song, even when, as very often today, the instruments perform without a voice. The small scale of such resources allows the individual greater freedom within prescribed limits, and well befitted musicians who had to travel over long distances in the service of numerous patrons.

The foundations of the classical system had been laid as early as the work of Bharata (second century B.C.) mentioned above. But for evidence as to the form taken by it in the Middle Ages, especially from the eighth century to the seventeenth, we must turn to the *Brihad deshi* of Matamga (eighth century), the *Naradiya Shiksha* of Narada (tenth century), and the *Sam-gita-Ratnakara* ('The Treasury of Music') of Sarngadeva (early thirteenth century). These theoretical treatises are based on the musical practice current in their times, and the dates of Narada and Matamga may well be earlier by some centuries than those given here.

Theory

Indian theory recognizes the octave (*saptaka*, lit. 'set of seven', i.e. seven intervals) as representing the complete cycle of sounds. Its primary division is into two disjunct tetrachords (*angas*, 'limbs') or intervals of a fourth (cf. Pythagorean Greek music theory). Mathematical proportions found in this funda-mental division are intimately linked with those found in Hindu temple architecture throughout the Middle Ages. As in the western scale seven main notes (*svaras*) or steps are recog-nized within the octave, and the names of the notes are abbre-viated in an early Indian system of sol-fa (*sa, ri, ga, ma, pa, dha, ni*).

The octave is further divided into twenty-two *srutis*, that is, microtonal steps of less than a semitone, nearly equal in size. The *srutis* (popularly called 'quarter-tones') are not used con-secutively in melody as in a chromatic scale, but are grouped variously in twos, threes, and fours to form the various scales (scale = *grama*; cf. Greek *gamma*) whose pitches are exactly fixed by means of them. This system has the advantage of enabling accurate intonation in a way denied to systems having fewer intervals, like the twelve semitones tuned to equal tem-perament in Europe.

In classical theory there are two fundamental seven-note (*sampurna*, lit. 'complete') scales having also six-note (*shadava*) and five-note (*audava*) forms. Written as a sequence of steps in *srutis* these scales are today interpreted as follows: *Sa grama*, 4 3 2 4 4 3 2 (cf. western major scale 4 3 2 4 3 4 2), and *Ma grama*, 4 3 4 2 4 3 2. According to the note on which a scale is made to start it can, as in western music, obviously have seven modal forms. From the two scales of *Sa* and *Ma*, fourteen theoretical *murcchanas* ('extensions') were thus formed. Indian theory always explores all theoretical possibilities in this way for the sake of clarity, but Indian practice is invariably simpler. Indeed, only seven of the fourteen possible *murcchanas* are regarded as suitable foundations for eighteen more complex structures called *jatis* (species or genera). Each *jati* – and there are seven principal and eleven mixed *jatis* – is already more than a scale. It has its own internal organization of notes, emphasis on particular notes, and other classified characteristics. It is, in fact, a kind of melodic germ-cell, having something of a parallel in the modes (*tropoi*) of ancient Greece.

Raga

By further elaboration, the *jatis* become *ragas*. The *raga* (lit. 'colour', 'feeling'), the true foundation of the classical system, is a melody-type having numerous characteristics. It must, for instance, use both tetrachords (i.e. both 'limbs' of the octave-scale), and any given *raga* is defined, *inter alia*, by its particular scale (whose descent may be different from its ascent); by the emphasis given to a particular note (*vadi*) and to its fourth or fifth, as a contrast with the tonic; by the frequency of certain notes and intervals; by a characteristic melodic pattern; by the pitch range (tessitura) in which the melody mainly lies; and by the particular types of movement between notes. These types include the important *gamakas* or 'ornaments'. *Gamakas*, which embrace slides, echoes, trills, and a wealth of other refinements, are the soul of Indian melody and give to it a more subtle and flexible character than the somewhat rigid melody of the ancient Far East. The use of *gamakas* in song calls for some remarkable techniques which would repay study by western musicians.

Each *raga* is thus far more than a technical entity. It is a musical and aesthetic organism of great potentiality. Having long observed and classified the qualities and moods of all the *srutis*, notes, intervals, modes, and other elements, Indian musicians gained enough experience to arrange their *jatis* and *ragas* so as deliberately to excite and sustain a given emotion or mood in the listener. Indeed each *raga* has a different and unmistakable ethos, and *raga* music is, from the aesthetic viewpoint, music that expresses different shades of thought and feeling.

Although *raga* as such is first mentioned by Matamga (eighth century), the idea of music capable of evoking definite moods is older by far. Matamga describes certain *ragas* as already out of vogue by his time; the ancient *jatis* are based on a similar idea; and nine moods were already recognized as fundamental by the Aryans in antiquity (*Ramayana*, *c.* 400 B.C.). These early settlers perforce adopted many of the seasonal agricultural rites of the previous inhabitants and it was natural that the songs sung at each of their six seasons should be able to articulate the prevailing mood, such as delight in spring or merriment in autumn. There were in fact at first six generic *ragas*. No doubt many of the pre-Aryan ritual tunes were taken over with the festivals and adapted by the Aryans. Though the steps by which this process was accomplished are unknown, many *ragas* must have originated in tribal melodies. The very title of Matamga's *Brihat desi* (*desi*, 'regional') suggests as much, and evidence is still preserved in the names of several *ragas*, such as *Malvi*, after the war-loving Malavas who fought against Alexander the Great, and *Dravida*, still current in the Dravidian south.

Matamga's object and that of other theorists was evidently to collect all these melodic idioms (as well as those from religious chant) within a general framework both technical and aesthetic. The aesthetic aspect was the true *raison d'être* of the system, and we can pursue its development along these lines. An appropriate *raga* was for instance assigned to each hour, to be sung with the object of heightening its particular mood, such as morning adoration and evening merriment. Though treatises

31

and traditions disagree about *ragas*, in all cases there appears to be one common factor: the minor element (more flat notes) imbue the *ragas* of the quieter hours (midnight to the heat of the day), and a major character those sung between six o'clock and midnight. Aptly then have *ragas* been described as celebrations of different moments in the ritual of living, and in this sense we can understand that extensive mythology which illustrates the benefits flowing from the right use of *ragas* and the misfortunes attending those who dare to sing them at the wrong time. And so through the centuries there developed a whole system of correspondences which related music not only to moods, hours, and seasons, but to heavens, zodiacal signs, planets, days of the week, elements, colours, voices of birds, human complexions, sexes, temperaments, and periods in human life as well.

The number of *ragas* in use has varied at different periods and in different parts of the country. They are said to have reached as many as 11,991 among the ancient Tamils! But normally there are considered to be 132 ultimately referable to a small number of classes, and of these about one half are more generally in use.

Tala

Melody necessarily includes rhythm. Thus each *raga* (melody-type) is associated with a *tala* (time-measure). One *tala* may serve for several different *ragas*, since the *talas* are fewer in number. About 108 have been known, but only a small number – in the south, seven main *talas* (each having five forms) – are in general use. A given *tala* has a fixed number of beats (*matras*) arranged in distinctive groupings. The pace or tempo of these beats, determined by their duration (*laya*), is slow (*vilambita*), medium (*madhya*), or quick (*druta*), each tempo being normally twice that of the preceding. If periodical stresses be added (as in a cycle of bodily movement), then according to where these stresses fall and the total number of beats counted before the whole pattern (i.e. bar) recurs, we get musical *time*. The organization of beats in multiples, that is, in terms of longs and

shorts (as in word-syllables) gives rise to metre or *tala*. *Talas*
may be relatively simple (like a four-bar phrase in common
time) but more usually strike the western ear as being of some
complexity. Whereas groupings of beats by bar and metre tend
in western classical music to be powers of either 2 or 3, or combinations by multiplication, in India they tend to be combinations of 2 and 3 by addition. Thus the south Indian *tala triputa
tisra* is 3 + 2 + 2. The mathematical framework of beat, pace
(tempo), time (bar), and metre forms the anatomy of music's
flow, though the last element already brings a definite significance into what was merely a forward movement in time.
Even the *tala*, however, is only a point for departure and return. When beats are divided, accents come unexpectedly, syncopation occurs, and phrases go across the expected boundaries,
we experience rhythm – music's vital flow. Though having
body-born (time) and word-born (metre) elements, rhythm
needs the emotional element for its completion, and this
finds its expression in the asymmetrical features just described.

The *talas* having longer periods give more scope for interplay
between voice and drum, or solo instrument and drum, and
tension can mount considerably between the two before they
come together again as they are required to do on the first beat
of the next complete period. Periods frequently go up to sixteen
beats and may be very much longer (e.g. *boradoshkhushi*, fifty-
six beats). Many of the *talas* originated in the Vedic texts and
vocal music but, as with the *ragas*, some began in the more
popular music of various regions and periods.

The recurrent period of the *tala* underlies the larger formal
basis of the performance. A song, however, falls into three main
sections. First is the *alapa*, a prelude in free but slow time,
without drumming and without words; this prelude feels its
way into the mood and establishes the main melodic features of
the *raga* in deliberate manner. Next comes a stanza announcing
the theme and sentiment of the song. And finally follows the
body of the work; at which point the drum joins in to establish
the *tala*; this section is in medium (and sometimes quick) time
and develops the mood in a continuous structure following the

rules of verse and strophe. The proportion between the un-measured prelude and the body of the work is rarely the same: in the south the *alapa* may be short; in the north it may be even longer than the succeeding section.

Kharaja (*drone*)

These two elements, *raga* and *tala*, giving direction to sound in time and space, are completed by a third: *kharaja*, a drone or 'pedal' note which, by sustaining the tonal centre, acts as a guide throughout the piece. In songs it is tuned to a pitch comfortable for the voice. The drone is believed to have originated in folk music (where it occurs in the single-stringed *ekata* and *tuntina*; cf. bagpipe), but the four-stringed drone of classical music, as found in the *tambura* (long-necked lute without frets), emerged some time after the ninth century. The tuning (left to right and in order of striking) is fifth, eighth, eighth repeated, fundamental; or, for a few *ragas*, fourth, eighth, eighth repeated, fundamental.

These strings are sounded in a continuous cycle at a pace unrelated to that of the time-measure, and the overlapping notes give the impression of a continuous sound. By dividing the (geometric) interval of the octave at the interval of the fifth (arithmetically) or fourth (harmonically), the four strings form a harmonic reference-frame for the art of *raga* and *tala*. They provide a ground rich in partials which blend with various notes in the *raga*, in whose structure a subtle harmony is already implicit. From this, and the development of the melody and rhythm to a high degree of subtlety, it may be seen that further added harmony is not merely unnecessary, but would indeed obscure and virtually destroy the fine melodic-harmonic balance of the system. Moreover, modulation in the western sense is actually incompatible with any modal system, since the latter is founded, not on constant change, but on the contemplation of an immovable tonic. The effect of this music in performance is complete and satisfying and, at its highest level, a triumphant blend of melodic and rhythmic art.

Raga-music

The three elements – tonic, *raga*, and *tala* – are variously divided in performance. In a song, and many types of instrumental piece, the *raga* belongs to the voice or instrument; the *tala* to the drums – and to the hands clapped according to a conventional system; and the tonic ground to the *tambura*. All three may be combined as in the *vina* which has both melody-strings and drone-strings.

These three elements then engage the attention of the performer. Selecting the appropriate *raga* (with its *tala*), he subordinates his individual creative power to it, yet he must be more creative than the western performer who is simply a channel for expressing a composer's ideas. The performance is affected by his own mood and the reactions of the listeners with whom he is in intimate contact from moment to moment. The composer–performer–listener relationship is thus in fact quite different from that of the west. And if he is a master he may finally crystallize his 'realization' of the *raga* into a composition, and this will serve as a model to his pupils and be learned by them. Then, since the profession is more hereditary than not, such music will be heard from an early age by the members of his own family.

The traditional Indian musician, thus trained (over never fewer than six years) to learn fifty *ragas* at least, has at his disposal a stock of musically pregnant formulas having well-tested moods suitable for extemporization on any given occasion. And when musicians meet, even for the first time, they have at once a mutual understanding which enables them to play together without rehearsal. In these ways the Indian musician has much in common with the western *bard* or poet-musician of the Aryan Celts whose tradition persisted in Celtic Britain into recent times.

A piece does not start or finish in any formal way; neither is there a set duration for its performance. It may last twenty minutes or, more often – as in the full unfolding of a single *raga* – an hour and a half, and the performers will imbue it with all the subtlety they can devise. It would be wrong to look for great external contrasts or vehemence of expression in such a performance or, taking it out of its context, to attempt to judge it according to western musical standards.

On the contrary, it can only be understood in terms of Indian philosophical thought. This thought, which is essentially contemplative, has, along with considerations of an artistic and purely practical nature, played a decisive part in shaping and maintaining the classical musical system. The tonic, beginning before a piece, continuing throughout, and still being heard after it, is no separate element, but the ever-present guide; in the language of music it expresses the timeless, eternal, unchanging background of all things – their origin, sustainer, and goal. The *ragas* as melody-types give variety in tonal space, the lower tetrachord reflecting the sensual world, the upper tetrachord mind-consciousness. Similarly the *talas* provide variety in tonal time. And this variety in tonal time and tonal space looks, not as in western music outwards, but always inwards towards the unity of the tonic. The interaction and interplay of the dual factors about the third gives a virtually infinite number of possibilities for musical expression whilst always preserving the sense of law. Thus it is that the *ragas*, like the *mantras* or sacred formulas, are regarded as aspects of and hence as approaches to *Shabdabrahman*, that is, the Absolute (*Brahman*) conceived as sound (*shabda*).

TRADITIONS OF NORTH AND SOUTH:
MUSLIM INFLUENCE
(*c.* 1000–*c.* 1700)

The classical *raga* system belongs to the whole of India. But throughout history there have been local and regional differences, especially noticeable between the north and the south since early times. For this the racial movements and cultures, like the Indus Valley and the Gandhara already described, were partly responsible. But there were other factors. Following the campaign of Darius in 518 B.C. India was added to the Persian Empire and remained part of it for two centuries; the Parsee fled to India in A.D. 717; and the Arabians occupied Gujarat in

A.D. 725. Thus north India was not untouched by Persian-Arabian influence before the eleventh and twelfth centuries when the Muslim conquest began.

At first the Muslims in India disfavoured music as no small part of Islam frowned upon its use. But the Sufis fostered it, and the Muslim rulers began to act as patrons from the time of Altamash (1210–36). Later it was assiduously cultivated at the Indian Moghul courts (from the early sixteenth century) and it reached a high point under the Emperor Akbar (1556–1605) whose musician, Tansen, is still a household word in north India.

The contribution of Islam to Indian music remains to be properly assessed, but one thing is clear beyond any doubt. The Muslim influence completed the division of the two musical traditions which are clearly distinguishable in Indian music to-day: the northern or Hindustani, and the southern or Carnatic. The former derives from the absorption by an ancient Aryan culture of new and rich influences coming through Persia from the Middle East; the latter is Aryan in form but largely Dravidian in content. The traditional Hindu music, strong, sublime, and restrained, was in the north fertilized by a Muslim tradition of elegant, decorative, abandoned music with more than a suggestion of romanticism. Because the Hindu tradition was soundly based, it successfully received the best elements in the other to produce a wonderfully vital art. A blend of strength and elegance is indeed apparent in all north Indian arts of the Moghul period. The culture of the Moghul courts brought in a more secular atmosphere; this is to be seen, for instance, in the *Kathak* dance of the north by comparison with the more religious *Bharata Natyam* of the south. Carnatic music also remained more intellectual and metrically more austere; whereas Hindustani music developed the more intimate and subtle features of note and melody, receiving and transforming many new Persian and Arabic tunes and *ragas* (e.g. *Huseini, Hejaz, Kafi, Bahar*). From Muslim influence date also the different names given to identical *ragas*, and the longer and more flexible time-measures, not to mention a decided preference for certain instruments.

South India leans towards the *vina*, which attained its present form about 1400, north India towards the *sitar*. This latter shows the fusion of the two cultures: it resembles the Persian *'ud* (lute) in shape and the Indian *vina* in principle. While the south favours a later importation in the European violin, the north prefers the *sarod* which, though most likely of indigenous origin (*vina*-type), reached its present form under Muslim influence (cf. Persian *sarud*). The name of the instrument which plays the tonic or ground-tone in *raga*-music, the *tambura*, or unfretted long lute, is like Persian *tanbur*. Among wind instruments the oboe called *shahnai*, used in temples and on all auspicious occasions (weddings, ceremonies, processions, festivals), reached the north from Persia and its name is from the Persian. The comparable oboe of the south is quite differently called *nagasuaram*. As regards drums, the *mridamga* is more widely used in the south than the north, while the north inclines to the *tabla* – probably named after the Arab *tabl* and representing a Muslim refurbishing of an instrument they found already in use.

THE MODERN PERIOD
(Since 1700)

When the Moghul Empire began to decline soon after 1700, Indian classical music was already showing signs of change. As music was cultivated more under aristocratic patronage than among the people it had diminished in popular appreciation. Vocal and instrumental music came more and more to need different performers.

Meanwhile, British interest had been growing since about 1600 and India was entering a new phase. During the British period, which lasted from the mid eighteenth to the mid twentieth century (1757–1947), the old feudalism gradually diminished and music began to lose its principal patrons. It fell in social status, and began to lose in artistry and force. And so began that slow degeneration which was already widespread at the beginning of the twentieth century.

Indian music received at least one happy contribution from

Europe in the late eighteenth century – the violin, which lends itself well to the subtleties of Indian intonation. By giving it a tuning different from that in the west and adapting it to their own techniques, Indian culture successfully assimilated it as it has, without losing its own identity, assimilated many new resources from time to time. The clarinet has been successfully adopted in the south. In the nineteenth century misguided missionaries, Indian admirers of the west and others, took a fatal step for Indian music. They popularized the harmonium tuned (and not always well tuned) in western equal temperament. This instrument all too often takes the place of the *tambura* today, and this has tended to blunt the Indian's sensitivity to notes. Moreover, with little appreciation of either system, these enthusiasts attempted to foist western harmony on to the already fully developed Indian modal system with results which are all too apparent. Latterly film music and light music have been enjoying a vogue, and the radio has helped to spread them. The better levels of European music reach India through gramophone records, but fundamentally, it must be honestly recognized, European music finds little response in the Indian heart. Concert performance finds no place in Indian classical music, although latterly, chiefly under the influence of radio, it has made some headway, some centuries after the rise of public concert-giving in Europe.

Believing that modern life calls for new developments, however, some Indian musicians look for new forms. Schools of thought range from the out-and-out traditionalists to those who seek modernity at all costs, not to mention those who have replaced their gods by the masses and pin everything on the creation of a folk art. The best considered trends are those of individual poet-musicians who, like Rabindranath Tagore (d. 1941) in Bengal, deeply imbued with the tradition of the classical *raga* have turned to folk-music for new inspiration, thereby repeating a process with ample precedent in musical history. More recently, some classical musicians have been feeling their way towards expression along more polyphonic lines.

The modern period has seen some attempts to write down music in notation. For the Vedic chant notation has been a convenience, and a number of different systems are used according to the locality. Various rudimentary systems have grown out of the ancient sol-fa and are used as aids to memory. But beyond this, in *raga* music which is differently extemporized each time, notation would serve very little purpose and might even discourage the creative element and that remarkable sense of balance between law and freedom which has kept the system so vital and flexible over the centuries. The Indian classical system is probably, of all the great musical traditions in the East, artistically the most important that has survived into the present age.

INFLUENCE OF INDIAN MUSIC
UPON EAST AND WEST

The existence of a melodic-rhythmic system (*raga-tala*) in India more than a thousand years before a comparable one in Mohammedan countries (*maqam-iqa*) has never been explained. It might suggest Indian influence on Persia at an early stage, and though, as we have seen, there was ample contact, the evidence is obscure.

The influence of Indian music has been chiefly upon the Far East. In the wake of Buddhism (early centuries of the Christian era) instruments and musical influences passed into China, Korea, Japan, and Tibet (see Chapters 4, 5, and 6); and, in the wake of Hinduism (around eighth century), into south-east Asia and Indonesia (see Chapter 7).

Some music has reached Europe through the gipsies. This Aryan people originated in India and, though they tended to take on the colours of the countries through which they passed during the Middle Ages (sixth to fifteenth centuries), they brought to Arabia and Europe certain *ragas* – the *Indiana* of the Spanish gipsies corresponds to the Hindu *Bhairavi* – many melodic ornaments which remain wholly Indian, and an instrument known as the *svara-mandala* which in the form of the gipsy *cymbalum* is of interest as one of the ancestors of our keyboard instruments.

Early in the present century some European music was

inspired by Hindu scriptures and drama, e.g. Gustav Holst's (1874–1934) *Hymns from the Rig-Veda* and opera *Savitri*, and incorporated certain Indian musical features, like Albert Roussel's opera-ballet *Padmavati*. Indian music is perhaps nearer to western taste than any other music of the East. Latterly Indian musicians have visited Europe and America and some good recordings of Indian classical music are becoming available in the west. These must, along with recordings of other oriental music, be accounted among the more important materials to which contemporary music is open at the present time.

4. China

IN the third millennium B.C. life in China was still largely that of a semi-nomadic and hunting folk living in a New Stone Age. During the course of the millennium agriculture gradually developed, especially in the valley tracts of the rivers Yangtze-kiang and Hoang-ho – the fertile loess region – and this period is remembered in the myths of semi-divine beings and legendary Emperors each of whom is said to have had a musical system. But of these systems only the names survive. By the turn of the millennium, high civilization may be said to have emerged. Arising near to the eastern terminus of the steppe-corridor connecting the Far East and the Near East, Chinese Megalithic culture could possibly have been set off by foreign influences – Mesopotamia was ruled by Sumerians and Egypt was under its Old Kingdom. However this may be, it appears to have been fostered largely by Mongoloid peoples.

After a first dynasty called Hsia (2205–1766 B.C.)[1] Chinese civilization entered on a long dynasty called Shang (1766–1122 B.C.) from which survive the first tangible musical remains. Excavations have brought to light two kinds of musical instrument, the sonorous stone (*ch'ing*) and the globular flute (*hsüan*); their type links them with Neolithic tradition. Two further instruments, drum (*ku*) and bell (*chung*), are mentioned in a source of the twelfth century B.C.; these are essentially instruments of the Bronze Age. The Ode referring to them comes from the *Shih Ching* (*Book of Songs*), a compilation begun towards the end of this dynasty, which embraces material over a millennium from about 1600 to about 600 B.C., and offers scattered information about music in early times.

1. Though the Chinese have an excellent historical sense, dates before about 850 B.C. cannot be scientifically checked, and the early dates adopted here follow convention.

During the agricultural year important festivals were held at the junctions of rivers in the intervals between seasons. On these occasions choirs of boys and choirs of girls from different villages challenged one another by singing sequences of distichs accompanied by gestures. Each half of the distich usually consisted of eight words, that is, eight syllables, a form well known in Chinese poetry. The contest of the sexes and the alternate singing (antiphony) were said to symbolize the two polar principles of the universe, *Yang* and *Yin*, and the sexual rites which followed brought harmony with nature and human harmony through the reunion of the two principles in the world. Musical form was closely connected with some such symbolism, for at one of the festivals two companies of musicians played one after the other and then both together. As we shall see in Chapter 7, certain musical customs surviving in Annam may form a link with these times.

While some odes were sung at the festivals, others were for singing at the Courts. The ancient *Shu Ching* (*Book of History*) says that one of the legendary emperors (third millennium B.C.) 'took odes of the Court and ballads of the village to see if they corresponded with the five notes.' Here perhaps we can see 'folk'-song in the process of originating in higher forms – its new traits rarely if ever originate among the peasants – and the impress of some of these ancient and higher forms survives in Chinese folk-song to this day.

The mention of 'five notes' is a reference to the five-note scale which since time unknown has been the principal basis of Chinese melody. According to one theory, this scale was widely diffused over Europe and Asia with the Megalithic culture (New Stone and Bronze Ages) but, with later cultures, survived only in fringe areas like the Hebrides, Lapland, and China which, as a sub-continent, has remained more separate from the rest of Asia than even India. The presence of the five-note scale in the Americas is, like that of numerous types of musical instrument, directly due to colonization from Asia by Mongoloid peoples, to whom both the Eskimos and the American 'Indians' belong.

In this formative epoch the foundations were firmly laid.

Though in the course of its history Chinese music has, like Chinese culture in general, absorbed many foreign influences, it has retained, and unfolded in accordance with, its own essential identity. And a persistent reverence for the past among the Chinese has assured a certain continuity of tradition.

ANTIQUITY
(11th–3rd centuries B.C.)

With the Chou dynasty (1050–255 B.C.) we enter at last a historical period when most of the institutions, manners, and customs of China found the pattern which lasted into modern times. We find music in three important centres: the agricultural festivals instituted in remote antiquity, and combining poetry, music, and dance; the ritual of the Imperial Court; and religious ritual.

Among the musical instruments used, three are of outstanding importance: the stone-chime (*pien-ch'ing*), a series of fourteen to twenty-four curvilinear or (later) L-shaped plates of stone suspended in a frame; the bell-chime (*pien-chung*), a comparable series of bells; and the reed mouth-organ (*shêng*), dating to about 1100 B.C., in which several bamboo pipes (usually seventeen today) rise out of a gourd wind-chest which is supplied with air through a lateral mouthpiece. No other cultures had such instruments at any corresponding period. Related to the reed mouth-organ is the panpipe (*p'ai-hsiao*). The first Chinese stringed instruments, important in religious and other ceremonial music, include the zither called *ch'in* (commonly five- and seven-stringed forms) and the zither called *sê* (originally twenty-six strings, now thirteen). To these must be added the older sonorous stones and bells and several kinds of drum. A recent catalogue of Chinese instruments describes over two hundred, and most of these go back to types already known in the Chou dynasty. As time went on, the Imperial Court, using many of these instruments, organized them into sizeable orchestras and noblemen maintained smaller bands.

During the last four centuries of this epoch, Chinese civilization reached its highest point, and the great philosophers Lao Tzŭ (604–517 B.C.) and K'ung Fu-tzŭ (551–479 B.C.) appeared. Lao Tzŭ, a semi-legendary figure, was the founder of Taoism (*Tao*, 'the Way'), a mystical philosophy which has tended to remain esoteric. As regards the place of music in its ritual little information is available, though the likening of the individual human essence to a musical tone is among Taoistic concepts. K'ung Fu-tzŭ, known to the west as Confucius, originated the philosophy which now bears his name. Tradition associates him with musical performance and the part played by music in the ritual of living. He it was who, describing himself as 'a transmitter, not a maker, one who knew and loved the ancients', edited China's most ancient books. In addition to those already mentioned (*Book of Songs, Book of History*), these comprise the *Record of Rites* (*Li Chi*) which includes an important chapter known as the 'Memorial of Music' (*Yüeh Chi*), and the meta-physical *Book of Changes* (*I Ching*) on whose cosmic elements the first principles of music are said to have been based. It was between the time of Confucius and the end of this epoch that the foundations of Chinese music theory were laid, forming a basis which contained the seed of all later developments. The chief source-book is the *Lü Shih Ch'un Ch'iu* of Lü Pu-wei (239 B.C.).

THEORY

The starting-point of Chinese theory is the foundation tone (*huang chung*, lit. 'yellow bell'). This was conceived simultane-ously as a sacred eternal principle, the basis of the state, and a note of definite pitch in music. Lü Pu-wei attributes it to the mythical Emperor Huang Ti (third millennium B.C.) who sent the equally mythical Ling Lun ('Music Ruler') to the western boundaries of the kingdom where, in a mountain valley, he cut a node of bamboo in such a way as to give the foundation tone – the pitch of a man's voice when he spoke without passion. It was considered important to find the correct pitch for each dynasty, or political disorder would be likely to ensue. More precise data on the pitches employed through the ages have yet to be assembled, but here the foundation tone will be conventionally taken as *fa* (F).

From the foundation tone, other higher notes were derived by taking a tube of length one-third less than the first, then a tube one-third more than the second and so on, that is, tubes alternately two-thirds and four-thirds the length of each preceding one. The resulting sounds thus have alternately vibrations of 3/2 and 3/4 times the frequency of the preceding, which gives, musically speaking, alternating series of ascending fifths and descending fourths. It will be seen from this that the vibration frequencies in the Chinese system are all based on powers of the numerals 2 and 3. 'Music expresses the accord of Heaven and Earth,' says the *Memorial of Music*, and according to the *Record of Rites* 'since 3 is the numeral of Heaven and 2 that of the Earth, sounds in the ratio 3:2 harmonize as Heaven and Earth.'

Taking the first five sounds in this series, *fa, do, sol, re, la,* and arranging them in scale order *fa, sol, la, do, re*, we reach the five-note scale of the Chinese. This already existed in the melodies of Chou times and was merely defined and rationalized by the theory. Chinese texts from the fourth and third centuries B.C. call the five notes *kung, shang, chiao, chih, yü.* Any of the five might serve as a locus for a new mode of the scale, the mode being characterized by this note as its principal and final. The scale is pre-eminently suited to melodic expression, to which it lends the greatest clarity.

The symbolism underlying Chinese ritual required music's fundamental note to move conformably with the twelve months (and the twelve hours). In other words, the key-note (and the scale based upon it) had to be *transposed* for each successive period. To regulate this movement a series of twelve notes was generated by the method of ascending fifths and descending fourths already mentioned; and each of the twelve notes so generated became in turn the starting-point of the scale.

In order to show all the notes in their musical firmament together the Chinese next arranged the twelve notes in stepwise order. The resulting arrangement has all the appearance of a chromatic scale, but it was never used as such, only as a system for transposing the five-note scale.

The components of the twelve-note series were further grouped into two six-note series, according to whether they were generated by ascending fifths or by descending fourths. The two six-note series are in appearance whole-tone scales, but again, they were not used as such. They were, as interlocking series, designed as classifications of the notes which might be sounded together in ritual harmony, namely, those subtended by the intervals of the fourth and the fifth.

Such, briefly, is the original theory. It is incomplete because a series confined to twelve notes does not allow accurate intonation for all twelve positions of the five-note scale. Realizing this, some scholars made efforts to find a system of equal temperament; others, asserting that temperament goes against nature's law, elected to keep their system perfect if incomplete; while others again made numerous experiments in the further division of sound by extending the series of notes related by fourths and fifths.

Although the five-note scale has always been fundamental in China, a seven-note scale may have existed alongside it since Chou times, because among the Chou instruments the cross-flute (*ti*) is capable of producing a seven-note scale. A seven-note scale with five principal and two auxiliary degrees was certainly in use by the first century before Christ at latest. By transposing the seven-note scale and its modes in twelve positions, a system of eighty-four modes was formed (from the sixth century) which came to be adopted in ritual music.

Through the centuries the practice and the theory of music were sometimes in agreement and sometimes out of it, but however far scholars might go, the original theory was not only securely founded in mathematics, but also deeply rooted in Chinese philosophy and metaphysics in such a way as to prevent excesses, and to stabilize and establish the system in Chinese tradition. Throughout the centuries it has inspired the speculations of the finest minds among musicians, mathematicians, astronomers, and philosophers, and has always acted as a guiding force.

THE EARLY MIDDLE AGES
(3rd century B.C.–7th century A.D.)

A short dynasty of the Ch'in people (221–206 B.C.) succeeded that of the Chou, but its Emperor Shih-huang-ti ordered a destruction of all books, music, and musical instruments. Some materials survived, however, and the Han dynasty (206 B.C.– A.D. 220) was a time of reconstruction.

From this time and during various dynasties (Han, Wei, Chin, The Six, Sui) there were some important new advances in music. An Imperial Office of Music (*Yüeh-fu*) was founded under the Emperor Wu (141–87 B.C.) for standardizing pitch, supervising music, and building up musical archives. The Chinese had long previously recognized the relationship of musical pitch to the length and capacity of a tube, and so it was that this organization was attached to the Office of Weights and Measures. Music also flourished at the Imperial Court, and in Han times the orchestra maintained there employed more than eight hundred musicians in four sections.

In the first century A.D., Buddhist monks from India reached China, where Buddhism was to become a vital force between A.D. 200 and A.D. 600. These monks brought their chant with them. As found today, the Buddhist rite, given by a precentor and novices, includes intoned utterances and responses, with occasional interruptions by single instruments. The chant tends to focus upon notes within a small compass and includes characteristic trills. As the chant proceeds, the pace increases, overlaps occur, and instrumental interruptions become more frequent. The accompaniment consists entirely of struck instruments (large drum, large bell, gong, cymbals, triangle, small bell, and 'wooden fish'). As we saw in the previous chapter, Indian melody is characterized by its decorative features (*gamakas*) which these early monks, adopting the Chinese zither (*ch'in*), introduced where there had formerly been only a more static and restrained music. The music of the zither has into modern times been played in a descriptive and impressionistic way – whence the style which uses glissandi, portamenti, staccati, open and stopped notes, harmonics, and no less than twenty-six kinds of vibrato.

The word *ch'in* literally means to 'prohibit', that is, 'to check the evil passions, rectify the heart and guide the actions of the body'. It became, *par excellence*, the instrument of philosophers in their meditations: for it embodied a whole system of cosmological knowledge which governed every detail of its measurements and construction; to learn to play it was, moreover, a comprehensive discipline and it might never be approached without due ritual preparation. Whilst its five or seven strings are tuned in the five-note scale, that is, agreeably to the cycle of fifths, these same strings are stopped according to a quite different principle. Along its fingerboard are a number of studs so disposed as to draw from any given string a series of notes which derive not from the cycle of fifths, but from an ascending and a descending harmonic series. Historically speaking, we associate the two systems, the cyclic and the harmonic, with different civilizations: the cyclic with Chinese, Pythagorean, and perhaps Megalithic generally; the harmonic with Mesopotamian, Indian, and European. It is therefore interesting to find them combined in a single instrument. This could have been the result of the Indian Buddhist influence. Some *ch'in* music is traditionally assigned to remote antiquity (e.g. to Confucius' time), though it is difficult to substantiate the claims made because no early notation survives. There was, however, apparently some kind of notation for the zither (*ch'in*) as early as the second century B.C.

During this period the tones of Chinese speech were first classified by Shen Yüeh (441–513). The Chinese language is ultimately referable to a limited number of monosyllables and, according to the inflection given to it, a given monosyllable may have several different meanings. The chief neumes (directions of pitch in the pronunciation of a monosyllable) are level, rise, fall, and enter, and a heightening of these tonal accents encouraged the development of the art of melody in song.

Around the same time (A.D. 485) dancing became an official part of the Confucian ceremonies. In a surviving Confucian hymn of six stanzas, we know that the dancers performed during three, holding a flute or wand in the left hand and a pheasant's feather in the right. In each stanza they took up thirty-two positions. These positions were based on the calligraphy of the poem in the sense that the calligraphic symbols were really the neumes of the words and hence in their own way repeated the shape of the melody inherent in the words. It is difficult to imagine a more highly integrated art than this, in which words, music, and dance come so closely together. As the ancient *Record of Rites* says: 'Poetry expresses the idea; song prolongs the sounds; dance enlivens the attitudes.' Words, music, and movement also combined in the Chinese marionette plays. These imitated early ritualistic ceremonies, but were secular entertainments, and represent an early stage in the growth of Chinese music-drama.

Meanwhile, from the fourth century, Chinese musical resources were considerably enriched by foreign influences. Following the destruction of the kingdom of Kucha in Turkestan in 384, China imported the Persian harp, the cymbals, and some new forms of drum. The Court developed a special taste for foreign national music and by 581 was entertaining 'the seven orchestras'. Bands came from Kucha, Bokhara, Samarkand, Kashgar, and elsewhere. Indeed the Court began to maintain permanent ensembles playing in foreign national styles, and between the middle of the sixth century and the end of the ninth the music in favour in Court circles was usually 'barbarian'. To some extent this served as a stimulus to China's own music, but more so to that of Japan, as we shall see in the next chapter.

THE LATER MIDDLE AGES
(7th–13th centuries)

With the T'ang dynasty (618–907) China entered a peaceful period when her arts thrived and, after some upsets during the period of the Five Dynasties (907–60), reached a high point of refinement during the great cultural age of the Sung (960–1279). This whole period was indeed something of a golden age in Chinese music.

Confucian ritual melodies of these times survive only in the editions of a later period. They present much the appearance of the medieval European *canti fermi*, striding along as it were in equal semibreves, usually in groups of eight. The treatment of such material naturally varied according to the resources of a particular shrine or temple; these resources sometimes reached elaborate proportions for, in addition to voices, we read of one hundred and twenty zithers (*ch'in*); one hundred and twenty zithers (*sê*); two hundred mouth organs (*shêng*); and twenty oboes, together with drums, bells, and chimes.

Judging from data gathered and reconstructed by the famous Chinese musical scholar Prince Tsai Yü in the sixteenth century and from other sources, we can form some idea of how this music may have sounded. The choir sang the hymn to a melody consisting of the semibreves or holding-notes, each syllable being sung to one note. In unison with the voices the wind instruments and bell-chimes were played, the reed mouth-organ (*shêng*) perhaps playing one inhaling minim and one exhaling minim. To each of the semibreves, the two types of zither (*ch'in*, *sê*) played sixteen semiquavers, thus helping to define the duration (*tsao-man*). This strictly-measured music is in great contrast with the rhythmically elaborate Hindu music. The mouth-organ, and to a lesser extent the zithers, played in two-part harmony whose intervals were always confined to fourths, fifths, and octaves in a style not unlike that of the earliest medieval European organum. Between and before the verses of the ritual hymn (and sometimes between lines), other instruments were added to punctuate, and to transmit sounds, including the stone-chime; large bell; large drum and 'tiger box'. When all these instruments were sounding together, with the voices holding the long notes, the tone-quality must have attained a subtlety completely unknown to us. For the Chinese ritual music was essentially a music of timbre or of the interplay of tone-qualities, which can help to explain why in Chinese music there is no harmony but the very simplest; because the sonorities would be obscured by further harmony, which would seem crude as compared with the inner harmonies – or harmonics – already so richly present.

The total effect of a Chinese classical hymn, performed in its proper surroundings, with every instrument constructed and played in accordance with the demands minutely prescribed by symbolism, must have been a profoundly impressive experience. To extraordinary subtlety was undoubtedly united great clarity, and clarity is one of the outstanding features of Chinese music as a whole. It was indeed the tonal expression of the Confucian maxim: 'the noble-minded man's music is mild and delicate, keeps a uniform mood, enlivens and moves. Such a man does not harbour pain or mourn in his heart; violent and daring movements are foreign to him.'

Though melodies for the *Book of Songs* reach us only through manuscripts of a later period, a single manuscript survives from the T''ang dynasty and was found in the Thousand Buddha Caves. It is the earliest Chinese music manuscript yet to have come to light. It includes what looks like a ritual orchestral suite in eight continuous movements built on an 'extended melody' (*ta-ch'ū'*) – a structure not unlike a rondo and found in music from T''ang times onwards.

During this period the Chinese empire was of great extent and it was open to all kinds of foreign influences. The music of the Courts was further enriched by 'barbarian' music and now included orchestras from India, Bokhara, East Turkestan, Mongolia, Tibet, Cambodia, Burma, and Annam. In the time of the Emperor Hsüan-tsung (713–56) there were six standing and eight sitting orchestras indoors as well as an outdoor ensemble of over thirteen hundred men. A troupe of three hundred actors known as the 'Pear Garden' was founded by the Emperor Hsüan-tsung in 714, and some melodies still found in the Chinese theatre are attributed to him. One from the music drama *The Little Shepherd* is a kind of dramatized folk-song in the five-note scale and two-four time.

The T''ang poets, as well as writing poetry to be sung, adopted the short lute (*p'i-p'a*), an instrument of central Asiatic origin which had first reached China during the Han dynasty. They composed programmatic pieces of a kind which China has long favoured in its chamber music. Such pieces are still popular and *The Last Battle of Hsiang Yü*, which survives in the current repertoire, makes use of slides and strange percussive sounds brought about by crossing the strings to depict the various phases of the battle. Its many different kinds of technique are said to have been derived from the zither (*ch'in*), and the short lute is indeed the only instrument to have rivalled the zither in popularity. It is now far more commonly found. It employs the seven-note scale, and among its resources are chords played in repetition, and an accompanying bass part (more or less serving the purpose of a ground-tone).

A notation for the short lute survives from the Sung Dynasty (960–1276): it was written by the Taoist poet-musician Chiang Kuei, who also left *Nine Songs for* (*the people of*) *Yüeh* in which he employs both seven-note scales and – new to Chinese music – nine-note scales in which some microtonal intervals occur. This is the earliest period from which printed music survives, including some melodies for twelve poems from the *Book of Songs* which their transcriber, the Confucian philosopher Chu Hsi, attributes to a T'ang source.

During the Sung there were some moves towards a popular theatre. Imitating the puppets, entertainments by 'flesh puppets' consisting of singing and dancing began to appear in the streets. The Songs of the South (*Nan-ch'ü*), as they later came to be called, derived their words from the banquet music of this epoch, gave them strictly five-note scale melodies of their own, and in the music (*chin-yüeh*) chiefly employed the cross-flute (*ti*) to support the voice. The Songs of the North (*Pei-ch'ü*) derived both words and music (in seven-note scales) from the banquet music and were open to the foreign musical influences of the north; the voice was chiefly supported by the short lute. The lyrics of both types of songs were in a special verse-form (*tzu'*), whose lines were of irregular lengths and whose syllables succeeded each other in an ordered pattern of tones which employed the four neumes mentioned previously. The form provided a variety of types of melodic structure which could serve as moulds for new poems. From these elements the true opera or music-drama of China was soon to develop.

MONGOL INFLUENCE
(13th–14th centuries)

Early in the thirteenth century China was attacked by the Mongols under Genghiz Khan, though it was not until the time of his grandson Kublai Khan that the conquest was anything like complete. China paid a heavy price for its Yüan Dynasty (1283–1368) in terms of lives, but among the benefits received was the encouragement given by the Mongol Emperors to music; moreover, they introduced new musical instruments and new scales.

The theatre also grew apace and its ensemble came to be known as *Yüan ch'ü* ('Music of the Mongol dynasty'). During this time the first complete music dramas or operas emerged, settling down in the northern and southern styles which have remained more or less fundamental into modern times. At first the northern school (*tsa-ch'ü*) was more prominent until the closing years of the thirteenth century. Its dramas often had four scenes consisting of action (mime and pantomime), declamation in recitative, and metrical songs. The verse-form for each song was indicated by means of a song-label (*ch'ü-p'ai*), and was chosen as appropriate to a particular dramatic situation.

Since the verse-form was associated with a particular scale-mode, it developed a kind of association not unlike that which we found in the moods of the Indian *raga*; and as the number of melodies was smaller than the number of lyrics, a given melody gave the listener a broad clue to the dramatic situation. In the closing years of the thirteenth century the northern and southern styles became mixed and a work might include acts in both styles, whilst towards the end of the Yüan dynasty the southern school became dominant. Five works from this dynasty survive and are still played, especially by amateurs. In these dramas, a particular theme (*ya-ti*, lit. 'elegant flute') is used something in the manner of a leading-motif, to express a certain feeling, such as joy or anger, and its related situations.

THE MING DYNASTY
(1368–1644)

In due course the Chinese overcame the Mongols and continued with a new dynasty of their own, the Ming (1368–1644). A system of equal temperament was successfully worked out in 1596 by Prince Tsai-Yü, a great scholar who left a most valuable nineteen-volume *Handbook of Music* covering the art in theory, practice, and history. His formula for equal temperament appeared a full century before the same formula was reached by Werkmeister in Europe. It seems, however, to have attracted little subsequent notice in China.

There are many editions of zither tunes extant from the Ming dynasty. By the beginning of it many of the most famous seven-stringed zither tunes were already in existence, though most of them are played in later (Ch'ing) versions today, where some of the note-values are altered. These are very charming pieces having that same pictorial and programmatic sense which we have already noted. They are of two main types. The structure of the smaller tunes (*hsiao-ch'ü*) follows that of the *ch'ü* melodies which we have discussed in opera, and words are commonly sung by the performer as the tune is played. The larger tunes (*ta-ch'ü*) are purely instrumental and in these compositions, which may last as long as twenty or thirty minutes, the melody is of a higher order, the structure having something in common with that of the rondo. As the player dwells on the different notes of the melody he creates the sense of different tonal centres, so that to the western ear there is no monotony in this music. Actual modulation from one key to another is rare, but it is occasionally used for a special effect; this is brought about by introducing notes outside the five-note scale so that a five-note scale at a different but related pitch temporarily holds sway. The rapid scale-passages in the five-note scale can evoke a harmonic effect, rather like western arpeggios. The various tone-qualities of the instrument are constantly brought into play: sliding notes are characteristic, and harmonics are much used, especially in the coda (as in the short pieces) and at the climax where they help the music to take flight.

In the latter part of the dynasty, towards the middle of the sixteenth century, drama was enriched by a new style of singing founded by Wei Liang-fu. His *K'un-ch'ü*, that is, the songs of the men from Kunshan, are still occasionally played by professionals in Nanking and Peking. Revising the works of the southern school, Wei Liang-fu superseded the previous music dramas by introducing operas lasting several hours and consisting of well upwards of thirty acts, mostly in the southern style. The length of the work was matched by the number of its singing roles, which might be as many as six. The successive acts were planned with due regard for alternating the narrative declamation (prose recitation) and the song (metrical poem). *P'i-p'a Ch'i, The History of Lute-playing*, composed or recomposed about 1530 and still a very famous play with music attributed to Wei Liang-fu himself, has more than a hundred arias alternating with sections in dialogue. The harsh attack of the voice in performance is characteristic, and the *falsetto* style assumed by men singing female parts, dating from the creation of separate troupes for men from the end of the dynasty, became a normal feature of the classical style. Men and women actors were in fact kept separate in China until the end of the Empire (1911).

The melodies sung in the Ming dynasty were not always syllabic, as had been the case with Chinese song since antiquity, but were sometimes melismatic and possibly of more popular origin. The time was two-four or four-four, each with a strongly accented first beat. The principal instrument of the *K'un-ch'ü* style is the cross-flute (*ti*), which continues to play between stanzas in a kind of *ritornello*, while the voice picks up the melody again at the next stanza. The flute may be supported by guitar (*san-hsien*) and short lute (*p'i-p'a*); and other flutes, a mouth-organ, and oboe-type reed are sometimes added. Percussion instruments always play an important part, the ensemble being led by a hoop-drum (*pan-ku*). There are also gongs, cymbals, and percussion sticks. Changes of scene and beginnings and ends of acts are indicated by energetic interludes for percussion alone, these being used conventionally to mark off one section or even stanza from another.

THE CH'ING DYNASTY
(1644–1911)

The progress of drama apart, the Ming dynasty was not a very creative period. Indeed the ritual music of Court and Temple had degenerated and, despite one or two attempts by various emperors to reintroduce something of the ancient splendours, it seemed as though China had completed a cultural cycle and her musical life continued to decline until the end of the Empire. Even the classical drama had reached a low ebb by the nineteenth century. During this century a more popular and more vigorous movement became active. Drawing to some extent upon the northern classical tradition, it created a body of operas called *ching-hsi* ('plays of the capital', i.e. Peking, the Manchu capital). These are the most commonly found of the pre-Republican operas in China today. The *tz'u* verse-forms were replaced by symmetrical melodies and in addition to the two-four and four-four periods of Chinese classical music we find music in three-four time, no doubt of folk origin. The instrument of accompaniment is a one-stringed fiddle, usually a *hu-ch'in* of some kind.

Long before this, however, Europeans had begun to visit China. Even late in the previous dynasty, a work on the clavichord by Matteo Ricci had appeared in China. During the Ch'ing dynasty various Europeans visited the Imperial Court, Pereira and Pedrini among them, and the latter built musical instruments for the Chinese. Père Joseph Amiot was the first European to write a work on Chinese music in 1780. Western music also began to be heard in China, though it was a long time before it came to be appreciated by the Chinese.

During this dynasty there appears to have been at least some influence of Chinese music upon European. In the eighteenth century a Chinese mouth-organ (*shêng*) was brought to St Petersburg and its free reed was introduced into Europe generally by a German organ builder. At the beginning of the nineteenth century a new group of western instruments was based upon the free reed principle, of which the mouth-organ and accordion are in current use. Later, the principle was applied to the keyboard, and the harmonium (1840) is indebted to it. During the rise of Romantic music in Europe, chinoiserie was one of the results of the exotic influences to which composers were open, and we find Chinese 'local colour' in works even from the time of Weber, whose overture *Turandot* (1809) makes use of an actual Chinese five-note melody from the work of Père Amiot.

But the extent of China's musical influence in the west has been nothing as compared with that in the east. Its stimulus and legacy to the whole of the Far East has been paramount, and on this we shall have frequent occasion to remark during the course of the next three chapters.

REPUBLICAN CHINA
(From 1912)

The year 1911 saw the end of the imperial house which had ruled China and fostered her music for several thousand years. Her traditional music was then far decayed and now is in danger of disappearing. There is no court music; the ritual Confucian music exists only, if at all, at the temple of Chenchu, the home of Confucius. As regards Taoist music we have hardly any information, though Buddhist celebrations are still to be met with here and there. The serious study of folk-song has hardly begun. The classical plays are still occasionally found, though more among amateurs today; the nineteenth-century drama is far more frequent. The minstrelsy of the streets and music-halls provides light fare of very doubtful value. Instrumental music is rarely to be found in its classical forms. Players of the philosophers' zither (*ch'in*) are rare indeed, and some other forms of zither are getting rare, though the short lute (*p'i-p'a*) is still to be heard.

And such traditional music as now survives tends to come more and more under western influence. In Imperial China western music was still hardly appreciated. But many of the now passing generation were educated in Europe and returned to China to teach there; European teachers followed; western artists toured the main cities. China has now a number of symphony orchestras on western lines. At last the Chinese came to accept western music, very often in place of their own, and this has no doubt hastened the decay of the traditional forms. Moreover, at a popular level western music has mixed with Chinese music to produce hybrid forms, especially in music for the films.

The Japanese occupation of Manchuria inspired various new forms of music. Songs were composed for bricklaying, road-building, and other occupations, and patriotic students created China's first unison songs. Choral singing was in fact completely new to Chinese secular music, but it rapidly grew in favour and has latterly found its way into opera. The new operas also include both male and female singers, producing their voices in a variety of styles, not infrequently including that of the west. Western instruments have been added to the accompaniment, especially strings, and western harmony has been adapted, not altogether unsuccessfully, to the five-note tunes.

But as well as combining with Chinese music in its lighter forms, western music has evoked different reactions from those who feel a responsibility for their own higher culture. It has stimulated them to record some of the surviving classical music and to seek out and begin to transcribe ancient manuscripts. Among serious composers, some see the future in using their own instruments, others in a national school of music using international instruments. The Chinese composers writing music on western lines have as yet made little or no mark internationally; and those who are serious about their traditional theory will have to face the problem of reconciling its demands (those of a cyclic system) with those of the quite different (harmonic) system of the west. But Chinese musicians have an ancient tradition and a highly distinctive mode of musical speech and should, in the long run, have something important to contribute to the modern world. Throughout their history, their capacity for absorption has always been great, though the influences now reaching them seem different in kind from any which have previously come their way.

5. Japan

INDIGENOUS TRADITION

IN the New Stone Age Japan was peopled chiefly by a non-Mongoloid race called Ainu (perhaps from about 2000 B.C.) whose descendants still linger in the North Island; and later (first millennium) by a people who early separated off from the Mongoloids of north Asia, the true ancestors of the modern Japanese. Ancient Japanese society was tribal, its religion spirit-worshipping; and its ritual observances contributed much to the religion later known as *Shinto* ('Way of the Gods').

Shinto chant, sung chorally in the austere temples, within a narrow melodic compass, was at first apparently in free recitative, though it became more formal in later times. It is characterized by a slow trill between notes a tone apart, a feature still to be found in Japanese recitative. Since antiquity Shinto chant has been accompanied by a bamboo flute, *yamato-bue* ('national flute'), and a mellow-toned six-stringed zither, *yamato-goto* ('national zither') – instruments which, in contradistinction to their other flutes and zithers (differently constructed and of Chinese origin), the Japanese regard as indigenous. The origin of this flute they trace to their sun-goddess Amaterasu who, ravished by the sounds of a zither made by a god from six long-bows, came forth again from her cave to restore light to the world, bringing dance and music to mankind. This myth underlies the scenes enacted in the Shinto temple song-dance called *kagura*. At least since the time of the Emperor Ichijo (A.D. 987) this has been performed to the accompaniment of the two instruments and a diminutive oboe called *hichiriki* ('sad-toned tube'). Later forms of the *kagura*, such as the modern temple benedictory dance, have added large drums of Tibetan origin (*o-kakko*, braced spool drum) and of Chinese orgin (*o-daiko*, cylindrical drum). The Shinto ritual preserves the earliest traditions in Japanese music and its style has always tended to remain distinct.

Indigenous tradition may also be sought in the songs popularly known as *Saibara* (*Saiba-gaku*) which, though performed at the Imperial Palace in historical times, originated in early Japanese folk-music.

One of the three five-note scales of Japan, and perhaps the least used, is found especially in the folk-music and may also go back to ancient times. This scale divides each of its two disjunct fourths into a tone and a minor third, thus (ascending): do, re, fa – sol, la, do. It could easily be mistaken for the Chinese scale of the Ming Dynasty, but such a scale was not prominent in China until after the early Chinese influence on Japan (now about to be described) had ceased.

FOREIGN INFLUENCES
(3rd–8th centuries)

The Stone Age in Japan ended with the arrival of metal from China (at first through Korea) from the latter half of the first century A.D. The Japanese early showed a capacity for adopting the useful features of other civilizations and this has helped to mould their musical history.

As early as A.D. 291, it is believed, Chinese musicians and instruments reached Japan following the conquest of Korea by the Empress Jingo. In the early fifth century there was some influence from Korean music itself, and in the mid sixth century Japan began to adopt Chinese ceremonial music through the Korean court. This started with the teaching of Buddhism, which had centuries previously reached China from India, and the Japanese Buddhists had a chant from their earliest days. Buddhist cantillation includes the singing of elaborate groups of notes to single syllables. From the end of the sixth century and at intervals until as late as the twelfth, young Japanese musicians went to China and Korea to seek out music in these countries, and early in the eighth century a Musical Office (*Gagaku Rio*) was attached to the household of the Emperor Mommu for studying the music they brought back. In 728 there is evidence of Manchurian influence, and in 736 Indian dances found their way from China to Japan.

Ancient forms now extinct in India are still played in Japan, including those of Siladitya, King of India – among the earliest instances of music-drama in the world still to survive. In 752 some hundreds of these foreign musicians performed at the unveiling of a huge Buddha at the Todaiji temple of Nara; and many of the instruments actually used by them on this occasion are still preserved in the Shôsôin Treasure-House at Nara. Buddhism was a strong organizing force and there seems little doubt that the orchestras of Japan were first developed in connexion with it.

LEFT MUSIC AND RIGHT MUSIC
(9th century)

By the ninth century foreign music and dance in Japan was so varied – Indian and Chinese, Korean and Manchurian – that Japanese musicians began to classify it and to adapt it to their own needs. Material of Indian and Chinese origin they called Left Music, and material of Korean and Manchurian origin Right Music – left and right in reference to the direction from which the dancers entered the stage. Both kinds of music employed three percussion instruments. Two of these they had in common, namely a large drum (*taiko*) and a gong (*shôko*), whereas for the third Left Music had the drum *kakko* (Chinese) and Right Music the drum *san-no-tsuzumi* (a Korean form of the same instrument). Similarly both kinds of music used two stringed instruments: a lute (*biwa*; cf. Chinese *p'i-p'a*) and a zither (*sô-no-koto*), their function being to embroider the melody. The melody itself was played by a third group, the wind instruments, and these differed very much in the two classes of music. Right Music had only two: a small flute (*koma-bué*, from Manchuria) and a diminutive oboe (*hichiriki*); and these played different melodies together somewhat in the style of medieval European organum. Left Music, on the other hand, had three wind instruments. Two of these, a medium-sized cross-flute (*ôteki*, from China) and oboe (*hichiriki*), performed in unison, whilst a reed-mouth-organ (*shô*, cf. Chinese *shêng*) added harmonies with six-note chords. Used as multiple drones, these create a soft ambience, rich in harmonics, in which the notes of the melody move and find their right emphasis.

EMERGENCE OF THE COURT DANCE
(10th–12th centuries)

The aristocracy much favoured the Buddhist music of foreign origin. And during the Age of the Court Nobles, Buddhist music became the music of the Court itself, both for ceremonial use and for diversion at imperial banquets and on other occasions. This aristocratic and elegant art was known as *Gagaku* ('graceful music'). It came to embrace several different classes, of which *Bugaku* is the classical court dance of severe character, and *Sōgaku* a form of orchestral music with or without dancing. *Bugaku* survives in Japan and is still occasionally performed there publicly today.

When music is transplanted to a foreign environment, as much of this had been since early centuries, it tends to stand still and largely to preserve its original character, and there is no doubt that Japan still keeps some of the oldest musical traditions in the east, long since obsolete in India, China, and Korea. But when music remains in its own environment, it normally continues to unfold. And so it was that the foreign music so popular in Japan at this period gave a new stimulus to the ancient Japanese indigenous forms. The music of the Shinto temples took on a new lease of life with the song-dance *Kagura* already described; and the monkey dance (*Sarugaku*) was connected with it as a sort of parody from the early eleventh century.

It was not long, however, before the formal music of the aristocracy began to decline, and new forms found favour. During the next six centuries, under the conditions of a military government and the cultural leadership of the Buddhist priests, there developed a music of the Japanese people which evolved many of the characteristic forms surviving today.

THE GROWTH OF MUSIC DRAMA
(13th–17th centuries)

The Nō Plays

The Age of the Warriors (*Samurai*) from the thirteenth to the fifteenth centuries brought a new cultural environment, and towards the middle of the fourteenth century emerged the dramatic performances called *Sarugaku no Nō*, a name commemorating their origin in the monkey dance (*Sarugaku*) already mentioned. *Nō* (lit. 'talent', i.e. display of talent) or *Nōgaku* was from the beginning a serious form of music drama played variously in the Shinto temples and open-air theatres in river-beds. The Nō plays are Buddhist in underlying intent but make use of scenes from ordinary life. They are, in fact, intermediate between the sacred and the secular, restrained and idealized in presentation, and some of the actors are masked. Among the most famous texts are those of the fifteenth-century writer Seami (e.g. his *Atsumori*), written around the time when this art was reaching its peak. The extant Nō texts include about 300 from before the seventeenth century, and some 250 plays are in the current repertory.

The music of the Nō plays is called *Yokyoku* or *Utai*. It consists of solo song by the actor-singers, unison choral song, and instrumental accompaniment by a cross-flute (*yokōbué*) and three drums. Its distinctive style of dramatic song (*naga-uta*) alternates recitative with aria. The rhythmical basis is provided by the various drums: a small hand-beaten shoulder-drum (*kotsuzumi*); a large hand-beaten side-drum (*ōtsuzumi*); and a large stick-beaten drum (*taiko*). Throughout the play a measure of eight beats or sixteen sub-beats is maintained or implied, and into these beats (*hyoshi*) all the words have to be fitted. As the verse-structure tends to a distich of twelve syllables unequally divided into seven- and five-syllable lines (a standard metre of Japanese poetry) the voice frequently moves across the ground rhythm, syncopating it and varying it in many ways. The voice may be accompanied in unison by the flute, and at the close of an aria it slides down from the finishing note to make a conventional ending.

The recitative favours a note of constant pitch; the aria is based on standard melodic patterns comparable in some ways with the Indian *ragas*. The scale is five-note in its major-third form – one of the important scales of Japanese music later to be described – and the traditional vocal style, containing features of ancient Buddhist origin, varies the main intervals of the scale with smaller intervals, through the use of slides, vibrato, and other refinements.

The Kabuki

In about the seventeenth century, Nō drama became essentially an art for the aristocrats, and in the early years of that century, O Kuni, a woman dancer from the shrine at Izumo, began to expand and popularize the Buddhist dances, to the accompaniment of flute and drum. The new popular form was called *Kabuki*, and around the year of O Kuni's death (1610) a women's Kabuki theatre was formed. To the flute and drum was added a guitar (*samisen*). This gave the music an entirely different character; and it may have been thence that three guitars were later added to the 'orchestras' of the Nō plays.

The Kabuki theatre had at first an interrupted career. The women's acting could not have confined itself to artistic appeal as in 1629 the women's Kabuki was suppressed on grounds of immorality. About 1630 it was succeeded by a young men's Kabuki. In 1652 this suffered a similar fate. Kabuki, however, continued in various forms; about 1680 playwrights began to write specially for it, and around the turn of the seventeenth century this people's theatre reached its peak.

THE RISE OF CHAMBER MUSIC
(16th–18th centuries)

During the sixteenth century new forms of music became prominent, and these forms had deep roots in the past. As early as 1254 a Japanese Buddhist priest brought a vertical bamboo pipe (*shakuhachi*) and its music from China, and with the help of this instrument his successors travelled spreading the

Buddhist gospels at street corners. Warriors (*samurai*), endangered by the civil wars, came to join these wandering monks for the protection it assured them, and the instrument became widely used from the end of the sixteenth century. It has five holes and its scale is identical with the ascending form of the 'hard' scale in Japan, later to be described. By means of special blowing techniques, largely dependent on the angle of the lips, subtle shades of pitch and sliding sounds are also produced.

The chief influences in Japanese music of this period lay, however, in a quite different direction. The decline of the warrior class following a prolonged period of peace, and the growing influence of the bourgeois class favoured the rise of a purely secular art. Vocal and instrumental music became the order of the day.

Japan had already enjoyed solo songs long before the sixteenth century. It could look back to the songs on Chinese poems in the Age of the Court Nobles, and still enjoyed the Buddhist recitations of long romances and war-stories to the sound of the lute (*biwa*) which flourished especially during the Warrior Age. But after about 1560 a new instrument reached Japan. The long-necked three-stringed guitar (*samisen*) was introduced from the Loochoo Islands which had received it from China about two centuries earlier. Japan gave the guitar a large plectrum (*bachi*), and used it not only to pluck the strings (variously tuned in fourths and fifths) but also to produce percussive sounds (*bachi-oto*) by striking the skin-covered 'box'. Musicians, inspired by literature and folk-music, soon used the guitar as an accompaniment to the voice, and in this role it quickly overshadowed the lute. It is perhaps the most popular of instruments today, being found especially among street musicians and accompanying the ballads and dances of the geisha girls.

KOTO MUSIC AND JAPANESE SCALES

The third instrument to become important at this time was the *koto*, a zither some six and a half feet long, having thirteen

strings, played with ivory plectra attached to the thumb and
the index and middle fingers. The instrument is laid on the
floor and the player squats on his heels before it. This instrument, quite different from Japan's own *yamato-goto*, had been
long previously imported from China and in a form known as
sô-no-koto associated with the court dance. After some improvements in its form, it suddenly rose into popular favour in
the seventeenth century through the genius of a blind musician
called Yatsushashi (1614–85) whose piece *Rokudan no shirabe* is
still extant. It was first much played by women who were
learning it about the time when English girls were practising
the virginals.

The *koto* rapidly became the national instrument of Japan.
It is played solo or as an accompaniment to the voice. The solo
pieces take the form of variations (*dan-mono*). Each variation
(*dan*) has fifty-two bars (*hyoshi*) though the first may have
fifty-four and the last fifty. More common (until recently) than
the solo music were the compositions for *koto* and voice (*kumi*);
the *koto* is really the basis of these; it continues throughout and
in the stanzas (*uta*) on which the form is based the voice part
accompanies the *koto* rather than vice-versa. The *koto* and the
voice are essentially in unison, though some interplay occurs,
for instance the *koto* keeps the rhythm going when the voice
holds a note. Two-note chords (*awaseru*, lit. 'to put together')
at almost any interval in the scale are occasionally added, not
for harmony as we know it, but rather to increase the sonority
and by way of emphasis.

The *koto* tuning is based on a five-note scale spread out over
about two octaves. The fundamental form is seen in the strings
of the koto from string no. 5 (the tonic) to string no. 10 (its
octave) when tuned in *hirajōshi*, the normal tuning. This is the
'soft' scale made up of two disjunct tetrachords (intervals of
a fourth) each of which is, in descending, divided into a major
third and a semitone – a principle of division known to the
Greeks as enharmonic. The notes are (descending): *do*, *la♭*,
(*si♮* in ascent), *sol – fa*, *re♭*, *Do*. This, Japan's chief musical
scale, differs from the Chinese five-note scale with its tones
and minor thirds.

In the 'hard' scale (as found in the Japanese national anthem) the tetrachords are divided differently: ascending, *Do*, *mi♭, fa – sol, si♭, do*; descending, *do, la, sol – fa, re, Do*. The bridges over which the strings of the koto pass are movable and thus re-tuning is easily effected. On a koto tuned in semitonal five-note scales ('soft' scale) the 'missing' notes are filled in by varying degrees of pressure on the strings. The style of playing is severe but includes three types of melodic graces involving shades of pitch of less than a semitone. Thus the two notes dividing up the tetrachords, apart from changing their positions according to ascent and descent in the soft and hard scales, have a flexible and movable character according to the need of musical expression. This is characteristic of Japanese music and can lead the listener to mistake the five-note scale for seven-note scales. True seven-note scales nonetheless also exist in Japanese music: the minor *ritsu* (with *mi♭* and *si♭*) and the major *rio* (with *fa♮*) – an ancient scale having early affinities in Mongolia.

MODERN FORMS AND WESTERN INFLUENCES
(From the 19th century)

In 1868, the military rule, now very corrupt, was banished. The feudal system was brought to an end. The changes which occurred around this time profoundly affected the existing musical traditions. The *Nō* became less exclusive and the *Kabuki* less traditional. The wandering monks ceased to be a protected class and their bamboo pipe (*shakuhachi*) became more widely used, and is now found in trios with the guitar (*samisen*) and zither (*koto*). Buddhist ritual music and folksong (*Oiwake*) continued, though the latter again influenced classical singing at the end of the century.

At the same time, the Meiji Restoration aimed deliberately to open up Japan to the influence of the modern world, and musically speaking the results have been far-reaching. The Japanese army organized its bands on British army models. Western vocal and choral music were taught in schools. The piano and organ were adopted. A Government Academy of

Music was founded in Tokyo for the teaching of western music, and latterly western aesthetics and musical history have found a place in the curriculum. There were at first many Americans among the teachers; Europeans followed; Japanese musicians studied in the west. Tokyo and the larger cities have built up western symphony orchestras and now most if not all types of western instruments are being manufactured in Japan itself.

Many Japanese composers have adopted western styles and some are writing works of real promise which have found their way into European music festivals. The seven-note scale has naturally assumed greater importance, equal temperament has been perforce adopted, and the twelve-note system has been imaginatively treated in a way that could hardly have been foreseen from a study of its use among western musicians. Kojiro Kobune (b. 1907), Yoritsume Matzudaira (b. 1907), Makoto Moroi (b. 1930), and other Japanese composers, while wholeheartedly adopting western methods and materials, have managed to remain thoroughly Japanese in spirit as to some extent in their use of forms, and thus to be true to the essentials of their own culture. Japanese musical culture appears in fact to be repeating its own history and to be undergoing a cross-fertilization at least as remarkable as that which took place between the seventh and ninth centuries.

But not all Japanese musicians look towards the west. There are two important schools for the teaching of traditional music. And between the two poles – the wholly western and the purely Japanese – yet other possibilities are being realized. Traditional musicians are trying to evolve new media of expression, and are experimenting with orchestras consisting wholly of Japanese instruments but inspired by western methods. This too is paralleled in the revival and renewal of indigenous Japanese forms under foreign stimuli a millennium ago.

Japan is the only country in the Far East where such a marriage of cultures appears to be taking place knowingly and on a significant artistic level. Its full results have yet to appear.

6. Tibet

INDIGENOUS TRADITION

THE Tibetans are a Mongoloid race more nearly akin to the Mongolians and Burmese than to the Chinese. Living away from the trade-routes of the ancient world, in a country whose average height is three miles above sea-level, they have developed a musical culture unique in the civilized world. The tradition which regards the Tibetans as originally a pastoral people is not belied by their love for that most pastoral of all instruments, the whistle-flute (*glin-bu*).

Their ancient religion was a form of shamanism (spirit-worship) known as *Bon* and it still has many adherents called *bon-po* in eastern Tibet. Its priests, today regarded as mere sorcerers cultivating demons and celebrating fertility rites, employ simple incantation and chant, make eerie calls on a trumpet (*rkan-dun*) of human thigh-bone, and clapper hand-drum (*rna-ch'un*) formed of two half-skulls in the shape of an hour-glass. The Tibetan word *dun* means equally 'trumpet' and 'bone'; and since these instruments are virtually unknown elsewhere in Asia, they are most probably indigenous. The Tibetan frame-drum (*lag-na*), whose relatives are found among shamans in India, Siberia, and the Arctic (Greenland), doubtless also originated in what was for Tibet a prehistoric time.

INDIAN INFLUENCE AND THE LAMAIST LITURGY
(7th–13th centuries)

Tibetan history becomes clear from the time of King Strongt-sam Gampo (613–50) who married two princesses: one from China and one from Nepal. Both were Buddhists, but Lamaism, the present religion of Tibet, grew chiefly from Buddhism of Indian provenance, with a liberal assimilation of *Bon*. The contact was at first through Nepal, and perhaps through ancient Khotan where a grotto carving of the small Indian cymbals could equally have been one of the cymbals (*rol-mo*) still used in Tibet. Direct Indian influence, from the eighth century to the thirteenth, brought into Tibet another hour-glass drum (*damaru*) – this time a wooden variety; the hand-bell (*dril-bu*; Indian *ghanta*), held in the left hand by lamas to symbolize wisdom; the conch (*dun-dkar*), used as a ceremonial signal; and the ram's horn (*rwa-dun*) of exorcism.

On the other hand, the monastery oboe or shawm (*rgya-glin*) is, outside the monasteries, called *surna*, a name which connects it with Persia, and it plays a seven-note scale; and the shape and decorative style of the 12- to 16-foot-long monastic trumpets (*rag-dun*) compare with those found in thirteenth-century Arabian and Persian manuscripts. Iranian influence certainly reached Tibet through Muslim elements in neighbouring countries and (perhaps from the eleventh century) through India.

At some stage the developing Lamaist liturgy brought together all these instruments (aboriginal, Indian, Iranian, and perhaps east Asiatic) and, probably with elements from Indian Buddhist chant, created a music suited to the services in the monastic temples. Today this music consists of prayers and scriptures, hymns and psalms, sung variously in rapid syllabic recitative and slow sustained metrical chant. The singing is in unison, and deep voiced – fully an octave lower than one would normally expect; and it is sometimes supported by a choral drone (like some Byzantine chant), no doubt based on an idea of Indian origin. The singing is supported or varied by orchestral accompaniment and interlude.

In contrast to Chinese ritual music, there are no stringed instruments in the orchestra at all, only wind and percussion. Two long trumpets, blowing in alternation, hold a drone like an eternal solemn organ-pedal; the oboes play an expressive melody like the panorama of events in passing time; while the percussion instruments lend their grave measures to the sound. Add to this the sudden calls of the smaller trumpets, thigh-bone trumpets, and conches, and the result is a timbre unique in music. The monks move their arms in gestures, and by the light of butter lamps a highly ritualistic atmosphere is evoked. The sound is far from sensuous in appeal. On the contrary, the seven or eight classes of instruments are said to portray the different sounds heard inwardly by yogis in meditation and so, in ensemble, they are said to aid devotion. The Tibetan name of the Tibetan Book of the Dead, *Bardo Thodol*, literally means 'Liberation by Hearing on the After-death Plane', and it is unfortunate that so few details of the Tibetan science of music (*rol-mo rig-pa*) are available.

The Book of the Dead (or rather Craft of Dying) goes back in essence to the eighth century, but exactly when the classical temple music emerged as the tonal expression of Lamaism it is impossible to say. But its notation, a highly decorative system of neumes, was most likely first introduced at Sakya (perhaps from India) about the twelfth century.

MONGOLIAN AND CHINESE INFLUENCE
(13th–17th centuries)
AND THE MYSTERY PLAYS

In 1270, Kublai Khan, the first Mongol emperor of China, adopted Lamaism to help unify his empire, and in due course the Tibetan musical notation found its way to Mongolia and elsewhere. The large cymbals (*sil-snyan*, lit. 'the pleasant music') used by monastic abbots came from east Asia and have still been imported into Tibet from China in modern times.

Sometime during the following centuries mystery plays, popularly miscalled 'devil dances' (no doubt because of the masks worn by the dancers), began to be performed annually by the monks in the courtyards of the monasteries. These impressive spectacles, about nine in number, are designed not as entertainments but, like the medieval mysteries of Europe, for religious instruction, depicting as they do the growth of Lamaism and its triumph over the 'demons' of the pre-Buddhist religion of *Bon*. Lasting as long as three days, these music-dramas bring together many forms of vocal music, instrumental playing, and dance. A vast and probably exceptional number of performers was seen at Tin-ge in recent times: six pairs of thigh-bone trumpet players, five censer-swingers, two pairs of long-trumpet blowers, numerous skull-libationers, 100 maskers with small drums, 100 maskers with cymbals, 100 maskers with large drums, followed by ordinary monks shouting and clapping, and laity armed with guns and other weapons, forming a procession over a mile in length.

There is perhaps here an echo of the vast Imperial Court orchestras of ancient China; and Chinese influence, no doubt more vital after its own drama reached a peak under the Mongols (Yüan dynasty, ended late fourteenth century), can be traced in the costumes worn by characters who are historically Indian. The most likely time for these plays to have originated is following the efforts of Tsongkapa (founder of the Yellow Hat sect) to reform Lamaism, which by that time (early fifteenth century) had degenerated in the direction of sorcery and magic. *Trchimekundam*, the most famous of these plays, which concerns the Buddha yet to come, is attributed to the sixth Dalai Lama (late seventeenth century) who was a gifted poet, and the tales of the others are variously of Indian and Tibetan origin.

Chinese influence on Tibet, largely political and civil, has continued on and off into modern times. Musically speaking, Chinese affinities are therefore more marked in the secular than in the religious sphere. Small itinerant lay troupes perform scenes in sheltered gardens and willow-groves and the actors are, as the actors were once in China, all male, or occasionally (like the Kham troupe) all female. Their performances comprise historical scenes about the lives of kings (*rnam-t'ar*, 'biography') and dance-dramas (*achhe lhamo*). Though these are more popular than the mystery plays their subjects are nonetheless religious in intent. Dialogue and songs (solo or concerted) alternate, being usually accompanied by drums and cymbals in a style reminiscent of Chinese drama. In the 'two-men's songs' (such as 'The Pearl King') one man answers another in alternate but not identical phrases, using a specially harsh yet strangely exciting tone of voice. Sometimes one holds a drone and when, as occasionally happens, their phrases overlap, splendid open harmonies alternate with sudden impressive unisons (as in 'The Lion of the Moon'). The dance-dramas show marked Chinese influence, and even direct borrowing as in the dance based on that most Chinese of creatures the dragon.

POPULAR FORMS

Household occasions call for music in Tibet and troupes of professional musicians often provide for them. The songs of welcome, good wishes, and love are of an expressive and lively nature and well reflect the gay-heartedness of this lovable race. Their little bands which accompany, or play alone, comprise drums and, in complete contrast with the temple orchestras, flute and stringed instruments (fiddle, lute). Typically the melody is outlined on a plucked string (lute) and elaborated or embroidered by flute and fiddle each in its own way. This creates a kind of variegated unison ('heterophony') also to be found in music of the Arabs and indeed over a large area of the East. The lute of Tibet (*pi-wan, pi-ban*), like those of China (*p'i-p'a*) and Japan (*biwa*), is linked by its name with the Arabic world, though the Tibetan four-stringed fiddle is carved with a horse's head which connects it with a legend still current in Mongolia whence, perhaps through China, it originally came.

Song-dances (*glu-gar*) enliven the Tibetan calendar festivals, and are found among caravanners there. Folk-music flourishes everywhere. Grass-cutters, coolies, log-carriers, winnowers, and field labourers all have their own songs, and the solo (leader)-and-chorus structure is not infrequently to be found in them. Short melodic phrases of restricted compass are (with endless variants) repeated over and over again; with that inherent circular quality which leads not to a final note but inescapably back to the first, they help to carry the labourers on over long and weary stretches of time.

While the religious music favours the seven-note scale (Indian or Iranian) of the oboes, the secular and folk music prefers the five-note scale (Chinese type) in its various modes. Some old tunes may actually be traced to Mongolian and Chinese origins.

Though western-type bugles, a legacy from British military

bands, are found in Tibet alongside the native bugle *mag-dun* (from *dmag*, 'army' and *dun*, 'trumpet'), Tibetan music has so far been less affected by western music than that of most countries in the east.

In high isolation, and under the guiding hand of Lamaism, Tibet has fused together many elements from Islam and the Near East, from China and the Far East, from the sub-continent of India, and from her own aboriginal tradition, and in so doing has made a distinctive contribution to the world.

7. South-east Asia

SOUTH of China, and east and south of India, lies a further sub-continent – south-east Asia – which has developed a distinctive and genial music of its own, best known through the chime-orchestras and dances of Java and Bali. This immense region is part mainland – Indo-China (Annam, Cambodia, etc.), Siam, Burma, and Malaya – and part island – the East Indies of Indonesia (including Sumatra, Java, and Bali). Racially speaking the area is exceedingly complex, and as early as Middle Stone Age times (perhaps 5000 B.C.) was already the home of three racial groups: Australoids (aboriginal), Melanesoids (from central Asia), and Negritos (possibly from India). These primitive strains which still underlie the present population are more conspicuous in the dark-skinned flat-nosed peoples of isolated areas, such as the Temiar people of the Malayan jungles, whose spirit-inspired songs and dances are among the most primitive in the whole region.

The upper racial layer is due to two main immigrations. The first of these peoples (variously called Indonesian, Nesiot, or pre-Malay[1]) originally came from further west, chiefly via central Asia (incorporating Caucasoid and Mongoloid elements on the way) and brought with them a New Stone Age, a bamboo culture, and agriculture. Their type predominates in the various Miau peoples scattered over the high plateaux of south China and Annam, whose antiphonal courtship songs, in which boys and girls answer each other in alternate phrases, challenge comparison with those in the ancient Chinese Book of Songs (Chou dynasty 1050–255 B.C.) to which we referred in Chapter 4. Their stone-chimes also link them with ancient China, and their reed mouth-organ (*khen*) is related to the Chinese *shêng*.

1. Also called by some authorities 'proto-Malay', thus confusing them with the Southern Mongol people, mentioned below, to whom the term otherwise refers.

The latter instrument is frequently four feet in length; its six pipes are played in groups of two or three at a time in a kind of primitive organum of fourths and fifths. The Laos of Annam play fourteen-piped instruments in melody, or in rudimentary polyphony with a strong harmonic feeling.

The mouth-organs are but one of a whole armoury of bamboo instruments found in many parts of south-east Asia. Perpetuating a very ancient tradition a number of these instruments are connected with the agricultural methods and rites of peoples who have depended on rice for their survival since prehistoric times. Such, for instance, is the tilting bamboo (Jav. *taluktak*), made to sound by running water in the terraced Javanese paddy-fields. A hollow bamboo-tube, carefully cut as to its node, is arranged on a pivot so as to fill with water from the irrigation channel of the field above and, when full, topples over to supply the field below. Then, after discharging, it regains an upright position and its lower end hits a stone, thereby emitting a definite ringing note at regular intervals. The chief purpose of this is to warn the field-owners of any interruption in the flow, but the sound, appealing to the innate sense of beauty in these peoples, has caused them to erect whole series of bamboos of different sizes, so as to give notes of different pitch and, owing to the different frequencies of tilting, of varying periodicity. The result is a very melodious and rhythmically fascinating series of sounds. Here already we have a pointer to the modern south-east Asian orchestras of chimes and the fundamental texture of their music: sounds and rhythms so varied and combined as to weave an intricate pattern and in so doing to lose their separate identities like threads in a cloth. And if, falling under the spell of such sounds continuously heard throughout long days in the fields, man lends his voice to the ensemble in freely improvised melody – and for anyone with musical susceptibilities it is difficult to resist – a free creative element is added and the composition is complete.

The Sedang tribes (Annam) have gone further and, wishing to charm the spirit-guardians of their rice-fields, have made more elaborate hammer-struck hydraulic carillons (*tang koa*) of numerous bamboos in a frame, which sound out an enchanting music for months without ceasing.

After the rice has grown, it is stamped. In Siam and Indonesia a log or tree-trunk is laid on the ground and carved out with holes, into which the rice is put; and the village women stand around stamping it with their pestles. As the holes are of different sizes and shapes and the women pound with different speeds and stresses, the result is a charming symphony of tones and rhythms echoed by a native poet in the line: *tintung tutunggulan gondang*. Here too we have the musical elements of the orchestra (*gamelan*), and a suggestion of how music might have come to be so important in the structure of south-east Asian society. Delighted with such sounds and rhythms, and perhaps seeking out those which gave most pleasure, the natives in early times no doubt found a rudimentary musical system. There are already signs of this in the stamping-block music (*bendrong*) connected with the fertility rites and performed even when there is no rice to pound! On moonlight nights and at times of eclipse the women stand round a hollowed trunk and beat it at different points where, owing to different thicknesses in the wood, the sounds are different and combine in an intricate but purposeful pattern susceptible of formal rhythmical analysis.

Other bamboo instruments, though no doubt under the influence of later cultures, have taken the selective process further: the flute (Jav. *suling*); tube-zither (Jav. *ketung-ketung*, Balin. *guntang*); rattle-chime (Jav. *angklung*) and wood-chimes or xylophone. The xylophone is found throughout south-east Asia in various forms (Ann. *tatung*; Camb. *rang nat*; Siam. *ranat*; Burm. *pattalar*; Jav. and Balin. *gambang*) and it is the near relative of many chime instruments played today in the Indonesian orchestras. Its older traditions may be sought in the xylophone-playing of the music-loving Bataks of Indonesia. The xylophone has wandered far and wide, and its presence in Africa is directly due to early immigrations from south-east Asia in about the fifth century of the Christian era, as of the Hova people now living in Madagascar.

The bamboo culture was continued to some extent by a later

race (variously called southern Mongols, Paroeans, or Proto-Malays), an early offshoot of the Mongols of Asia who found their way from south China to Indo-China about the fourth century B.C. One of the two principal scale-systems of Indonesian music, called *pelog*, was evidently known to these Proto-Malays. Like the other system, to be described later, it is a five-note scale based upon a recognition of the octave; it divides the octave into five unequal steps, though it has seven loci for three different modes of the five degrees. The five steps are variable within certain limits, but the scale tends to two disjunct tetrachords each consisting of (descending) a major third and a semitone. Its chief mode is the form using conjunct tetrachords. At first *pelog* may have existed over the whole south-east Asian area, but as regards the instrumental music it is now dominant only in Bali and Java. Owing to lack or non-survival of a music theory, the principle behind this scale-system and the other main south-east Asian scale-systems related to it is unknown, though their intervals may be connected with the properties of struck chime-instruments. Certainly they are more strange to western ears than anything in the Orient. Yet they are just as natural to the people of south-east Asia (and their relatives to the peoples of north-west Brazil, Peru, Melanesia, and Polynesia), as are those based on the cycle of fifths to the peoples of China, Japan, and Pythagorean Greece, and those based on the harmonic division of a string to the peoples of ancient Mesopotamia as well as to those of India, Islam, and Europe.

These Proto-Malays are believed to have brought the first Bronze Age to south-east Asia over a millennium later than it reached China's Yellow River, and to them, no doubt, are due the earliest known instruments to have been excavated in Java and the islands, the large bronze gong-drums brought originally from Indo-China and south China and used as magic 'rain-makers'.

THE HINDU MILLENNIUM

The influence of China and the influx of instruments from the north has continued on and off throughout history with the southward expansion of Mongoloid peoples. Already, however, on the threshold of historical times, a new and important influence was to make itself felt.

From the second and third centuries A.D. Indian merchants, seeking spices, sandalwood, and gold, began to explore the vast territory from the border of China to the Indies and had, by the fourth and fifth centuries, turned the greater part of it into an Indian colony. Hindus and Buddhists followed, bringing their music with them, and from the fifth century petty Hindu kingdoms began to rise, each with its cultural and artistic life, raising these peoples to high civilization which in some cases lasted over a thousand years.

Annam

The early musical influences are sometimes very difficult to trace, especially in the north. Annam, for instance, while preserving evidence of Hindu influence (sixth to seventh centuries in the plastic arts), appears musically to have had more affinity with China, to which it was annexed from a century B.C. till the tenth century A.D. It had court orchestras like those of China for a long time, and its surviving instruments are largely descended from those of the T'ang dynasty (608–906) and later times.

Cambodia

The Khmer civilization of Cambodia (early sixth–early fifteenth centuries) more clearly owes its impulse to Indian culture. Its arts flourished when Hinduism and Buddhism existed peacefully side by side, especially during the first three centuries (early ninth to twelfth centuries) of the period of Angkor. The temples of this capital city, conceived as an image of the universe, tell us through their reliefs that numerous instruments, including the angle-harps, were played there in the cult of the God-King. Traces of this civilization survive in festivals and intricate dances, though Cambodian music keeps few Indian features today. It came under Annamese culture to some extent, but is more akin to that of Siam which, as we shall see, developed at a somewhat later time.

Burma

On the other hand, Burma, despite its Mongoloid racial affinities, is of all countries on the south-east Asian mainland culturally as well as geographically nearest to India. Its history as a unified people begins late in Indian times with the so-called period of Pagān (eleventh to thirteenth centuries). This ancient capital city, whose hundreds of ruined stupas and pagodas now lie half-hidden in a tangle of cacti, jujubes, and tamarisk trees, was once the scene of intensive building, great religious fervour, and strenuous military activity. All these are commemorated in the old war-dance *Kar-Gyin*, a solo-and-chorus song believed to date back to this time. To Buddhism, always its principal religion, Burma owes its liturgical chant – a form of a non-metrical recitative, half-spoken and half-sung, partly in Burmese and partly in an ancient derivative of Sanskrit. At puberty every Burmese boy participates in a novitiate ceremony followed by a period of separation, usually nominal today, from his former life. The ceremonial song is sung in a seven-note scale with a sharp fourth degree (a kind of Lydian mode) – a marked characteristic of Burmese music found also in the conical oboe (*Hne*) which, together with the drum, small cymbals, and circle of twenty-one gongs, accompanies the song. The little bands of Burma are reminiscent of India and the instrumental music keeps some features which long ago disappeared from the homeland. Especially important is the boat-shaped harp (Burm. *saun*; Siam., *soum*, lit. 'boat') of thirteen strings (seven strings until the eighteenth century) which plays in octaves, more or less decorated, and occasionally varied by fifths. Historically this elegant instrument is connected with the roots of Burmese music theory. It is directly descended from the 'celestial' arched harp, brought by Buddhists through Bengal in the Gandharva period (see Chapter 3). It evidently once found its way as far south as Java, though it quickly disappeared there if we may judge from ninth-century temple reliefs. The only similar harp today is found in some parts of Africa, where it evidently descended from Egyptian proto-types. The type of Gandharva times was already known in the earlier Indus Valley ideograph (third millennium B.C.) which we connected (see Chapters 1 and 3) with Sumerian civilization. Remembering the close affinity between Egypt and Mesopotamia in ancient times (Chapters 1 and 2) we no doubt have, in the surviving south-east Asian and African harps, distant links with musical life in the Near East upwards of four thousand years ago.

Java and Bali

Hindu influence was at first strong in Indonesia also, where it gained force rather later than on the mainland. Under the Sailendra dynasty of Sumatra the famous kingdoms of Java rose and the reliefs in Hindu temples and shrines from the later seventh or early eighth century up till 1375 well illustrate the musical instruments of the period. These, and especially those at Borobudur around the year 800, contain not only most of the native instruments which went to make up the orchestra (*gamelan*) of more recent times, but also numerous Indian instruments of the day, many of which appear to have gone quickly and completely out of use. There is little doubt that the instruments or ensembles found in the households of the ruling classes bore at first a largely Hindu character and in the tenth century there is other evidence for the existence of small ensembles such as drum, conch-horn, and crooked trumpet.

As regards the tuning, some instruments continued in the native (*pelog*) scale already described. Others adopted another scale, the *slendro* (or *salendro*), named after the Sailendra dynasty, and this is found in areas where this dynasty and its successors were a living force. Said to have been invented by the deity Batara Éndra by order of the Hindu god Siva, it was possibly adopted by Buddhists coming from Sumatra in about the eighth century. It is a five-note scale (with three different modes) which divides the octave into more nearly equal parts than *pelog*, namely into intervals of about six-fifths of a tone.

The intervals of *slendro* are still stranger to the western ear than those of *pelog*. To say that it tends to equal temperament may be to exaggerate; the excavation of older Javanese instruments relates it (as does the ear) more closely to the major pentatonic (five-note) scale (with intervals of a tone and minor third) which is not only Chinese but existed in the *raga*-music of India also. The two scales are, however, far from identical. While the Indonesians think of *slendro* as masculine, exalted, and severe, *pelog* appears as feminine, friendly, and sad.

One of the most influential factors in organizing music was the Sanskrit drama brought by the Hindus. The great epic *Ramayana*, already mentioned in Chapter 3, was freely adapted and translated into many south-east Asian languages and the performance of scenes from it early became popular in many parts of the sub-continent. It appeared in Javanese from the ninth century and there is evidence that plays were acted in Java from the eleventh century at latest. Alongside the performance of these dance-dramas were other performances called shadow-plays (*wayang*), believed to have originated before the Hindu came, the shadows of the puppets being thrown on to the ground (or a screen). These performances are still popular today, and, like the Indian *kathakali* dance, give scope for dancing and narrative song.

To a Javanese, singing and poetry are virtually inseparable. Poetry is classed according to its mood, and each mood-class (such as love and fighting) has its own metrical form. In Javanese songs many of the ancient Indian metres are still current.

Dancing has found its highest expression in Bali. The dances there are acts of worship or part of traditional ceremonial as well as figuring in the plays.

The dramas were not always drawn from religious mythology, however, and sometimes they presented romanticized or imaginary local history. A dance-drama called *gambuh*, played in fourteenth-century Javanese, still survives in one village (Batuan) in southern Bali and its orchestra may be somewhat like the orchestras of that early period: flute (*suling*), drum (*kendang*), metal drum (*kenong*), and gongs (*kempul*), though its fiddle (*rebab*) is ultimately of Muslim origin (through India).

POST-INDIAN PERIOD

Siam

Hindu kingdoms existed as late as the fourteenth century (Majapahit in Java; Angkor in Cambodia) but by the end of the first millennium there were signs that Hindu influence was on the wane and that new movements were coming from the north. The Thai people, who had a flourishing kingdom of Nan Chao in China during the T''ang dynasty, gradually filtered into the land we now call Thailand or Siam during the Sung dynasty. During the period from the middle of the thirteenth century to the sixteenth, two kingdoms arose in Siam, which now became an important centre of musical culture. The Siamese scale-system has certain affinities with the two Indonesian systems already discussed. The octave is divided into seven more or less equal parts (seven-eighths of a tone) which serve as seven loci for a five-note scale. The melodies composed in it are structurally not unlike Chinese melody, and the likeness is greater when they are sung, since the singers tend to depart from these intervals in the direction of the Chinese five-note scale. The Siamese orchestras were of two main kinds whose pattern exists today: an indoor ensemble (*mahoori*) of softer-toned instruments including strings and used for wedding and other celebrations, and an outdoor ensemble (*piphat*) of louder-toned instruments (with more drums, but no strings) used for festivals and Buddhist ceremonies as well as on martial occasions.

The Thai may have absorbed something from the Khmer culture of Cambodia which from the ninth century extended to the Siamese plains, but in turn the Siamese subjugated the Khmers in 1431 and the orchestras of the present Cambodian court are similar to the Siamese, though smaller, and possibly representing an earlier form of them. Of the eleven instruments in each orchestra, five are chime-instruments and the remaining six are stringed instruments for the indoor ensemble (played by women) and percussion with one flute and one stringed instrument for the outdoor (played by men). The stringed instruments are very close to the Chinese and Mongol type (two- and three-stringed fiddles), and the male and female division is reminiscent of the Chinese Court of the T'ang dynasty (618–906).

The Mongol conquest of south-east Asia by Kublai Khan affected Burma more than most parts, and following the fall of Pagān, the Shan period (thirteenth to fifteenth centuries) saw the fealty of the Burmese to the Tartars. The Burmese have a class of 'Chinese airs' and their fiddles are similarly of Chinese and Mongol type; and a class of 'Siamese' airs which post-date their military struggles with Siam from the sixteenth century.

Of all regions in south-east Asia, the Sinic influence has remained most conspicuous in Annam, which again came under direct Chinese domination in Ming times (1368–1644).

Indonesia

Muslim influence was, on the contrary, stronger in the Islands. A Muslim state existed in Sumatra in the late thirteenth century and by the end of the fifteenth Java was predominantly Muslim also. The chief musical legacy is the *rebab*, a two-stringed Perso-Arabic spike-fiddle. This instrument leads many of the Indonesian orchestras today and is found very generally throughout the sub-continent. Other Muslim instruments had little influence on the art of music, though some were assimilated at a more primitive level. Islam is the principal religion of the Islands today and Bali alone has remained Hindu. Thus while Javanese music very quickly modified or lost its Hindu elements, Balinese music has kept much from older traditions. In the sixteenth century Javanese, who fleeing from Islam reached Bali, created the first musical notation native to south-east Asia. This is based on the vowels in the names of the five notes of the scale (*ding, dong, deng, doong, dang*); and indicates the rhythmical disposition of notes by giving the names of the metres.

But Muslim musical influence did not penetrate very deeply. The force of the Hindu culture was largely spent well before Islam appeared, and this no doubt enabled native Malayan elements to come forward and the more completely to assimilate and digest all that had been received from elsewhere. One aspect of this activity was the imitation of some of the newer metal instruments in bamboo. Exactly when the Indonesian orchestras (*gamelan*) began to assume their present form is very difficult to say, since we have no written descriptions devoted specifically to music until as late as the eighteenth and nineteenth centuries. The process is likely to have been gradual, perhaps from the time when, between the eleventh and thirteenth centuries, bronze casting began to show a sudden advance. All the main features of this native phase still appear unchanged in the orchestras of today which provide music for ceremonial, festivals, dancing, shadow plays, and martial activity.

The orchestras are, musically speaking, of three different types. Since the two scale-systems have only one note in common, different orchestras are needed for the *pelog* and *slendro* scales. Rich nobles of the Central Javanese principalities can afford to maintain two such gamelans (together with a third designed to play a 'royal arrangement', that is, to play a gamelan composition alternately in the two scale-systems). Villages can afford only one. Though humbler, the village orchestras are identical in principle with the largest court orchestras and are tuned in *pelog* or in *slendro* according to history and tradition rather than aesthetic preference.

THE GAMELAN AND ITS MUSIC

The most classical form of orchestra, the *gamelan angklung* of Bali, consists, with the exception of the drum (*kendang*), of tuned chime instruments: a curved xylophone (*gambang* – of metal or sometimes of wood); various bronze celestas (*gender*; *saron*; *demung*); gong-chimes (*bonang*); a pair of kettle-gongs (*reyong*); and a bamboo rattle-chime (*angklung*). All these instruments have fixed pitches. The larger Javanese orchestra known as *gamelang gong* adds to the above further instruments of percussion, namely single-tuned gongs and untuned cymbals, and a quite different group of more flexible melody instruments: flute (*suling*) and spike-fiddle (*rebab*). And for the singing of poems, a solo voice or chorus or both may be added as occasion demands.

A gamelan composition (*gending*) – of which there are over five hundred in the Court repertoire of Jogya (Java) alone – is always based on a broad nuclear theme, rather like a medieval European *canto fermo*, moving so to say in equal minims. This theme forms the lowest moving part of the texture and is played by celestas (*saron*) and sometimes by a gong-chime (*bonang*). Such melodies are based on the various modal forms of the five-note scale organized in a particular tonal pattern. In Bali a more severe four-note scale is often used. Each pattern (*patet*) is related to particular moods and shows some likeness to the Indian *raga*. Some patterns are believed to have a magical potency and their performance requires suitable preparation such as the burning of incense; such is the case with the *gending Kidung* which gave back speech to a hero in one of the shadow-plays. Some of these tunes are reminiscent of the most ancient Chinese ritual melodies and there are some strikingly close comparisons to be made. The main periods of a given nuclear melody are punctuated by the deep boom of the great gong (*gong ageng*) which serves as a kind of full-stop (regularly or irregularly) every several bars, while the smaller divisions are punctuated by the smaller gongs (*kenong*, *ketuk*).

The second element in the structure of a gamelan composition is the paraphrase of the main melody by various chimes (incl. *gambang*, *gender*, *bonang*), played at a pitch higher than that of the original melody. These chimes may keep fairly close to the main theme (e.g. repeat each note in half-time); or they may play a sort of hide-and-seek with the theme (by anticipation and delay), or vary the theme more decoratively with flourishes around it. The method is more or less prescribed by tradition, but it does allow scope for creative improvisation within certain limits. When played simultaneously, the several variants of the same melody create a kind of harmonic texture, though the harmonies are incidental rather than a separately conceived element of the music.

The texture is further enriched by a group of instruments forming a third and highest-pitched part in the ensemble.

These play figurations which help to fill in the texture and create a kind of ambience round the main theme, circulating round its strong striding notes like films of mercurial satellites round the planets.

To these three elements, which are normal in the orchestral compositions of Bali, the Javanese *gamelan* adds a further and more freely creative line. This is indeed a more or less independent counter-melody delegated to the flute and spike-fiddle (*rebab*) which, according to the special requirements of Javanese (and especially west Javanese) aesthetic, bring out intermediate notes and subtle variations in pitch. In large orchestras the zither also plays an important role.

The instruments playing the various elements in the composition may be divided differently from those given in the scheme above, for there is great variety in this music and they do not always play the same role.

The structure as so far described normally falls into a framework of two-time. Rhythmical variety is produced by subtle cross-accentuation by various means on the half- and quarter-beats. In this function a drum plays an important part. It indicates the changes in pace and moreover holds all the players together by its rhythmical initiative. In Bali the leading instrument of the *gamelan* is in fact usually the drum; in Siam and Cambodia it is the xylophone; while in Java it is the spike-fiddle (*rebab*) which usually plays the prelude and announces the melody on which the composition is based. Thus the *gending* proper is preceded by a kind of introduction where the players feel their way into the atmosphere with anticipatory fragments – a sequence reminiscent of Indian *raga* music.

The full range of sound of the largest gamelans covers six or seven octaves from the deep boom of the big gong to the tinkling of the highest celesta's smallest keys. In strong contrast with the solo vocal and chamber music of India (strings and drums), and far from the solo music of the Chinese zither or lute, the effect of an Indonesian orchestra is totally unlike anything else in music. Saturated yet translucent, vital yet subtle, it can be deeply mysterious or magnificently festive, and like running water is always changing yet always the same.

THE MODERN PERIOD

It may be surmised that the *gamelan* music of Indonesia reached its peak around the end of the eighteenth century or beginning of the nineteenth century. However this may be, it is certain that already long before that time south-east Asia was first touched by European music. Portuguese sailors of the sixteenth century have left popular melodies known as *kronchong*, so called after the small narrow five-stringed guitar of Portuguese origin.

By the seventeenth century Dutch merchants dominated the whole Malayan archipelago, and Dutch melodies and children's games from this and the following centuries are still sung, though this forms a very small part of music in the area.

Already in the mid eighteenth century there was a tendency for music to break away from its original religious connexions. Native rulers encouraged this and new and more popular forms came into being, as in the court dramas of Bali. In some of these western influence may indeed already be detected. Court dramas also came to be given outside the courts and were imitated in more popular forms. Love, politics, and popular themes figure in Burmese comic opera at the present time.

The guitar, mandoline, ukelele, and violin have all been imported into the sub-continent and are sometimes played in combination with native instruments. The piano became popular in Burma under British administration.

There is no doubt that the impact of western civilization is different in kind from anything experienced by south-east Asia in the past. Cultural influences from China, India, and even Islam were, it seems, easily assimilated, but western music seems incompatible in principle. Latterly, it must be admitted, it has tended in many quarters to become a substitute for native music, but virtually only in its most popular forms. In some countries the native tradition is seriously in danger, as in Siam where most composers show the influence of this impact deeply and where very few traditional composers remain. The tune now accepted by the Republic of Indonesia for its

National Anthem bears all too clearly the stamp of the radical change.

Perhaps actuated by the realization that their music might ultimately be lost, and to some extent inspired by the west, south-east Asian musicians have been experimenting with notation for some time. Musicians in Siam and Burma have tried to adapt western notation to their needs. In Java, seven or eight different native systems have been evolved during the last seventy years, all of which aim at fixing the nuclear themes of the great *gamelan* compositions. In some systems the parts of the paraphrasing instruments have been added, and for instrumental music in central and east Java the *Kapatitian* system is now almost exclusively used. The objection that these instrumental parts would, if not so fixed, become too free seems unlikely in the stream of a vigorous tradition, and it is equally possible that fixing such parts rigidly might destroy the capacity to create beautiful paraphrases though the use of written notation by players in performance is in any case unusual.

Certainly there is still a great deal of orchestral music in Indonesia today; a census carried out only a few years ago revealed the existence of some 17,000 orchestras in Java and Madura. In Bali the number is probably relatively as great and every village has its own orchestra and its dance-group. And the music is still an entirely traditional and communal art, accessible to all, understood by all, loved by all – a striking element in the very structure of society, and with no recognizably individualistic traits as in the west. But, as the years go on, the sound of pounding, whether it be of rice or chimes, grows perceptibly less.

Legacy to Europe

The musical influence of south-east Asia on Europe, though slight, has had happy results. In the seventeenth and eighteenth centuries Dutch bell-founders, perhaps with some knowledge of the metal chimes in use in their recently won colonies, re-placed the bells in their keyboard carillons by bronze slabs, thus creating the *glockenspiel* which was already used in the orchestra by Handel's time (1738). In the late nineteenth century (1886), perhaps inspired by the resonant bamboos of a Javanese metal *gender* seen in Paris, Auguste Mustel invented the *celesta*. The *xylophone*, first referred to in 1511, was known of old among the Russians and Tatars, and its provenance in Europe cannot be connected with south-east Asia in any obvious way. The marimba of the Bantu Negroes in Africa, however, may be traced directly to the xylophone of the Malays.

As regards the influence of south-east Asian music on western composers, a *gamelan* was heard at the Exposition Universelle in Paris in 1889, and Debussy is said to have been deeply impressed by it. Latterly recordings of Indonesian and other south-east Asian music have been available in Europe and America, and European composers have visited Indonesia. The music of Benjamin Britten's ballet *The Prince of the Pagodas* makes much play with chime instruments and has come noticeably under this influence.

8. Ancient Greece

THE Greek-speaking peoples first arrived from Europe about 1900 B.C. and developed a Helladic culture. Fusing later with the Minoan culture of Crete, a country which had formerly been open to Egypt, this was succeeded by the Mycenaean culture in Greece, which after about 1400 B.C. became independent. The period from say 1400 to 1100, later referred to as the 'Heroic Age', was thus one of absorption, and to it we can possibly attribute the formulation of a number of myths concerning the origins of music which connect it with Egypt. Among these myths is that of the earliest lyre, *chelys*, said to have been invented by the god Hermes. The Cretan *hyporchemata*, or songs to be accompanied by dancing, gave rise to the Greek *paeon* (originally a magic cure dance) to Apollo.

Similarly the culture of Mesopotamia had, through Asia Minor, reached Thrace, and about 900 B.C. Greeks (Ionians, Dorians, and Aeolians) crossed the Aegean and settled in the islands off the Asiatic coast. The myths of the hero Orpheus, 'father of songs', came from Thrace; that of Linus, who gave verse and music to the Greeks, has a Mesopotamian parallel; while the semi-mythical originators of flutes and reeds, Hyagnis and Marsyas, as well as the legendary 'founders', 'inventors', and organizers of Greek music like Terpander and Olympus were all Phrygians from Asia Minor. Olympus is indeed said to have introduced about the year 900 B.C. the *nomoi* (plural of *nomos*, lit. law) or traditional melodic formulas on which the music of the reed-pipe (*aulos*) was based. Though it is difficult to distinguish the historical elements in such myths and legends, when taken together they nonetheless indicate an extensive Egyptian and Asiatic contribution to the foundations of music in ancient Greece.

THE AGE OF THE EPIC
(8th–7th centuries B.C.)

By the eighth century B.C. the Greek alphabet was already in existence; the epic poems attributed to Homer (about 850 B.C.) appeared – the *Iliad* is regarded as the beginning of European literature; and a new national culture arose in Greece. Taking the epic poems on the exploits of the gods and heroes as their materials, bards who were privileged minstrels resident in the houses of aristocratic families sang them to the sounds of the lyre in a conventional recitative style which made the poetry and music one in execution as it must have been in conception. They used the traditional melodies (*nomoi*), which may have been short phrases repeated with suitable variations over and over again.

The lyre, played by the fingers or a plectrum, doubtless served to pitch the voice and inspire the singer by playing a prelude and interludes, though it is unknown whether or not it provided an accompaniment during the actual recitation. This instrument (*kitharis*, later *kithara*) consisted of strings (from 3 to 12) of equal length, stretched vertically between a lower sound-chest and an upper cross-bar supported by two curved arms inserted at their bases into the sound-chest. A less elaborate form (*lyra*) was common among amateurs for domestic music-making.

Alongside the poetic declamation by the professional bard, there is evidence for the existence of a folk-dance and music, typified by the shepherd playing the pastoral panpipes (*syrinx*) to his flocks. But we know more directly of the music of the community at large, represented by the choruses of citizens (variously men, women, boys, and girls). These choruses sang in the cults of the gods (paeons, dithyrambs, and procession-als); wedding-hymns; funeral-laments; pieces in celebration of famous men and victorious athletes; and for every social occasion. Amateurs, these singers were accompanied by the professional bard on his *kithara*. In place of this instrument, or sometimes in addition to it, might be found the reed-pipe called *aulos*. This instrument was especially associated with the worship of Dionysus (Bacchus) whose cult spread throughout Greece with the cultivation of the vineyards. An oboe, often found as double oboes set at an angle and originally coming from Asia, this instrument had an exciting sound which stood in marked contrast with the restrained music of the lyre.

In ancient Greece music embraced both poetry and dancing, and the stress of the dancers' feet was intimately reflected in the rhythms of the music. Not only dancing but also athletics are known to have had their musical accompaniment in Homer's time.

Musical competitions are said to have formed part of the festivals and games held from very early times, though the first undoubted fact is that Sacadas of Argos won the reed-pipe contest in the Pythian festival held in honour of Apollo at Delphi in the early sixth century. Similar competitions in music and poetry were included in the Carnea at Sparta as well as at the Panathenian Festivals.

THE RISE OF LYRIC POETRY
(7th–5th centuries B.C.)

While the poets long continued to praise their gods and honour their heroes, it was not long before they also began to sing of love, war, politics, and other popular themes suitable for the occasions of private and social life. Their lyric poems were so called from their being sung to the lyre, and the music to which they were sung was created simultaneously with the poems. The lyric poet-musicians are now known only to us as poets, because unfortunately not a trace of their music remains. The lyric impulse came from Ionian Greece and found an early champion in Archilochus of Paros (*fl.* about 714 to about 616 B.C.) who sang convivial, colloquial poems into which, possibly drawing some inspiration from folk-song, he introduced triple rhythm and quick tempo.

The lyric movement found its first centre in the Dorian culture of Sparta whose strong community life favoured choral forms. Tyrtaeus (*fl.* till 668 B.C.), as well as singing poems in

elegiac metres, composed patriotic marching-songs (*embateria*)
for the Spartans who took reed-pipe players with them into
battle; while Alcman (*fl.* about 615 B.C.) is remembered for his
Parthenia or choral dances for Spartan maidens. Stesichorus
(632–552 B.C.), however, devoted himself to more formal poems
which still harked back to the old mythology.

The Aeolian dialect was favoured by the lyric poet-musicians of Lesbos, a Greek island in the Aegean Sea off the coast
of Asia Minor. Their art was more personal and was usually
composed of monody, that is, for the single voice. The noble-
man Alcaeus (*fl.* from about 611 B.C.), first of the Aeolian poets,
was a soldier who sang warlike odes and, like Sappho (*fl.* about
600 B.C.) who wrote in a great variety of metres and Anacreon
(about 550 to about 465 B.C.), may have drawn upon the materials of local folk-song.

How exactly the lyre was used in accompanying the poems
in this and the succeeding period it is very difficult to know,
though a description written in a later period by Plato (429–
347 B.C.) suggests that the instrument elaborated the vocal
melody, a practice which may well go back to this time. The
sung poem was the essential part, but the lyre, starting from
the same melody, might either play it literally or embroider it
melodically and rhythmically according to artistic sensibility
and skill.

In addition to their lyres the Greeks had a harp (*magadis*) of
trumpet-like tone and, with its twenty strings, large enough to
be played in octaves. When boys' and men's voices sang in
octaves it was, after this instrument, called 'magadizing'. The
magadis, and its smaller forms the *pectis* and *barbitos*, could play
the finer intervals of Greek music.

CLASSICAL MUSIC AND THE RISE OF DRAMA
(6th–5th centuries B.C.)

Towards the close of the sixth century and early in the fifth,
Athens became the main centre for poet-musicians who created
a classical style, which during the fifth century found its principal outlet in dithyramb and drama.

The dithyramb probably originated in the Dionysus cult, for in the sixth-century festivals the Birth of Dionysus was danced and sung to the reed-pipe by a circular chorus of fifty men or boys.

The earliest dramatic performances arose from the same source, and it was in the field of drama that music now found its most important development. The plays – tragedies and comedies – were essentially musico-dramatic pieces, their creators being poet-musicians who had been trained as such in the elementary schools. All three elements – poetry, music, and dance – were combined in them, and they were played by versatile actor-singer-dancers in the outdoor amphitheatres.

The poetry was accented tonally rather than stressed by syllable, and was variously rendered in speech, recitative, and song. The melody was partly conditioned by the pitch-accents of the words, that is, by the melody inherent in the words, and the musical rhythm was based on the quantities of the syllables. It is in fact very doubtful if there was any real distinction between the musical rhythms and the poetic metres.

At first the music consisted exclusively of choruses. These were either unaccompanied or were sung with the reed-pipe (*aulos*) or, occasionally, with a single lyre, since great care was taken to avoid obscuring the value of the words. Later monodies, that is, parts for solo voices, were added, especially in the tragedies. As regards the dance (*orchesis*), this was performed by the chorus in a special place in front of the stage. This place was called *orchestra* and when, with some supposed remains of Greek drama before them, Italian poets and musicians gave birth to opera around the year A.D. 1600, the term *orchestra* came into general use in Europe for the first time.

Important among the classical dramatists was Aeschylus (524–456 B.C.), composer of the *Persae*, who was the first to introduce a second solo actor into tragedy, thus creating dialogue. This naturally tended further to limit the choral parts. The tragedian Sophocles (495–406 B.C.) was a good dancer and musician, while in Euripides (480–406 B.C.) we find a more realistic and rationalistic art; of the music of his *Orestes* (408 B.C.) we are told that it did not rise and fall with the speech accents, and that the melody of its paired verses, strophe and antistrophe, was identical. Perhaps the greatest Athenian composer, and certainly the greatest comedian, was Aristophanes (*c.* 444 to 380 B.C.). His plays parody the composers of his own and former times; he virtually describes the decline of the classical style due to modulation, chromatic tuning, and laxity as seen in the unstable style of playing on the reed-pipe; and he introduces popular metrical forms into his own works, as may be seen in the rhythmical refrains of some of his choruses. *The Frogs*, performed in 405 B.C., while appealing against the intrusion of uncultivated ideas, is at the same time prophetic of the decline of music in Greece. It appeared only a year before Athens fell in the Peloponnesian War and underwent an intellectual revolution which was to have serious results for its artistic culture.

MUSIC IN DECLINE
(4th century B.C.–2nd century A.D.)

Already in the late fifth century there had been signs of unrest among poet-musicians, with a developing taste for the sophisticated, popular, and more theatrical forms. The poets sought to give immediate pleasure and sensation rather than to produce balanced compositions. The dithyrambist Timotheus of Miletus (446–357 B.C., *fl. c.* 400 B.C.), for instance, introduced chromaticism and the smaller (enharmonic) divisions of sound, created intimate forms of vocal expression, and, attracted no doubt by the larger and more elaborate *kitharas* of his time, employed more music for instruments alone. Philoxenus (430–380) quickly followed. Their innovations, at first condemned, rapidly created a new vogue. They had few successors, however, and creativeness soon reached a low ebb. To make up for this, greater stress was laid on the quality of the performance, and from the fourth century the musician began to regard himself as an executant rather than as a composer. He found his true metier in the rearrangement and parody of well-known themes. The rise of virtuosity and cult of applause were the inevitable results.

Plato (429–347 B.C.), a true child of classicism, became the great critic of his age. The two main branches of learning in the Greek schools, together designed to give man a liberal education, were gymnastic (*gymnopedia*) or physical culture and music (*mousike*) or mental culture. The latter, which included singing, poetry, instrumental playing, dancing, and oratory, was clearly in decline. Seeing the innate qualities or ethical significance (*ethos*) of the different Greek scales (*harmoniai*), Plato looked back to the time when these were appreciated at their true worth. With Aristotle (384–322) he recalls the days of the ennobling Dorian, headstrong Phrygian, and effeminate Lydian. Plato believed classical music to be truly mimetic of nature, that is, mimetic of *noumena* or the principles of nature, not *phenomena*, and hence to bear an inescapable *ethos* according to its mode. And in outlining the ideal musical education of youth he refers to Egypt for his models.

The actual cult music of Egypt must have been known to an appreciable extent in Greece by this time. The historian Herodotus (*c.* 484–425 B.C.) tells us that Egyptian gods, ceremonies, and litanies were passed on to the Greeks. The Isis and Serapis cults, complete with their liturgies, hymns, chanting, wind instruments, and sistra, spread through Greece and later through the Roman Empire right into the west of Europe. Sistra have indeed been found as far afield as France.

By the time of the great theorist Aristoxenus (about 320 B.C.) the classical styles of Greek music had almost passed from memory. But new popular styles came to the fore. Among these the pantomime had long been important and its mummers gave a sort of variety show consisting of parodies and comic scenes, ballet, acrobatics, and crude jokes. Under its influence the drama now tended to disintegrate further and by the latter part of the second century B.C. even the popular classics of Timotheus and Philoxenus had been virtually forgotten.

Unfortunately the change of taste in Greek music around 400 B.C. occurred before the Greeks found adequate means of writing the music down, and when musical notation at last came to be used, spasmodically perhaps from the fourth century, the popular styles were felt to be hardly worthy of preservation. Moreover, the custom of improvising on the basis of the traditional melodies (*nomoi*) would in any case militate against preserving the music in any static or crystallized form. In effect, fewer than twenty fragments of Greek music have come down to us on stone and papyrus, and none is older than the second century B.C. when Greece was already undergoing conquest by the Romans (*c.* 200 to 30 B.C.). The earliest of the surviving pieces still seems to show a close marriage between words and music, although the poet-musician of earlier times had been succeeded by poets and musicians who had a limited understanding of each other's arts. The notation of the First Delphic Hymn, a paean to Apollo from the late second century B.C., was found on a stone at Delphi; that of the Second Delphic Hymn is the work of one Limenius of Athens (*c.* 127 B.C.); while that of the 'Epitaph of Seikilos' to his wife comes from a tomb at Aidin in Turkey and may date from the second century B.C. or later. Like all the surviving examples, it consists of a single line of melody.

But in general it seems that music had become mere entertainment. Hence the musician lost a great deal in social standing. The teaching of music reached a very low ebb in schools, and upper-class Greeks and Romans thought it degrading to have too much to do with practical music-making. This cleavage between citizen and professional brought about a divorce from which musical Europe still suffers at the present time. And the snobbery which attended it is still a familiar feature of our musical life. Though the citizen might not perform, however, it was very fashionable to *talk* about music. If he were incompetent in practice, he could nonetheless expound the theory, and under this vogue extravagant notions were developed about musical *ethos* which would never have been countenanced in Plato's day. That theory, or rather theorizing, had usurped the place of the musical art is seen for instance in Varro (116–28 B.C.), who uses the term *musica* no longer to mean Music but Harmonic Science, that is, the theories of intervals and tuning of musical instruments.

THEORISTS AND THEORY

Tradition assigns the origins of Greek music theory chiefly to Pythagoras (*c.* 585–*c.* 479 B.C.) who is believed to have brought back the principles of it from the Egyptian priests and perhaps from the Mesopotamian schools of learning and, forming a brotherhood, to have taught these principles as part of a discipline designed to bring moral uplift. The Pythagoreans conceived the musical scale as a structural element in the cosmos. The firmament was, moreover, pictured as a kind of harmony – the 'harmony of the spheres' – and tonal space was divided with the help of a single stretched string (*monochord*) in such a way as to reflect this harmony. Tireless in their experiments, the Pythagoreans left a knowledge of all the intervals now known to western music and many more besides. The most complete data are given in a work attributed to Euclid (*c.* 300 B.C.), and much information may be gleaned from the works of Plato (427–347 B.C.), especially the *Timaeus*.

Practising Greek musicians, however, by no means unaware of the role of the mind in defining their materials, naturally placed more emphasis on the evidence of their ears than on the mathematics of the speculative theorists. The important and most practical theorist Aristoxenus of Tarentum (*fl. c.* 322 B.C.) was the son of a musician and himself versed in the fourth-century music and that of the earlier classical tradition. His analytical works on the theory of music are of unique value.

Amidst the numerous writings on Greek music theory there is much that is obscure and much that is confused not least through the inconsistent use of terminology, not to mention much that the authors themselves did not fully understand. Moreover, Greek thought had in any case a strongly mathematical bias and indulged in speculation for its own sake. Much music theory, connected with number symbolism and astronomy, mysticism, and metaphysics, was later, particularly from the second century A.D., developed along lines which could have had few bearings on practical music, particularly as music was known in classical Greek times. This is not to say that no interesting discoveries came out of these speculations, but the discoveries were chiefly in other fields.

The works of some later authors are important for certain information they afford, including Plutarch (A.D. 50–120); Nichomachus (second century A.D.); Claudius Ptolemy of Alexandria (second century A.D.); Plotinus (A.D. 204/5–70); Porphyry (third century) and Iamblichus (d. 363). But the difficulties outlined above are among the causes which have made the study of Greek music theory one of the most formidable and unsatisfactory of all studies.

The essential data may shortly be told. The Greeks knew of the octave interval, which they called *diapason* (lit. 'through all'). But the unit of their tonal space was the interval of the perfect fourth (ratio 4:3), which turns out to be the natural leap of the human voice. Called tetrachord (*tetrachordon*, lit. 'four strings'), it was embraced by four strings of the lyre. The two limiting notes were conceived as fixed (*histotes*), and the two notes between them as movable (*kinoumenoi*). The movable notes could occupy various positions according to three different genera as well as being subject to subtle variation within these genera. The four notes of the tetrachord were counted from the highest to the lowest and not, as is more usual in western music, from the lowest to the highest.

Four notes necessarily subtend three intervals. In the *diatonic* genus, the most common of the three genera, the three intervals (read downwards) were: tone, tone, leimma. Leimma literally means 'remnant' and refers to what is left over of the interval of the fourth after dividing off two equal tones; it is in fact an interval smaller than the western semitone. In the *chromatic* genus the sequence of intervals was minor third, semitone, semitone. In the *enharmonic* genus, much used in Greek vocal music, it was ditone (interval of two tones), quarter-tone, quarter-tone or, and perhaps originally, ditone, leimma – that is, two intervals only, as in each tetrachord of the Japanese 'soft' five-note scale referred to in Chapter 5.

The ditone is one of the main features which distinguishes Greek melody from later European melody. This interval is slightly larger than the western major third and sounds sharper to our ears. The western major third, based upon a quite different division of sound, may have been used experimentally in the time of Didymus (63 B.C.), though Ptolemy (second century A.D.) is more usually regarded as the first exponent of it. The quarter-tones, known in Greece at least in the fourth century B.C., suggest that the Greek ear may have been more sensitive than ours. This would not be at all surprising in a people who, like many in the orient today, had no harmony (only heterophony) and relied upon the finer possibilities of melody for no small part of their musical expression. Subtle vocal inflections played an important part in Greek melody and the movable notes of the genera were regarded rather as centres of gravity than as fixed points.

The Greek tetrachord was further classified by the order of its three intervals. Thus, in the diatonic genus, three primary modes were formed according to whether the (descending) order were tone, tone, leimma (Dorian); tone, leimma, tone (Phrygian); or leimma, tone, tone (Lydian). Each primary mode had secondary modes. Those which lay above the primary mode were called *hyper*-modes and those which lay below were called *hypo*-modes.

This then was the material from which the Greeks built their scales. When two tetrachords were put together, either disjunctly with a tone to join them, or conjunctly with a tone to complete their downward series, the result was a complete octave-scale (*harmonia*). An octave-scale has only seven different notes – the eighth repeats the first – and, if each be taken in turn as a starting-point, seven different modal forms of the scale are possible in a given genus. Taking the white notes of the piano as nearly equivalent, the seven *harmoniai* in the diatonic genus are as follows (descending): a to A (Hypodorian, later Aeolian); g to G (Hypophrygian, later Ionian); f to F (Hypolydian); e to E (Dorian); d to D (Phrygian); c to C (Lydian); and b to B (Mixolydian, later Hyperdorian). The names of the *harmoniai* were drawn from the different districts of Asia Minor where these modes are said to have been in use, but the classification was varied, the names were changed at different periods, and the associations were sometimes based on slender connexions. The most important note was called *mese*, which was the centre of the Greek scale-system.

So as to embrace all the diatonic, chromatic, and enharmonic notes of the three genera within a single octave, the Greeks had a theoretical scale of twenty-one sounds to include all the possibilities. And so as to relate the seven octave-scales and tetrachordal groupings to each other, they had also a theoretical continuous two-octave system. But since the lyre had only a limited number of strings, any given scale had to be transposed so as to come within its compass – the compass of the Dorian Harmonia given above. Any such scale when transposed was called a *tonos* (pl. *tonoi*).

The sequences of notes in the octave-scales are sometimes referred to as modes, and for our purposes this serves well enough. But the Greek word for mode (*tropos*, pl. *tropoi*) referred to something of which such a scale was only the bare bones: it connoted a melodic style or idiom having a particular *ethos*. It was most probably more akin to the melody-type which we have seen in the Indian *raga* and elsewhere.

Greece's chief musical legacy to Europe was her written theory, and this had an important bearing on the medieval church modes. It was transmitted in fragments through the late Latin writers Boethius (about 480 to about 524) and Cassiodorus (about 477 to about 570) and, as we shall see in Chapter 10, somewhat more abundantly through the Arabic writers from the ninth century, following the Arabic domination of Spain. But long before this transmission began Greek musical art was a thing of the past.

9. The Jews

DURING the third millennium B.C. both Mesopotamia and
Egypt were, as we saw in the first two chapters, centres of
advanced civilizations. In the desert land between the two
countries various Semitic tribes lived as nomads and shepherds, singing of their struggle to survive. The prayer for water
must have been constantly in their minds, as witness the 'Song
of the Well' in the Book of Numbers; and in the desert today
the Bedouins still sing: 'Spring, O water, Flow in plenty.' In
both songs, the ancient and the current, the form is terse, the
rhythm accentual. The music of the Biblical song does not
survive, but when they repeat (with variations) a short pattern
of melody over and over again the Bedouins may be perpetuating ancient custom.

Early in the second millennium B.C. the Jews first separated
from other Semitic groups under Abraham who in about 2000
B.C. is said to have emigrated from the Mesopotamian city of
Ur into Canaan (Palestine). Jacob his grandson took the Jews
to Egypt for pasture and there, in contact with the cultures of
the Middle and New Kingdoms, they remained for over four
hundred years, finally becoming slaves. Then, about the
fifteenth (perhaps thirteenth) century B.C., they were delivered
by Moses and led into Canaan. According to Philo, Moses was
instructed in the sciences and in music by the Egyptian priests;
no doubt his people brought instruments out of Egypt's New
Kingdom together with many songs and tunes. The description
of the 'Song of Miriam' in the Book of Exodus suggests that
rhythmical body movements were inseparable from the singing
of their women-folk, as in the song-dances of Jewish women in
the Isle of Djerba (North Africa) today.

Miriam's song was accompanied by a frame-drum (*tof*),
usually called timbrel or tabret, which Arabic tradition attributes

to Tubal-Cain, the worker in brass and iron. Tubal-Cain was a kinsman of Jubal and according to Jewish tradition this latter was, if we take the most likely interpretation of the passage in the Book of Genesis, 'the father of all such as handle the lyre (*kinnor*) and flute (*'ugab*)'. The small lyre may have come from a larger Egyptian or Sumerian form; the flute was the instrument of shepherds and herdsmen. These three, tabret, flute, and lyre, were the common instruments of the Jewish people in their nomadic days. A further three were connected with their cults: a ram's-horn (*shofar*) blown in times of danger and repentance; a loud trumpet (*hazozra*) used as a signal; and – reminiscent of the Egyptian cults – bells or jingles (*pa'amon*) worn on the garments of priests for their powers of protection.

During the period commemorated by the Book of Judges (1200–1050 B.C.) the Jews began to conquer Palestine and to settle there as shepherds and farmers. Their new life inspired new songs of labour; dirges over the fallen; and, like the 'Song of Deborah', songs of triumph. The cults of the Mesopotamians, Egyptians, Phoenicians, and Canaanites flourished side by side in Palestine, and their ritual music was heard by the Jews at the local shrines. Until the tenth century B.C., moreover, musical instruments were still not made in Palestine but only imported from the Lebanon, Ophir, and other places outside, and when Solomon married Pharaoh's daughter a large number of instruments is believed to have reached Israel from Egypt. But already by the turn of the second millennium many tributaries of foreign culture were meeting in Palestine, so that when conditions were becoming secure enough for the Jews to develop their own culture they already had a rich and varied background on which to draw.

THE KINGS IN PALESTINE AND THE FIRST (SOLOMON'S) TEMPLE
(11th–6th centuries B.C.)

Under King David (reigned 1013–973 B.C.), its second king, Israel became a large and united nation with its capital in

Jerusalem. The royal Court had its own musical tradition from the beginning, that is, from the reign of the first king, Saul (1050–1013 B.C.), whom the young David is described in the Book of Samuel as soothing with his lyre (*kinnor*). Vocal music also flourished there and male and female musicians sang songs as in the other oriental palaces of the time. 'Royal psalms' marked the many aspects of court life, not only the enthronement and its anniversaries, but the marriage of the king, and his departure to and return from war.

During the reign of David's son and successor King Solomon (*c.* 973–933 B.C.) the Temple was built, about the year 950 B.C., in Jerusalem as the great focus for Jewish worship, and its services were designed as the expression of that belief in One God which stands at the core of Jewish religion. The ritual consisted of regular morning and evening sacrifices, together with the festivals of the religious year. The ritual music is said to have been organized by David, who was not only a performer but also a composer and, according to the Book of Amos, an inventor of musical instruments as well. He it was who appointed the men of the tribe of Levi to look after the music of the Temple services, and the Levites were regarded as a caste of sacred musicians. Women played no part in the ritual music.

The central feature of the Temple music was the singing of the psalms. Most of the psalms of the Bible are not as old as David and came only to be attributed to him in later times. At the same time, the Biblical Psalter preserves types which go back to Solomon's Temple: especially the psalms of praise (e.g. cxli), petition (e.g. xliv), and thanksgiving (e.g. xxx). Unfortunately the ancient music of the psalms no longer survives, but the nature of the poetry affords some clues as to what it might have been like. The unit is a single line divided into two halves by a weak or strong caesura. The number of accents in a half-line is normally three, but the number of syllables is varied. This accentual character of early Hebrew poetry brings it near to prose. The unit of the music is likely to have been a melody pattern based on a given interval, which could be freely varied in length and stress so as to allow for the accents and the changing number of syllables. And more than one such pattern would have been required for the two half-lines.

At first the psalms were probably sung by priests and Levites alone, though the congregation might answer with *Hallelujah* (as in Psalms civ to cvi), and some processional psalms for festival use (e.g. xxiv) suggest actual antiphonal singing. Psalms of pilgrimage (e.g. cxxii) were clearly designed for choral singing.

The chief instrument associated with the psalms and played by the Levites was the *kinnor*, the small lyre from Israel's nomadic days; lovingly do the Scriptures refer to its sweet and gentle tone. The big vertical angular harp (*nevel*), having ten strings, perhaps of Phoenician origin, is also mentioned and doubtless reinforced the tone as required. The lyre and harp thus assisted at the services and their role must have been to mark clearly the intervals of the melody patterns chosen for the particular psalms. There are some grounds for believing that the word *Selah*, often found at the end of a verse in the psalms (as in the third psalm, verses 2, 4, and 8), is an instruction for the playing of an instrumental interlude. Moreover, the temple singing may have been actually accompanied by the stringed instruments. The pauses were marked by copper cymbals (*mziltaim*; later *zelzlim*) held by the singers.

The shrill trumpets (*hazozra*) were used in pairs by the priests as a signal, and the penetrating tone of the ram's-horn (*shofar*) served a variety of ritual purposes. This latter instrument was particularly associated with sacrifice, and a Jewish myth traces its origin to the horns of the ram caught in the thicket which Abraham sacrificed instead of his son Isaac.

We may gauge something of the splendour of the ancient music and its effect on its hearers from a famous passage in the Second Book of Chronicles. There we learn that at the dedication of Solomon's Temple, a hundred and twenty priests blew trumpets and two hundred and forty-eight Levites sang and sounded their instruments 'to make one sound to be heard in praising and thanking the Lord; and when they lifted up their voices with the trumpets and cymbals and instruments of music and praised the Lord, . . . then the house was filled with a cloud . . . so that the priests could not stand to minister by reason of the cloud: for the glory of the Lord had filled the house of God.'

Instrumental music was clearly much favoured in these times and was also employed by the Prophets to help inspiration and ecstasy. As the Prophet Elisha listened to the king's minstrel, 'the hand of the Lord came upon Elisha and he prophesied.'

In addition to singing and instrumental music, dancing (*machol*) was at first important in the religious ceremonies. The Second Book of Samuel tells us that 'David danced before the Lord with all his might', though the custom appears to have fallen into disuse.

AFTER THE EXILE
(6th century B.C.–3rd century A.D.)

For nearly four centuries the Temple music continued without interruption, and the Court music flourished under a succession of kings. But in the year 587 B.C. Jerusalem fell to the Assyrian king Nebuchadnezzar. All at once the Jewish state was ended, the Temple destroyed, and large numbers of Jews were exiled to Babylonia. Many of them remained there and for many centuries lived in complete isolation from other Jews. The chant which they have preserved shows some remarkable similarities with the chant of other isolated Jewish communities who during the early centuries found their ways to various parts of the east, such as Persia and Yemen (south Arabia). These Jews are thus likely to have preserved some very ancient forms and their chant may contain elements which go back to the days of the First Temple.

The Second Temple

After the period of the Babylonian Exile (586–538 B.C.) many Jews returned to Palestine during the period of Persian domination (538–332 B.C.), bringing back their household singers, both male and female, with them. Corporate Jewish life was resumed, though naturally on a more modest scale than in former times. There was of course no longer any Jewish royal Court, and so no Court music. The new life found its principal focus in the Second Temple whose building was completed about 514 B.C. Services were held with music, and the families of Temple musicians claimed descent, as in pre-Exilic times, from Levi. The musical tradition had no doubt some such links with that of the First Temple. It is to this period that most of the psalms of the Bible belong, and their expression now centres round the devotions of smaller groups and individuals, unlike those of older time. We even know the names of some of the melody patterns on which they were sung. Thus Psalm viii bears the instruction: "To the Chief Musicians: upon Gittith', which means 'to be sung to the strain "Wine-press"' or perhaps 'to be sung to the strain from the town of Gath'. Antiphonal and responsorial chant now became more usual, the Levites or a precentor singing the first half-verse, the congregation responding with the second. This is important as one of the forerunners of Christian Church music techniques.

Towards the end of its time in the first century A.D., the Second Temple still had a chorus of Levites to sing the Psalms and portions of the Pentateuch. The minimum number of men was twelve, aged between thirty and fifty, and their period of training was five years. These might be joined by Levite boys 'to add sweetness to the sound'. The Temple orchestra consisted of a minimum of twelve players, playing nine lyres, two harps, and one pair of cymbals. On each of twelve festal days two *halilim* were added. Though *halil* is now the name given to a flute, the old *halil* was a double oboe of oriental or Egyptian origin, unknown in the services of the First Temple. A small pipe-organ (*magrepha*) rather like the panpipes (*syrinx*) seems to have appeared around the beginning of the Common Era.

As in the days of the First Temple, the precise relationship between Temple choir and Temple orchestra is unknown; the orchestra may have accompanied the choir, or it may have alternated with it, and we cannot rule out the possibility of its having performed both functions. In the Second Temple, as in the First, the trumpets and ram's-horn were used as signals and formed no part of the actual music of the services.

Sectarian Music

Alongside the music to be heard in the Temple, it is probable that the separate Jewish sects had some ritual music of their own. The recently discovered Dead Sea Scrolls, for instance, contain psalms of thanksgiving and other liturgical materials of one such sect, now believed to be the Essenes, which existed in the first century A.D., and the manuscripts contain some signs which have the appearance of a musical notation in neumes. If, as from comparisons with certain other early notation systems, the identity should come to be proved, these signs would belong to the oldest system of Jewish musical notation extant, though it is possible that others existed before it.

The Greek and Roman Periods

By this time Palestine, having submitted to Alexander in 332 B.C., had become part of the Greek Empire. Hellenic influences were, it is true, not very marked in the sphere of Jewish sacred music, but in the secular music things were very different. As we saw in Chapter 8, from the third century B.C. to the first century A.D. Greek music was characterized by its emotionalism, and there is no doubt that this kind of music enjoyed a considerable vogue among the educated Jews of the time.

From the first century before Christ the Romans began to occupy the region and in A.D. 6 Judea (southern part of Palestine) became a Roman province. The Romans had no cultural influence on Israel and indeed took a step which proved fatal for the Jewish State. In A.D. 70 under Titus they destroyed the Second Temple. For the next century or more, Roman persecution, internal revolts, and economic stress combined to make conditions very difficult and after A.D. 200 Jewish settlements in Palestine decreased. The close of the classical period witnessed that great dispersal of the Jews throughout the East and West which brought entirely new conditions for Jewish life and music, attendant upon the development of its main centres outside of Palestine.

Jewish Christian Origins

One group of Jews active from the first century A.D. calls for special mention here, namely those who became followers of Jesus, the Christians. The earliest Christian precentors were brought up in Jewish houses of worship and the beginnings of Roman Christian music, described in a later chapter, may in some measure be traced to that of the Hebrew Temple. Although no theory of Jewish music is ever known to have been committed to writing, the descendants of the Jews taken to Egypt in the fourth century B.C. to help people Alexandria played an important part in the development of Judaism and Christianity and in the formulation and perpetuation of materials which furthered the music of the early Christian Church, particularly that of the Byzantine tradition.

UNDER THE WESTERN SETTLEMENT
(4th–16th centuries)

During the early centuries after the dispersal the spiritual heritage of Judaism was gathered and compiled in writing, and it is from this period that such works as the *Talmud* and *Mishnah* come. There was no longer a Temple, but before the destruction of the Temple centres designed for worship on a smaller scale had already begun to spring up. This was the origin of the Synagogue. Levites, who were music leaders and teachers in the Temple, performed the same office in the early synagogues, and retained the traditional musical forms. The liturgy, which was the responsibility of a precentor, gradually developed in Palestine and Babylonia. The Rabbis, knowing the effects of the degenerate Greek music on their people, discouraged any contact with secular music. For this reason, and also as a defence against the pagan cults in which Syrian and Mesopotamian Jews were wont to participate, they discouraged and even forbade the use of instruments in worship. Indeed, the one instrument permitted was the ram's-horn which – later European influences apart – is the sole instrument found in the synagogue today. It is moreover used only on special occasions as a signal, its role since the most ancient times.

Vocal music, on the other hand, was actively encouraged and became a corner-stone of Jewish worship. Until the seventh century in Babylon vocal music appears not to have been communal and hence choral, but individual, because, with the dispersal, communal worship was on a much smaller scale and more emphasis was placed upon the individual. Under this stimulus two forms of vocalization became more important: the cantillation of the Bible and the cantillation of prayers.

The cantillation of the Bible was already known in the days of the Temple, whence it found its way into the synagogue. It is the oldest type of traditional Jewish musical practice extant. The reading of the prose was given with the help of a chant so as to aid the memory in study, and the chant was made up of a succession of melodic formulas. Each of these was indicated by means of a sign (*ta'amin*, 'accent') written above or below the text. Each sign conveyed a melisma or group of notes to be applied to the vowels of the reading, and this constituted a *neume*, the rhythm being dictated by the words. Neumes may already have been known about the second century B.C. and were later used by the Christians, becoming the basis of the early Christian hymns. The signs now known originated between the fifth and tenth centuries A.D., the three main systems being the Proto-Palestinian (fifth century) which has some affinities with Syrian neumes; the Babylonian (late seventh and eighth centuries); and the Tiberian Masorite (ninth and tenth centuries) which shows Byzantine influence. As the meanings of the signs were orally transmitted over nearly a thousand years they were subject to considerable change, as a comparison of different interpretations will show. In cantillation, the scale modes to which the 'accents' were sung were usually based on tetrachords and as each book of the Bible had its appropriate musical mode, the performance of the 'accent' naturally varied in pitch, as well as in other ways, between the different books. The oldest authentic cantillation of the Bible uses scales of jubilant major quality.

The cantillation of prayers may also go back to the days of the Temple, although the evidence is indirect. Its chant is based on the eight modes (*octoechos*), which are believed originally to have been systematized in relation to the calendar. They are not, like the Greek *harmoniai* which we described in Chapter 8, octave-species, but more complex structures which serve as models for melody-types. Each service has its traditional melody-type, and the cantillation, taking such a melody-type as its outline, weaves a free vocal performance around it. The performance may call for considerable virtuosity. The melodies extemporized in this way take their name, *hazanut*, from that of the professional precentor, *hazan*, who occupied so important a position in Jewish worship from the middle ages until early in the present century and who played a part in the evolution of the highly embellished melody which we associate with Jewish chant.

The dispersal of the Jews in the Mediterranean and many parts of Europe naturally gave rise to differences in their musical practice, both in the synagogue and outside, chiefly owing to the influences to which they became subject in the countries where they came to live. The first important Jewish cultural centre resulted from the Jews following the Islamic conquest of Spain from the eighth century. The influence of Arabic music on Jewish is indeed more noticeable than any other single influence, though more so on the secular songs than on the religious chant.

The Jews who settled in eastern Europe during the fourteenth and fifteenth centuries are today the largest in number of all the Jewish settlements. They have developed a large repertory of domestic songs (love, lullaby, work, wedding, dance), many of which are in oriental scales. Among the melodic features of these songs is the characteristic tetrachord approximating to European *re*, *do♯*, *si♭*, *la* (or approximately semitone, augmented second, semitone). This tetrachord, found in the oriental Heijaz scale and well known in Tartaric-Altaic songs, is also of great importance among the Jews. Though they may ultimately have derived it from the east, it seems no less to be the tonal expression of their sadness and sufferings, their hopes and aspirations, and their nomadic life.

CONTACT WITH EUROPEAN MUSIC

As early as the ninth century the Jews began to employ a form of chant which was melodically fixed, unlike their cantillation, and this was no doubt largely inspired by their contact with Gentile music. The well-known tune *Kol Nidrei*, for instance, was partly borrowed from Gregorian chant. Gregorian chant especially influenced the music of the Jews of Central Europe, and the synagogal melody of medieval Europe made much use of the Church modes.

So long as the Church remained the great patron of European music during the Middle Ages, however, it was hardly likely that the contact between the two musical traditions, the Jewish and the European, would in any way be direct. But with the rise of secular music at the courts during the Renaissance, the Jews found it possible to get employment as musicians, especially from the second half of the sixteenth century in Italy, the country in which they first took part in life outside the ghetto.

Salomone Rossi, who was attached to the Court of Mantua for many years (1587–1628), and was there during Monteverdi's time, was a composer of some importance and the first to write polyphonic music for the Jewish service (1622), employing soloists and a chorus to sing it. Rossi had no immediate successor, though around 1700 German synagogues went a step further and introduced instrumental music. Through the use of the organ and more especially of Gentile choirs much non-Jewish music came to be heard in the synagogues. Israel Jacobson (1768–1828) adapted Christian material, including chorales, to Jewish words. Salomon Sulzer (1804–90) believed in limiting the material used to what was historically Jewish, though despite this his own work turned out to be very

European in character. The facile Louis Lewandowski (1821–94) followed. And it was not long before the synagogues in America began to imitate the synagogues in Europe.

Meanwhile, in the early eighteenth century, the Hasidim, a sect which followed the Pietist movement of western Europe, sprang up among the Jews in eastern Europe. The Hasidim employed music as a means to ecstatic union with God, and the typical Hasidic tune is built up in succeeding sections, usually beginning slow and ending quick. Hasidic song no doubt helped to delay the degeneration of Jewish music, but it was already too late to save it as contact with European harmony was beginning to destroy the modal sense of the traditional chant, and by the late eighteenth century disintegration was already well advanced. For much of the music adopted was very far from being religious in character and the lengths to which some of the innovators were prepared to go may be seen from the fact that one liturgical melody was borrowed from Verdi's opera *La Traviata*!

Latterly, composers, reacting against this state of affairs, have attempted to forge a truer link between the Jewish idiom and western music and have, like the Swiss-born Ernest Bloch (1880–1959) in America, begun to write for the synagogue music of better promise. Though the ancient musical tradition has virtually disappeared, there has nonetheless been a certain continuity of spirit in Jewish music and it still has all the appearance of being a definite cultural entity.

While Jews have thus drawn much upon the resources of European music, they have also contributed to its mainstream. Salomone Rossi, already mentioned above, was indeed active in both fields. Besides his polyphonic contribution to the Jewish service, he was a pioneer of violin music and among the first to adapt to it the principles of monodic song. Direct Jewish influence on European music was, however, slow in gathering strength, as during the seventeenth and eighteenth centuries the Jews were on the whole treated as foreigners and practised the lowest trades. Gentiles, however, attracted by what they heard in the synagogue, were not averse to using Jewish traditional chant as a basis for their compositions, as is the case with the choral psalm settings of the Italian composer Benedetto Marcello (1686–1739).

After the French Revolution (1789–95) Jews were received as citizens in European society and found a place in the mainstream of European music. Having enthusiastically embraced their new social life, however, they not unnaturally tended to turn away from everything connected with the ghetto, and thus it is difficult to discern in their works many features that are distinctively Jewish, though technical facility is a noteworthy accompaniment. First come Mendelssohn (1809–47), Meyerbeer (1791–1864), and Offenbach (1819–80); and, at the peak of the Romantic Movement, Mahler (1860–1911) and Schoenberg (1874–1951). The literary texts chosen by the last are much concerned with Jewish problems, and his concept of the serial tone-row has given a new though highly controversial direction to much of western composition.

In general, however, Jewish musicians appear to have been better performers than composers and no mean proportion of the great performers of the western world bear Jewish names.

Among non-Jewish composers who have been influenced by Jewish musical material are Bruch (1838–1920); also Mussorgsky (1839–81) and Rimsky-Kòrsakov (1844–1908), in whose works traces of Hasidic melodies may be found.

THE MODERN PHASE
(Late 19th–20th centuries)

Since 1882 the Jews have begun to 'return' to the Holy Land from all over the world. They have come from Europe, Egypt, Asia, and elsewhere, having a modern form of Hebrew as their common tongue. With them they have brought songs and dances, many of which they learned in the countries of their age-long sojourn, together with modern musical techniques. The building of the towns of modern Palestine has inspired new occupational songs. During the 1920s and more especially the 1930s opera companies and orchestras became active. Jewish operas were written, Jewish theatre music was commissioned, and community singing began within the framework of the Sabbath festivals. A Hebrew University dates from 1925 and research into older Jewish cantillation and the collecting of Oriental Jewish music, latterly helped by recording techniques, is greatly enriching the background of composers. Jewish composers and other musicians have found their greatest opportunity since the Palestinian Broadcasting Service was opened in 1936.

Palestinian composers react differently to their musical environment. At first the assimilation of European styles was complete and the results conventional. The leading composers of the older generation, such as the German Jews Erich-Walter Sternberg (b. 1898) and Paul Ben-Haim (*né* Frankenburger, 1897), stem from the modern idioms of central Europe. Some composers are deliberately cultivating oriental melody, both old and new. Some are steeping themselves in the spirit of the Biblical past, allowing the medium of expression to take care of itself; while other younger composers born in Palestine and trained there absorb their many-coloured background without effort.

The liturgical style of the synagogue music is at present a mixture of tendencies and forms, and Jewish composers have as yet hardly been attracted to that field. The rural labour settlements on the other hand are inspiring new musical 'services' and the festivals are linking the new with the old.

The foundation of the modern Jewish State of Israel in 1948 may prove to have been an important turning-point. There is clearly a desire to regather and re-link cultures; and what is happening in the Israel of today in some way echoes what was occurring in the Canaan of two thousand years ago. East and west are meeting on a scale without precedent. It is as yet too early to expect definitive results, but just as Japan is becoming an important melting-pot of music in the Far East, so Israel is becoming one in the Near East, and, in some measure, a musical gateway between east and west.

10. The Arabic World

THE Arabian peninsula, lying between Egypt and Mesopotamia, was a centre of civilization as early as the third millennium B.C. From archaeology we know that south Arabia had important cities by the early first millennium. But the origin of the Arabs and their relationship to other Semitic peoples remains a matter of controversy, and nothing very precise is known of their music in prehistory, though we do know something of the factors which went into its making.

In a myth not unlike the Biblical myth of Jubal and Tubal-Cain mentioned in Chapter 9, Arabic tradition ascribes to Tubal b. Lamak the invention of the tambourine (*duff*) and drum (*tabl*), to his sister Dilal the lyre (*mi 'zaf*), and to Lamak himself the lute (*'ud*). The mention of a sister suggests the importance of women in music-making among the Arabs from the earliest times.

Since ancient days the Bedouins have sung their simple caravan song (*huda'*) to cheer their long monotonous treks across the desert; its metre, *rajaz*, is said to correspond to the movements of the camel's feet, and consists of six metrical feet each of which comprises two longs, a short, and an accentuated long. It is regarded as the prototype of all Arabic metres, and Bedouin music, like that of the various pastoral and agricultural tribes in Arabia, has undoubtedly been a source upon which poets and musicians have drawn throughout the ages.

As an important trading centre of the ancient world, Arabia was much in contact with the surrounding peoples, the Mesopotamians, the Jews, and, later, the Greeks among them. Arabian influence helped to shape their cultures, but in turn received much from them, especially from Mesopotamia. The influence is to be noted in the names of certain Arabic instruments which find counterparts in other languages. Thus the drum in Arabic is *tabl*; in Jewish *tibela*; in Syriac *tabla* and in Babylonian-Assyrian *tabbalu* (cf. Indian *tabla*; Turkish *dawul*; Persian *duhul*).

The first traceable reference to Arabian music occurs on a seventh-century B.C. Assyrian inscription in which Arab prisoners sang their songs of toil and made music which so caught the fancy of their Assyrian masters that they were asked for more.

Among the Arabs of the first millennium the art of music is likely to have played a role somewhat similar to that which it played in the early Semitic civilizations of Mesopotamia. The cults no doubt had their own music and dance, for Dhu' l-Shara, an ancient deity of the Nabataean Arabs, was worshipped 'with hymns'. We only know of such things through later writers with different faiths who saw fit to condemn the earlier 'pagan' practices, but the very condemnation attests a survival into later times. The soothsayer (*sha'ir*) could conjure up a genie (*jinn*) by means of music, and tradition still remembers the genie as the inspirer of verse or melody. The soothsayers were poet-musicians and from their incantations stems much of the poetry and music of later times. What the Court or household music is likely to have been is difficult to say, though most probably singing girls (*qainat*) like those of later times provided gay songs and good company.

THE CENTURIES BEFORE ISLAM
(1st–7th centuries A.D.)

Already before historical times the ruin of the ancient Mesopotamian cities had repercussions on the Arabian kingdoms. In south Arabia, it is true, the kings still fostered music and poetry, and even today the Arabs further north (Al-Hijaz) look south to Al-Yaman as the true home of Arabian music. But the Arab kingdoms never recovered and large-scale migration took place. Even from the second century Arabs began to migrate northward where they stimulated the development of music in three important new centres: Syria, Mesopotamia, and the west of Arabia itself.

At this time Syria still kept much of the earlier Semitic culture, and the culture of the immigrant Nabataean Arabs blended with it, especially at the important music centre of Ghassan. The Arabic world may have borrowed a reed-pipe (*zanbaq*) from this region.

Mesopotamia (Iraq), similarly a repository of ancient Semitic culture, had been under Persian cultural domination since the sixth century B.C., and the kings of the Sasanid Dynasty (A.D. 224–642) were very fond of music. The conquering Lakhmind Arabs made their capital near ancient Babylon, at a city called al-Hira, which became the most important centre of Arabian culture in early historical times. It was through this centre that many features of Persian music came to be adopted by the Arabs. Thence passed into Arabia the upper-chested harp (Persian *chang*, Arabic *jank*) and the long lute or pandore (*tanbur*; Arab. *tunbur*), and the shawm (*surnay*), and other influences during a later period. Among the musicians of the time was the theorist Barbad of Fars, whose melodies were still played in Merv in the tenth century. It is recorded that there were seven modes before his time, and at least twelve during it, as well as his own three hundred and sixty melodies. These numbers suggest sidereal connexions of a kind which, as we saw in the first chapter, were popular among the Mesopotamians of earlier times. As regards the musical scale of the period we have to rely on the evidence of a tenth-century theorist who says that the pandore of Bagdad of his day was fretted in accordance with a pre-Islamic scale arrived at by dividing a string (finger-board) into forty different parts. Such gives a division into quarter-tones, though how these were grouped to make up the scale is unknown.

In western Arabia music centred especially in two towns in Al-Hijaz, namely 'Ukaz and Mecca. 'Ukaz was the site of a fair where poets and musicians came together for contests; here they recited and sang the 'treasured poems', just as entire odes were still sung in the desert in modern times. Mecca on the other hand became a centre of Arabian cults and a place of pilgrimage. The pilgrims had a primitive chant whose type may still be heard in the *tahlil* and *talbiyya*. A similar chant may have been used for the hymn which Arabs of the North are said to have sung whilst encircling sacrificial stones, and such chant might have been part of their ritual.

Little is known of the cult music, however, and since the early Arabs were more given to diversion than to religion, it is small wonder that we have more data on their secular music. In this music female musicians played an important part. Singing-girls (*qainat*, pl. of *qaina*) were found wherever Arabs appeared, in Arabia, Syria, Mesopotamia, and also Persia, and probably included Greeks and Persians among their number. In addition to figuring at the courts, where they became the favourites of kings, they were attached to all households of standing as well as to taverns and encampments.

Song was and always has been of prime importance among the Arabs. At this period it included refrain (*tarji'*) and antiphon (*jawab*), and the final vowels were prolonged with high trills (*tudhri*). The metres were marked by the instruments of percussion: drum (*tabl*), tambourine (*duff*), and wand (*qadib*). Ornate melody and rhythmical vitality are among the outstanding characteristics of Arabian music as we still know it, and it is interesting to find at least some indications of it at this early period.

Dancing was part of entertainment, and in addition to the percussion instruments accompanying it, the dancers wore little bells (*jalajil*). Women are described as joining in the family and tribal music with their instruments including the tambourine (*duff*). And other instruments of the period include a vertical flute (*qussaba*) and a reed-pipe (*mizmar*).

Such then was the tradition of music up to Islamic times: a cult-music of which little is known; a secular music of charm and no doubt markedly sensuous quality; and a folk music into whose lore the art dipped from time to time.

THE RISE OF ISLAMIC MUSIC IN THE EAST AND THE ARABIAN CLASSICAL SCHOOL
(7th–9th centuries)

It was in Mecca, the centre of Arabian cults, that Muhammad (571–632) was born, and in the Hijaz that the religion (which started in 622) bearing his name first flourished. There is evidence both that he favoured music and that he did not favour music! This admits of only one valid interpretation: he had a sense of discrimination. But this sense of discrimination was dictated not so much by purely musical considerations as by religious and ethical ones. The singing-girls represented no small part of the forbidden pleasures and even the primitive pilgrim chants led devotees back to their pagan ways. At the same time, Arabs had music in their blood, and where Islam could not eradicate the music of the ancient shrines, it adopted them, especially the *tahlil* and *talbiyya*, and some pilgrim songs, being given a new form, were even permitted to be accompanied by fife (*shahin*) and drum (*tabl*).

Islamic Sacred Music

But more important was the music arising from the new faith. There has never been a service in the mosque comparable with the services in Christian churches, and consequently Islam has had no actual liturgy. But music has always been employed in a variety of ways. Early in Islamic times the call to prayer (*adhdan*) was chanted in the streets by the muezzin and shortly afterwards from the minaret of the mosque. Its cantillation (*talhin*) was at first dirge-like, though it became more melodic as time went on and today may be heard in a variety of different styles ranging from simple chant to florid melody. The Koran (*Qu'ran*), or sacred book of Islam containing the revelations of Muhammad, has a cantillation (*taghbir*) of its own. The assonance of its rhymed prose lends itself to reading (*qira'a*) in modulated sounds. This cantillation was also at first restrained, but it later developed melodically and by the ninth century the melodies used even included those of popular ballads, no doubt associated with the spread of cantillation far beyond the actual places of worship. In fact it became a secular pleasure, as did also the singing of hymns (*nasha'id*).

With the advent of Islam secular music appears at first to have suffered something of a setback. From Islam's earliest days it has always had its purists and the legists who, finding it convenient to remember only Muhammad's strictures, condemned all music whatever, not only the secular but also the sacred, and a large and controversial literature sprang up on 'listening to music'. No doubt some actual measures were taken against the singing-girls under the Orthodox Caliphs (632–61) who, following Muhammad's death, made their capital at al-Medina. And it was here that, about the middle of the century, male musicians came to the fore, and Persian influence resulted from the songs of the Persian captives sent to the Hijaz.

The Classical Arabian School

It was not long, however, before secular music received new encouragement under the Umayyad Caliphs (661–750) who, unlike their predecessors, were more concerned with the imperial side of Islam. They made their capital not in Arabia but in Syria at Damascus, maintaining at their courts elaborate musical establishments not unlike conservatories. Under Yazid I (d. 683), 'appassioned of music', we first hear of a Court Minstrel.

The outstanding feature of secular music at this time was the solo song with lute. Singing indeed continued to be considered superior to purely instrumental music until the tenth century. The Arabic lute had been a skin-bellied instrument, but after the Persian lute (*barbat*) reached Mecca about 685, the former acquired its wooden belly and in commemoration its new name (*'ud*, lit. 'wood'). In the lute-song, the form of the music followed that of the poem and usually a single short melody, varied according to all the possibilities of ornament, was moulded to the words.

The most important musician of the time was Ibn Misjah (d. *c.* 715); he may be regarded as the father of Arabian classical music and perhaps the first codifier of its theory. Travelling in Syria, Persia, and elsewhere, he learned a great deal of theory, singing, lute-playing, and rhythmical accompaniment that was new to him. He digested much of what he learned, but also rejected much as being alien to Arabic music.

So we may regard the classical Arabian music of his school as being indigenous, but with Persian, Byzantine, and other enrichments.

Ibn Misjah's system, which we know only through later writers, embraced eight 'finger modes' (*asab'*) for the lute which dominated the Arabian theory used by performers till the eleventh century. With one exception they are identical with Greek and church modes.

On the basis of these were built the melody-patterns and melodies, being performed with shakes, graces, trills, slides, appoggiaturas, and all those forms of embellishment which make up the ornate melodic style known to Arabs as *zawa'id* (cf. *tahasin, zuwwaq*), and to western musicians as *fioritura*. The style has aptly been compared with that of surface ornamentation in Arabic architecture.

The rhythmic modes (*iqa'at*, pl. of *iqa*, 'rhythm') had also been codified by this time; at first four (third quarter of the seventh century), then six (in the time of the Ummayyads) and finally eight (ninth century). These measures each had a basic cycle (*daur*) and variant species (*anwa'*). The basic cycles varied in complexity: thus that of *Khafif-al-ramal* is simple and equivalent to a western $\frac{6}{8}$-bar of quavers (two groups of three), while that of *Khafif-al-thaqi l* is like an asymmetrical bar of $\frac{10}{8}$ made up of $3 + 2 + 3 + 2$ quaver beats where the last beat of each of these four groups is a quaver rest. Such rhythms, together with the modal melodies and their embellishments, comprise the three essential characteristics of Arabic music from early times.

The Arabian classical art continued to flourish under the early 'Abbasid Caliphs (750–847) and the centre of musical activity moved to Bagdad (Iraq), where it reached its highest level. Music, together perhaps with Arabian art and letters, now reached its 'Golden Age' under Harun al-Rashid (*fl.* 786–809) whose wide musical interests will be known to all readers of *The Arabian Nights*. Certainly the environment was Persian in many ways: the Persian Romantic School under the famous singer Prince Ibrahim (d. 839) vied with the old Arabian Classical School and its vogue lasted a century or thereabouts.

But the older art found a great protagonist in Ishaq al-Mausili (767–850), probably the most famous musician Islam has ever produced. A wonderful singer – we can picture him beginning his songs on a high note with an overwhelmingly sudden attack – he was no less an important theorist, though we know of his works only through his pupil Ibn al-Munajjim (d. 912), the author of the only complete treatise on the classical tradition to have survived, *The Book about Music (Risala fi'l musiqi)*. This treatise shows the Arabic classical scale (still found as late as the fifteenth century) to have been the same as the Pythagorean scale of the Greeks, but with its intervals read upwards and not, as among the Greeks, downwards.

THE DECLINE OF PRACTICE AND RISE OF HELLENISTIC THEORY
(9th–13th centuries)

From the year 847 Islam's political power began to dwindle. Bagdad still remained a great centre and most of the Caliphs still kept up elaborate musical establishments attached to their palaces, but their musicians never again compared with those of the previous splendid age and music went into a marked decline. At the same time various important counter-currents were at work: for music was adopted by the mystical fraternities of Islam, a rise of interest in instrumental music followed the arrival of new instruments from abroad, and some important theoretical works appeared.

At the core of Islam during this period two fraternities became important, the Sufis and the Dervishes (Islamic monks), and they gave to music a new lease of life. From about the eleventh century the Sufis have believed that the ultimate truth can only be apprehended through divine ecstasy – by 'lifting the curtain and witnessing the Watcher (*Allah*)' – and the most direct means to this is 'listening to music (*sama'*)'.

Rise of Instrumental Music

As we have seen, from early times the vocal music had been paramount. But from the earlier part of the tenth century

Persian, Turkomanian, Moghul, and Turkish tastes brought instrumental music to the fore. The chief form of the period, a kind of vocal suite called *nauba* ('succession'), consisted of several sections each of which was preceded by an instrumental prelude (*tariqa*), and this gave the instrumentalists a chance to play in succession. How the suites of this time sounded we do not know, for the first written music extant is not earlier than the thirteenth and fourteenth centuries and such fragments as there are unfortunately tell us very little. Later the suite was prefaced by an improvised instrumental movement called *taqsim* ('divisions'), a term still in use today.

The lute retained its popularity but other instruments became important. The psaltery (*qanun*) of trapezoidal form, well known in Arab ensembles today, is mentioned as early as the tenth century (Syria). The first definite evidence of bowed stringed instruments also comes from this century. Al-Farabi mentions a bowed *rabab*, and its bow was shaped like the warrior's bow, which is still the shape of Arabian fiddle-bows today. The Middle East also favoured the spike-fiddle (*kamancha*), a kind of viol with a hemispherical chest and long iron foot. Among wind instruments, the *surnay* (cf. Turkish *zurna*) became popular at this time; it has, as we have seen in so many previous chapters, become popular in one or another form throughout the East.

Hellenistic Theorists

By the middle of the ninth century, many of the treatises on Greek musical theory had been translated into Arabic, some of them through Syriac, and by the end of the century scholars at Bagdad had fairly complete remains of Greek music theory at their disposal. Much of Greek theory was assimilated to Arabic music, and new tunings for the lute were introduced in terms of the finer Greek intervals. The Arabic theorists soon became masters of Greek theory and it was not long before they went ahead of the Greeks in their knowledge of the physical bases of sound and the tuning of instruments. Music (*al-musiqi*), in fact, became an important course of study in the early universities.

Among numerous authorities and some two hundred works written between the ninth and thirteenth centuries, four are of outstanding importance. *The Treatise concerning the Inner Knowledge of Melodies*[1] by Al-Kindi (d. *c.* 874), whose manuscript is in the British Museum, is the earliest treatise on Arabic music theory extant; it is largely derived from Greek theory and includes a system of phonetic notation. It was not until the thirteenth century that numerical elements were added to convey mensural values. *The Grand Book on Music*[2] by Al-Farabi (d. *c.* 950) was the greatest book on music that had ever been written. Al-Farabi, philosopher, musician, and theorist, was of Turkish origin and worked at Aleppo (Syria) and Cordova (Spain). There is a very important chapter on music theory in the *Kitab al-shifa'*, of the Persian theorist Ibn Sina ('Avicenna', d. 1037), which summarizes all the scientific and philosophical knowledge of Islamic countries down to its time. Ibn Sina describes a feature of melodic decoration not previously mentioned: namely the occasional striking of the octave, fifth, or fourth simultaneously with the melody-note. He calls it *tarkib* (lit. 'organum') but this cannot be directly connected with medieval *organum* in Europe.

Hellenistic theory was still prominent in the time of the last Caliphs, but Safi al-Din (d. 1294) already appears as the pioneer of a new school of theorists ('the Systematists') who were much occupied with the problems of intonation in tuning and playing the lute; his important *Book of Musical Modes* (*Kitab al-adwar*) is quoted by nearly every theorist who came after him.

Maqam and Iqa

During this period the system of the melodic and rhythmic modes became more elaborate, and found the pattern which, in outline, it retains to this day. The melody-type came to be called by its present name of *maqam* (cf. Egyptian *naghma*; Tunisian *taba*; Algerian *sana'a*). Any given *maqam* has a distinctive scale, a certain register and compass, one or more

1. *Risala fi khubr ta' lif al-alhan.*   2. *Kitab al-musiqi al-kabir.*

principal notes, and typical melodic phrases. From the thirteenth century there were twelve such primary modes, seven of which have Persian names.

While the *maqam* controlled the melody, the *iqa* ('rhythm') determined the measure. In the ninth century there were eight such rhythmic modes or measures, based on alternations of a hollow sound (*doum*) usually of low pitch, and a dry staccato sound (*tek*) of higher pitch. These were beaten out on the tambourine (*da'ira*) and drum (*tabl*) and tiny kettledrums (*nuqarat*); and the plectrum (*midrab*) of the lute also followed the rhythm when convenient. Under Turkomanian and Turkish influence new rhythmic modes were introduced and by the fifteenth century there were as many as twenty-one.

The Arabic melody-types and rhythmic modes may be compared with similar types existing throughout the east and mentioned in many previous chapters. Whereas the Indian *raga-tala* system adds to these two elements a continuous ground-tone, such is not found in the Arabic *maqam-iqa* system, although a drone does occur in the music of the Arabic bagpipe (*arghul*), a folk instrument which came into prominence during this period.

Despite the musical advances of this time, the Caliphate had gradually declined, and the Islamic Empire grown gradually weaker. This civilization was finally destroyed when Bagdad fell to the Moghuls in 1258; and Persia and Mesopotamia fell around the same time. For a time Egypt and Syria became centres of culture, Egypt having received some Turkomanian musical influence from the twelfth century and Mamluk influence from the thirteenth, but, musically speaking, they never reached anything like the importance of Bagdad and both fell to the Ottoman Turks in 1517.

MUSLIM SPAIN AND THE MUSICAL LEGACY
TO EUROPE
(8th–15th centuries)

So far we have virtually confined our examination of Islamic music to that of eastern lands. One important centre in the

west, however, calls for special notice. Spain became Muslim
from 713 and an independent Caliphate was set up at Cordova
in 755, from which time Islamic Spain pursued a history separate from that of the Islamic East. The ninth-century schools
established by the Moors (Moroccans) in Spain rivalled any
that Bagdad could boast and Cordova became an important
musical centre. The great Ziryab sang at the Court of 'Abd al-
Rahman (d. 852), and the classical Arabian tradition flourished
there. The greatest figure in Islamic music in Spain is perhaps
that of Al-Farabi, better known to the west under his Latin
cognomen Alpharabius (d. c. 950), whom we have already
mentioned among Islam's important Hellenistic theorists. The
story is told of Al-Farabi that when on one occasion he played
the lute by his first mode he made his hearers laugh, then by
changing the mode he had them weeping, and finally he sent
them all into a deep sleep during which he left them – a tale
whose mythical content has many parallels, including one from
the Gaelic world.

The name given to the twenty-four melody modes (*tubu'*) in
Spain in the thirteenth century links them with the name given
to the four elements (*tubu'*), which the modes were believed to
reflect. The different operations of the elements were believed
to underlie the variety of nature and this variety was reflected
in the modes of music, which were thus naturally considered
to have each a different *ethos*. The four strings of the lute were
connected not only with the elements in nature, but with the
humours of the body, the reactions of the soul, the colours, the
seasons, the zodiac, and numerous other correspondences.
Such ideas as to music's *ethos* enjoyed a profound vogue at this
time, and the magical influence of modes is still a reality in
parts of Islam today. After Al-Farabi music in Spain never
again compared with that of its early Islamic times. Some new
musical influences reached Spain from North Africa through
the Berbers from the middle of the eleventh century, but it
was not long before Islam began to dwindle in Spain. At
Granada, the Court Singers again became important for a
short time and the ancient splendour of Moorish Spain to some
extent revived under the Nasrid rulers from 1232, but in 1492

this last Arabic stronghold fell to Ferdinand and Isabella of Castile.

Islamic Spain was, however, important not only for its own earlier musical achievements but also for its influence upon a large part of Europe. Islam was the chief animating force between Byzantium and the Renaissance, and it was from Spain that its culture was radiated to the rest of Europe, whose own culture by the eighth century was still 'barbarian' by comparison.

Whereas European music knew at first only a few fragments of Greek theory, the Arabs had whole treatises at their disposal and their scholars wrote treatises of their own as early as the eighth century before there was anything of the kind in Europe; they are known to have written some 260 works, including numerous theoretical treatises, between the eighth and early fifteenth centuries. There was indeed nothing of the sort between the sixth and ninth centuries in Europe, and there was even no Byzantine work between the fourth century and the tenth. Many of the Arabic works must have been known in Spain. The two treatises, *De Scientiis* by Al-Farabi and *De Ortu Scientiarum*, were translated from Arabic into Latin and became important textbooks in European educational institutions. The former inspired and is acknowledged by the English theorist Roger Bacon (1267–8) and by other theorists in their works, and there is no doubt that Arabic theory stimulated theoretical acoustics in Europe. In the colleges of Islamic Spain music became part of mathematical science as it was in the Islamic East and students came thence from all over the civilized world. The oldest music faculty of any western university is to be found in Spain, at Salamanca (thirteenth century).

Europe owes several instruments to Islam, though of these only the lute has survived; the Spanish *laud* came from the Arabic *al-'ud*. Its neck was fretted and it was tuned in the Pythagorean scale. The *rebec*, the principal stringed instrument in Europe before the days of viols, was a direct descendant of the Arabic *rabab*. It was in connexion with this instrument that the bow was first introduced into Europe and it exclusively retained its hunter's-bow shape in Europe until the fifteenth century and less exclusively into considerably later times.

Some forms of Arabic poetry characterized by a refrain before and after each stanza, such as the *zaqil*, which reached its peak in the early twelfth century, inspired the Spanish *cantigas* and may also have served as a model for the French *virelai*. Whether any surviving tunes were of Arabic origin has not been firmly established, though the form of the poetry certainly determined that of the music and the florid style of performance characterized by the gloss (*zaida*) of the melody, which has been likened to the arabesque style in Mudéjar art, is known to have reached Spain from the Moors. The troubadours of France came in touch with eastern oriental culture during the crusades and with the civilization of Muslim Spain, and it would have been surprising had they remained closed to all influences. At the same time the oriental minstrels wandered all over Europe and must have brought their Arab lays there. The music of the thirteenth-century *chante-fable*, *Aucassin et Nicolette*, has been thought to have some oriental elements. Some rhythms may have come thence and certain Moorish traditions survived in Spanish secular music and dance: the 'morris' dancers still painted their faces like the Moors as late as the sixteenth century.

THE RISE OF TURKISH MUSIC AND THE MODERN PERIOD
(16th–20th centuries)

Some forty years before Spain finally fell to Isabel and Ferdinand of Castile the Turks captured Constantinople. A non-Semitic race and perhaps largely of Alpine stock, the Turks are first heard of as early as the sixth century on the borders of China; but the Osmanli Turks who captured Constantinople do not come into history until the thirteenth century. From this time they became a rising power and it was they who created the Ottoman Empire; Constantinople fell to them in 1453, Egypt and Syria in 1517, and in 1529 they reached the gate of Vienna. Adopting Islam, the Turks became important exponents of its music. Their Sultans maintained outstanding musicians and singers at their Courts and their music had a wide influence in the Near East and the Balkans. Their theory was rooted in Arabic and Persian music, with its Graeco–Byzantine element, and many works were translated from Arabian and Persian into Turkish.

The Mevlevi Order ('dancing dervishes'), founded at Konia in Persia as early as 1240, maintained an important establishment at Constantinople until recent times, and has been responsible for preserving many of the older traditions and musical instruments. This order employs music and dancing in its ritual as a means of liberation. It numbers among its important composers Itri (1631–1712) and Dede efendi (1797–1864), many of whose pieces survive, and even claims to have performed in the present century some music composed by the great Al-Farabi (tenth century) who was, as we have seen, of Turkish origin. Certainly some of the rhythmic modes are found only among the dervishes, like that analogous to a $\frac{9}{4}$-bar disposed as follows: Minim (*doum*), crotchet (*doum*), crotchet (*tek*), minim (*doum*), crotchet (*tek*), minim (*tek*).

The Mevlevi orchestra (*mutrib*) consisted of singers and instrumentalists, usually being made up of two or three reed-flutes (*nei*, Persian *nay*) and two pairs of kettledrums (*qudum*) of a type peculiar to religious fraternities. Flute and drums had accompanied dancing long anterior to the foundation of the order and may possibly perpetuate shamanistic practices of an earlier time. The use of the reed-flute is said to be after Jallal ud din Rumi, the founder of the order who, at the opening of his great poem the Mathnawi, likens the homesick longing of the reed for the bed from which it was torn to the mystical love-yearning of the self for the Self. The complete list of their instruments, some nine or ten of them, shows types like the fiddle (*rabab*), frame-drum (*mazhar*), and cymbals (*halile, zil*), which have tended to disappear from the classical music. Mevlevi music shares with classical music the reed-flute, zither, and tambourine; though the classical short lute (*'ud*) and long lute (*tanbur*) are, as secular instruments, not found in dervish music at all.

Among the distinctive manifestations of Turkish music was that of the Janizaries, the military bodyguard of the Turkish sovereigns from about 1400 to 1826. The melody is played by reeds and the instruments of percussion include the big drum, cymbals, triangle, and crescent. The last consists of countless little jingling bells hung on a number of brass crescents on a long pole topped by a 'pavilion'. Composers began to imitate this music, as Mozart in his 'Turkish' opera *Il Seraglio* and Beethoven in the finale of his Ninth Symphony, and both composers remember it in their piano music where the style of certain well-known movements is indicated by the phrase *alla turca*.

By contrast with that of Turkey, the music of other Islamic countries tended to fall back and live in its memories, though the dervishes of these countries performed a similar function of fostering the older tradition. From the thirteenth century to the seventeenth the systematic theorists wrote a large number of works on the minutiae of tuning the lute. From the fourteenth century music reverted to the plain Pythagorean scale in Persia and later elsewhere, though the adoption of the modern quarter-tone (*rub'*) scale made a final break with the Arabian–Persian–Syrian system. There were no important theoretical works written at all during the eighteenth century.

CONTEMPORARY TRENDS

At the moment when Arabic music had reached its lowest ebb, the beginnings of a cultural revival became apparent in the Arabic world. The lead was taken by Egypt, and at first, in the time of Mehemet Ali who, brought up by a Janizary in Turkey, became Viceroy of Egypt from 1805 to 1848, this was of a technical nature. Later in the century there was a revival of interest in music theory beginning with the writings of Mikha'il Mushaqa (d. 1880) and this has grown during the present century, especially in Egypt. In various Arab lands scholars are beginning to take more of an interest in their older music. Artistic renaissance was a particular concern of Fouad I (Sultan of Egypt from 1917, King 1922–36) and a Conservatoire was founded at his instigation in Cairo. In 1932 a congress was held to collect and examine what remained of classical Arab music and to renew contact with Europe with a view to making available the best European methods.

One outstanding result of this examination was the difference it revealed between the Arab music of the west or Maghrib (Tunis, Algiers, Morocco) and the Arab music of the east (Egypt, Syria, Persia). While both areas use modes based on the degrees of a seven-note scale, the former tends to use a 'natural' scale, the latter intervals of less than a semitone selected from their twenty-four-fold division of the octave. While both have a complex sense of rhythm, this also differs in the two areas. The west usually employs relatively short metrical phrases with elaborate cross-rhythms between the percussion and the melody; the east has less cross-rhythm but often larger and more intimate metrical phrases, which can reach as many as eighty-eight beats. The asymmetrical rhythms have a very vitalizing effect upon the listener and may be compared with the bases of geometrical design in Arab architecture. Arab music is very generally confined to elaborate melody, though late in the nineteenth century some popular music of Upper Egypt for chorus, three rebecs, *tabl*, and *tar* showed a kind of harmonic writing which, though it is well assimilated, must ultimately be attributed to European influence.

European influence is of course now widespread as in most traditions of oriental music. At the conservatories now existing in the chief cities in most Arab-speaking lands both Arabic and European music are taught in theory and practice. Hand in hand with interest in the west, the east has of course lost much of its own. Ataturk suppressed the dervish orders in 1922 and for one reason or another they have either been forbidden in or are tending to disappear in most Islamic lands, though the Mevlevi, among the principal guardians of classical music, still exist in a very limited way.

The European music having the most appeal to the Arabic public is chiefly that in the more popular forms or at best the arias from romantic opera. Such materials underlie the songs of many singer-composers in Arabic lands, and by way of accompaniment there is much influence from European light orchestration.

The Arab composer in modern life is faced with a difficult problem. Shall he aim to compose in the European tradition and risk losing his own qualities altogether? Shall he seek out the music of his own past and cling to it entirely? Shall he compromise by imbuing what is essentially European music with 'local colour'? What kind of marriage can he effect between a traditional eastern style founded on the horizontal structure of highly embellished melody and elaborate rhythmical support on the one hand, and a traditional western style employing harmony and counterpoint on the other, or between an oriental medium favouring the individual instrument and voice and an occidental medium using numerous instruments and large choirs in ensemble? And how shall he reconcile subtle scales in just intonation and western scales in equal temperament?

In so far as he is aware of these problems, each Arab musician is trying to solve them according to his lights. Perhaps the most promising composers in the European style have come from the non-Arabic and no longer Islamic country of Turkey. But in no part of the region we have been discussing is there as yet anything to compare with the promising achievements of the Jewish and Japanese, and distinctive results may have to await a settlement of some larger problems.

II · PLAINSONG

Alec Robertson

1. Introduction: Christian Chant

IT is impossible to reach any clear understanding or true appreciation of Christian chant, whether of the East or of the West, without at least some appreciation and understanding of the animating spirit that brought it into being, nourished it, and enabled it to develop. This was the liturgical spirit. The Greek word for liturgy is derived from two words meaning 'people' and 'work' and in the Christian sense

it comprehended the whole prayer-life of the Church and of all Christians. . . . For the Christians of antiquity, the liturgy was not only a school of prayer, *the* school of prayer, but it *was* their prayer. In the collective prayer, each took his own part and so made it his own personal prayer.

The full reading of the Word of God, explained by the living tradition of the Church which spoke through the lips of the Bishop, led to prayer. This prayer was usually prompted and schooled by the psalms, and it was always finally summed up in the Collects, but this summing up took place only after everyone had been given time to pray his own personal prayer, not apart from the whole Church, but at the height of his communion with it. Then the Eucharist took the personal offering of the believer, and by means of the *Prex sacerdotalis*, that is the consecration, brought it into Christ's own sacrifice; and when that transfigured offering was given back in Communion, it was in order to take the Christian himself into the risen Christ. Then all the blessings of the sacramental order . . . filled the whole life of the Christian with the one perfect gift.

Therefore his life was to be, with that of the Church herself, at once that continuous festival of the Christian year, and that school of asceticism which Christian life should be when the presence of the Mystery in it is understood as it should be.[1]

Such were the high and brave ideals of the early and undivided Christian Church, persisting later through innumerable quarrels, dissensions, and heresies, and animating the rites and accompanying chants of her many liturgies.

1. Louis Boyer, *Life and Liturgy*.

It will be our task, with this background kept in mind, to explore, first of all, the beginnings of Christian chant; and that means a journey into a fog, musically speaking, that rarely lifts and is usually impenetrable.

A moment of illumination was provided by the discovery at Oxyrhynchus, in 1918, of a hymn to the Holy Trinity written down in Greek alphabetic notation in the late third century. Then the darkness again until we reach the era of the first complete manuscripts known to us. These date from the ninth century, but there are fragments belonging to the eighth century.

These manuscripts are written in a well-developed neumatic notation (a subject to be discussed later in this section) showing the number of notes and their melodic direction, but with no precise indication of intervals. Manuscripts with intervallic notation date from about the beginning of the eleventh century, and using these for comparison scholars were able, in many cases, to read the earlier manuscripts.

If, however, our knowledge of the music sung in the early Christian ages is minimal, there are abundant references from Apostolic times as to the texts that were sung and some to the manner of the singing and the occasions thereof.

The first Christians were Jews and, conforming to the practice of their founder and his disciples, continued to worship in the Temple and the Synagogue. Thus we read in the Acts of the Apostles that 'Peter and John went up together into the Temple at the hour of prayer, being the ninth hour' (3:1) and that after the descent of the Holy Spirit the newly baptized continued 'daily with one accord in the Temple' (2:46).

The early Christians (a name first given to the followers of Christ at Antioch, in Syria, the third city of the Roman Empire) had no need to invent a new music for their cult. At the end of the Last Supper, Christ sang a 'hymn' with his disciples which tradition ascribes to a portion of the Jewish Hallel (Psalms 113–18) recited at the principal Jewish festivals.[1] St Paul exhorted the faithful to offer to the Lord 'psalms, hymns,

1. The apocryphal Acts of St John speaks of Christ and his disciples engaging in a round dance at the end of the Last Supper. Gustav Holst drew on the text in his *Hymn of Jesus*.

and spiritual songs' and in the First Epistle to the Corinthians he writes 'when you meet together each contributes something – a song of praise, a lesson, a revelation, a "tongue", an interpretation'. The age-old Jewish melodic formulas (for they were that, rather than melodies) used in the Synagogue[1] provided the basis for the singing of the psalms and Old Testament canticles and would have been adaptable to the three canticles of the new faith, which we know as *Benedictus*, *Magnificat*, and *Nunc Dimittis*.

There are also fragments of hymns in the New Testament (Ephesians 5:14, 1 Timothy 3:16 and 6:15) based, however, not only on Jewish but also on Hellenic–Oriental models. In the Septuagint, the most influential of the Greek versions of the Hebrew Old Testament, the word Church (*ecclesia*) was used of the 'assembly' or 'congregation' of the Israelites and was so used by the Christians of their assemblies. They met in private houses of the wealthier converts with former Jewish precentors taking charge of the proceedings or, in Rome, in the funeral halls of the Catacombs during times of acute persecution.

One morning coming away from Mass in the Catacombs of St Callixtus I passed a band of pilgrims, candles in hand, chanting as they passed down the narrow corridors on their way to Mass, just as the early Christians must often have done.

At the assemblies, as the words of St Paul quoted above suggest, there was room for free improvisation as the spirit moved this or that person to testify; and with the influx of Gentiles foreign to Jewish tradition and laws, one may well believe that these converts sometimes used folk-songs familiar to them for their inspired utterances. However that may be, and whatever the influence of Graeco-Roman music, the formation of Christian chant, as scholars have long come to acknowledge, owes most to Jewish Bible song and to the practice of the synagogue.

1. 'In the early days of Christianity the readers may have preserved the rules of Jewish cantillation, which permitted a certain amount of improvisation as long as the traditional formulas and cadences were kept.' Egon Wellesz, *New Oxford History of Music*, vol. 2.

The non-sacrificial worship of the Synagogue was much simpler than that of the Temple, and consisted of readings from scripture, a number of set prayers, and the chanting of psalms. No instrumental accompaniment was used. The Christian *Synaxis*, or non-Eucharistic service, founded itself, but not slavishly, on synagogue worship, taking a shape that was officially described for the first time, by St Justin Martyr, in the second century. The original outline was as follows:

1. Opening greeting by the officiant and the reply of the church (i.e. assembly of the faithful).
2. Lesson.
3. Psalmody.
4. Lesson (or Lessons, separated by Psalmody).
5. Sermon.
6. Dismissal of those who were not yet members of the church.
7. Prayers.
8. Dismissal of the church.

The Eucharist (thanksgiving), the distinctive Christian service, had its origin in the custom of a common meal with a devotional purpose held by Jewish religious brotherhoods, but it must be remembered that the Last Supper, a meal of this kind, is the source – not the model – for the performance of the Eucharist.

'With absolute unanimity', Dom Gregory Dix says,[1] 'the liturgical action reduces the seven actions in the New Testament accounts of the Supper to four:

(a) The offertory: bread and wine are taken and placed on the table together,
(b) The prayer: the president gives thanks to God over bread and wine together,
(c) The fraction: the bread is broken,
(d) The communion: the bread and wine are distributed together.

In that form and in that order the four actions constitute

1. Gregory Dix, *The Shape of the Liturgy*.

the absolutely invariable nucleus of every eucharistic rite known to us from antiquity from the Euphrates to Gaul.'

These two separate services gradually fused together from the fourth century until they came to be regarded as inseparable parts of a single rite in the Mass. Their original separation is still hinted at in the Roman Mass when the officiating prelate goes to the altar to remain there only at the Offertory, and in the Byzantine rite when, at the end of the *Synaxis*, the deacon dismisses the people, who give the required vocal response but remain where they are. If to these two services we add the Jewish custom observed by religious people, of going up to the Temple to pray at morning and evening and at the third, sixth, and ninth hours, we have a foreshadowing of the eventual shape of the Mass and the Divine Office.

This is not the place for a detailed survey of the development of the many formed liturgical rites that came into being throughout the Christian world, East and West, after the persecutions were, in general, brought to an end with the so-called Edict of Milan promulgated by the emperors Constantine and Licinius in A.D. 313. But it should be borne in mind that in the preceding centuries there was no question of 'a species of Congregation of Rites' introducing and deciding the various elements of the liturgy. As a matter of fact such developments and changes were usually brought about by the Christian people itself in various places and in various circumstances, and later on were accepted and established by authority. Monasticism arose precisely in that way. The creation of the great basilicas at Jerusalem, Rome (both erected by the emperor Constantine after his conversion), Antioch, and Alexandria, and many of lesser rank, 'made it possible for the arts to be brought into the service of Christianity. The liturgical forms quickly developed and an artistic psalmody spread over the world.'[1] Eusebius (260-340), Bishop of Caesarea, gives a vivid picture of the results of this:

The command to sing psalms in the name of the Lord was obeyed by everyone in every place: for the command to sing

1. Peter Wagner, *Introduction to the Gregorian Melodies*.

psalms is in force in all Churches which exist among the nations, not only for the Greeks but also for the Barbarians . . . throughout the whole world, in towns and villages and in the fields, also, in short, in the whole Church, the people of Christ, who are gathered from all nations, sing . . . hymns and psalms with a loud voice, so that the voice of the psalm singers is heard by those standing outside.[1]

This is conclusive evidence, amply confirmed in other writings, that all the people took part in the singing, although the Arian Bishop Cyril of Jerusalem (fourth century) forbade women to sing loudly enough to be heard, and the Catechist Isidore of Pelusium (fifth century) grudgingly allowed them to take part on the ground that they would otherwise gossip during the service!

The general use of the Psalter is understandable; for, as St Athanasius (296–373) expressed it, 'the words of this book include the whole life of man, all conditions of the mind and movements of thought.' Many are the testimonies of the Fathers of the Church to its efficacy. The singing of the psalms, following the practice of the Synagogue, was responsorial and antiphonal. 'The strict parallelism, the fundamental principle of Hebrew poetry, was carefully preserved in all translations of the Bible. This dichotomic structure led to the establishment of such typically psalmodic practices as responses, antiphons, refrain-psalms, etc., all of which were taken over by the Churches.'[2] The number of psalms known by heart by the general run of the laity cannot have been large, and their part in the services was probably limited to responses such as *Amen* (So be it), *Alleluia* (Praise God), or a refrain, as in Psalm 135, 'For his mercy endureth for ever'. The most ancient book of liturgical chant that is known, the *Codex Alexandrinus* (fifth century) in the British Museum, was intended for the use of the precentor and contains the psalter and thirteen canticles, including *Benedictus* (the Song of Zachariah), *Magnificat* (the Song of the Virgin Mary), and *Nunc Dimittis* (the Song of

1. Wagner, op. cit.
2. Eric Werner, 'The Music of Post-Biblical Judaism', *New Oxford History of Music*, vol. 1.

Simeon). The psalms and canticles were sung responsorially by soloists with choral refrain, but antiphonal singing,[1] that is, primitively, the singing of verses of the psalms by alternate choruses of men and women, must soon have become the province of the liturgical singers or, in other words, professional choirs. This manner of singing the psalms was first begun at Antioch about the year 350 and soon spread over the whole Church. St Ambrose introduced it in the West in 387.

At the end of each psalm, as the monk Cassian (360–450) tells us, the people all joined in the 'small doxology', *Gloria Patri* (so called to distinguish it from *Gloria in excelsis Deo*, the 'great doxology'), in Gaul, about 420. We shall see later how antiphons, as we know them (a verse preceding and concluding the psalm or placed also between the verses of a psalm in the Divine Office), grew out of this early antiphonal singing.

It is worth noting here that by a decree of the 4th Council of Carthage the liturgical singers were given a blessing in the following beautiful words, '*Vide ut quod ore cantas, corde credas, et quod corde credis, operibus comprobes*' ('Take heed that what you sing with your mouths you believe in your hearts, and what you believe with your hearts, you show forth in your works'). This blessing has lost none of its relevance today.

It must always be borne in mind that the chant was designed for large buildings, and so scriptural lessons were not read but intoned in order to make them more audible, to lend them greater solemnity, and, by a strict system of punctuation, to make them intelligible to those who could understand the language used. Eric Werner, in the *New Oxford History of Music*, has pointed out the remarkable resemblance between Jewish cantillation and the Roman *tonus lectionis* (reading tone) giving the following examples: ·

1a

Jewish (Yemenites) (Syrian)   Roman

There is a similar resemblance between Oriental Jewish

1. The Greek word *antiphonon* means literally 'counter-sound'.

psalmody on the one hand, and Gregorian psalm tones on the other:

The *Peregrinatio Etheriae* (Pilgrimage of Etheria), a book discovered in a manuscript at Arezzo and published in 1887, contains a very interesting account by a Spanish abbess, written for her community, of a pilgrimage made between 385 and 388, to the holy places of the East, and in particular to Jerusalem from Christmas to Whitsuntide. She describes 'the regular singing of hymns and psalms, and antiphons at Matins and of psalms and hymns at the sixth and ninth hours, and of psalms, hymns, and antiphons (suitable to the day and place) at Vespers' and mentions also that 'it was customary to translate the lessons, where they were read in Greek, into Syriac and Latin for the benefit of those who did not understand that language.'[1]

With the Christianization of the Roman Empire the ancient world became more and more clearly split into two parts, East and West: and now that we are about to consider the chant of the West it is as well to remind ourselves that everything came from the East,

the faith itself, the first theology, the 'angelic' life of the monks, the devotion to the Cross and the Mother of God. Were not the Byzantines the direct heirs of Paul and John, whose letters were still heard in the original language by the same congregations to which they were originally addressed? Did not the majority of the bishoprics, and especially the most ancient, lie in the East? And where did the Christianization of the world begin? In the East, the land of the Holy Places, of the Desert Fathers, of the

1. Egon Wellesz, 'Early Christian Music', *New Oxford History of Music*, vol. 2.

Apologists, of the Councils, of the majestic liturgies, and of the decisive victories of orthodoxy over the agnostic and christo-logical heresies. To be sure, they had certainly accepted, first in their hearts and then with their lips, the prerogatives of Rome, the first apostolic see, and home of the innumerable martyrs whose graves lay like a wreath about her walls. But Rome had been abandoned by the Emperor and thrice plundered by the Barbarians. Always threatened, and totally impoverished, she was soon to become a far off city, great only in her monuments and her memories, and by the presence of the successors of St Peter. In the sixth century she came under the jurisdiction of the Byzantine church of Ravenna, but eventually the Holy See, the independent summit of the Church, escaped completely from the Greek *basileus*, and by what in Greek eyes seemed an act of treacherous desertion, turned herself towards the West, and even toward the ruler of the barbaric Franks.[1]

Before we turn to Western chant there must be added a brief account of the struggle of the Fathers of the Church against the secular music of their time, which constantly endangered the purity of a musical language fit to express 'the contemplation and love of God' and in which to sing His praises. Here narrowness, if it can be so called, spelt strength.

Restraint, tranquillity, nobility, solemnity were certainly not characteristics of the music heard in the theatre or at private entertainments. The cry of Clement of Alexandria (d. 215) was:

It must be banned, this artificial music which injures souls and draws them into feelings snivelling, impure and sensual, and even a Bacchic frenzy and madness. One must not expose oneself to the powerful influence of exciting and languorous modes, which by the curve of their melodies lead to effeminacy and infirmity of purpose. Let us leave coloured [chromatic] harmonies to banquets where no one even blushes at music crowned with flowers and harlotry.

St John Chrysostom wrote in the same strain, wishing to banish anything that recalled pagan cults and the songs of actors. For this reason, the early use of melismatic melody was frowned on in some quarters and, as a famous passage in the *Confessions*

1. F. van der Meer, *An Atlas of Western Civilization.*

tells us, it troubled St Augustine when he felt he was taking more pleasure in the singing than in what was sung.

If the chant remained, in general, a purely melodic art it was certainly not because the means of accompaniment were not at hand, but because of the associations of the instruments used at the theatres. The psaltery and the lyre, however, were permitted at private gatherings of the faithful and were introduced also into some churches. At Miletus, in Egypt, hymns – presumably metrical – were accompanied not only by hand-claps and bodily movements but also by bells.

The Fathers of the Church were certainly led into some tortuous symbolism in trying to explain away the references to instruments in the psalms, but their instinct was right, and accompaniment to the chant today remains an anachronism to be permitted only because of the weakness of the flesh! Sung as it was meant to be, 'Nothing elevates the soul [of the believer], nor gives it wings, nor liberates it from earthly things, as much as a divine chant, in which rhythm and melody form a real symphony' (St John Chrysostom).

2. The Roman Rite: History, Notation, Modes, and Rhythm

HISTORY

UP to the second half of the fourth century the language of the Roman Church was Greek, an international language that linked Asia and Gaul with Rome; but in the mid fourth century there appeared the Itala, or old Latin version, of the Greek Septuagint, which was itself superseded by the *editio vulgata*, or Vulgate, compiled in 382 by St Jerome at the command of Pope Damasus and finally completed at the start of the fifth century. The survival of texts from the Itala version of the Bible in Roman chant books is a valuable aid to dating the melodies, but we do not know what the original Roman chants, or those Rome received from the Churches of Jerusalem and Antioch – and many other sources – were like.

Greek texts and chants persisted for many centuries in Western Europe, and to this day Greek and Latin are used one after the other in the Trisagion ('thrice holy') and Adoration of the Cross on Good Friday, both ceremonies of the Church of Jerusalem. After the first of the *Improperia*, or Reproaches, one choir, as the people go up to venerate the Cross, sings *Agios O Theos*, and the other, in responding, translates the Greek into Latin, *Sanctus Deus*, two more such sentences following. The chants are said to have a Greek flavour.

At Solemn Papal Masses today in St Peter's the Epistle and Gospel are read first in Latin and then in Greek, by monks from the Basilian Monastery of Grottaferrata.

An interesting late survival of the use of Greek appears in the Ordinal of Barking Abbey (1404); this is an Alleluia verse directed to be sung alternately in Latin and Greek on the feasts of Christmas, Circumcision, Epiphany, and Transfiguration.

We have now to examine the part played by the Popes in regard to what, by long custom, became known as the Gregorian chant: and, in particular, what part Gregory I, Pope and Saint (540–604; Pope from 590), took in the work of revising and adding to the body of chant existing in his reign. The first of the *Ordines Romani* documents, which describe Roman ceremonial from the sixth to the eleventh centuries, is found in a ninth-century MS. of the Abbey of St Gall. The earliest part dates from the time of Pope Stephen II (768–72) but it is said to have drawn freely from a text of the sixth century.

A number of Popes of the fifth to the seventh centuries – Leo I, Gelasius, Symmachus, Johannes, Bonifacius, Gregory I, and Martinus I – are here credited with the editing of a cycle of chants for the entire year, and after Martinus, the names of three abbots of St Peter's are mentioned in the same connexion; but a very old tradition names Gregory 'the Great' as the author or compiler of chants on the evidence of the Pope's biographer John the Deacon, who devotes a chapter in his *Vita Sancti Gregorii*, written about 872 – that is nearly 300 years after the Pope's death – to this *Cento Antiphonarius*.

John's biography led to numerous pictorial representations being made of Gregory 'sitting on the papal throne and dictating to a scribe the melodies that a heavenly dove perched on his shoulder is whispering into his ear'.

The first witness, known to us, to the tradition of a Gregorian Antiphonary given such wide currency by John comes from Egbert, Bishop of York (*c.* 732), who alludes to Gregory's 'book of chants and prayers' and speaks of their being brought to England by his missionary, St Augustine; and the Venerable Bede, in his *Ecclesiastical History of the English People* (completed in 731), praises Putta, Bishop of Rochester, who died in 668, for his knowledge of the Roman chant which he had learnt from the pupils of St Gregory, and makes a similar reference to a singer named Maban, employed under Acca, Bishop of Hexham (d. 709), who 'had been instructed by the successors of the pupils of St Gregory in Kent.' This is, at least, evidence of Gregory's reorganization of the *schola cantorum* at Rome.

The long Gregorian tradition was first challenged, without result, in the seventeenth and eighteenth centuries, and more decisively by the Belgian musicologist Gevaert in 1890, again without lasting effect; but in the past five or six years the challenge has been renewed with startling results. These results are set out in detail in Dr Willi Apel's book *Gregorian Chant*,[1] and can only be briefly summarized here. We know what feasts were celebrated at the time of Gregory, but the earliest information as to the musical items used in the Masses of these old feasts comes only from certain manuscripts of the eighth century which, however, do not have any musical notation. Comparative study of manuscripts with and without staffs enables us to assume 'that the majority of the melodies existed about 900, or 850, in nearly the same form as they do in the later medieval sources and in the present-day publications.' What cannot be maintained is that the melodies are as old as the texts and feasts, the former dating back to the middle of the eighth century, the latter at least to the time of Gregory. If he did compile an Antiphonary of texts *and* music, we have to consider how the music was noted down: if it was not, how was it possible to preserve and revise an oral tradition extending over two or three centuries unless the melodies were of simpler character, and far fewer in number, than those found in the manuscripts? 'It is a matter of scientific caution and prudence to assign to the liturgical melodies, as we have them, a considerably later date than has generally been done before.'

Dr Apel points out that the early sources of the so-called 'Gregorian' chant all came from such places in western Europe as St Gall, Metz, Einsiedeln, Chartres, Laon, and Montpelier, in other words, from the Franco-German Empire, as contrasted with the exclusive Roman origin of other special sources he mentions. We know that the Frankish clergy stubbornly resisted the efforts of King Pepin and above all of his son Charles the Great to establish the Roman Liturgy in their land and tried to hold fast to their traditional Gallican rites. What happened is related by J. A. Jungmann in his standard work *The Mass of the Roman Rite*:

Unconsciously, of course, but none the less surely, profound alterations were made from the very outset in the Roman Mass – in fact fundamental transformations. . . . About the middle of

1. Willi Apel, *Gregorian Chant*, 1958.

the tenth century the Roman liturgy began to return in force from Franco-Germanic lands to Italy and to Rome, but it was a liturgy which meanwhile had undergone radical changes and a great development. This importation entailed supplanting the local form of the Roman liturgy by its Gallicized version, even at the very centre of Christendom.

It would certainly be strange if the melodies were not affected by these radical changes and developments. Some of them, such as lesson and psalm tones, litany chants, and simple antiphons, would be most likely to have preserved their primitive character and may date back to the earliest days of the chant. But the ornate or highly melismatic chants are, in their present-day form, Franco-Roman productions of the eighth and ninth centuries.

There is no need to assume that the new conclusions many scholars have arrived at should be taken to mean that St Gregory had no interest in the chant. Dr Apel does not quote a letter the Pope wrote, in October 598, to John of Syracuse in which he speaks of his preoccupation with liturgical chant and the ceremonies in order 'to re-establish the ancient traditions or to institute new practices'. When the Benedictine Abbot Augustine (later Archbishop of Canterbury) arrived in Britain with his band of forty monks, in 597, to convert the Anglo-Saxons he was uncertain what form of liturgical prayer and music he should offer these people. They had met with a different order of Mass, different texts and music in their journey through Gaul from those they were accustomed to in Rome, and had been much affected by their novel experience. The Pope, replying to Augustine's request for guidance, told him to make use, with circumspection, of anything in the Gallican, or in any other liturgy, 'that might be more pleasing to Almighty God, and to introduce into the Church of the English what you have been able to gather together from many churches'.[1]

We have now to examine in some detail the chant called Gregorian – its notation, modal system, rhythm, and melodies – with reference to the two main choir books in use today.

1. *Epistles*, Book x, 1,64.

These are (1) the *Graduale*, which contains all the solo and chorus chants of the Proper, the variable parts of the Mass, together with the *Kyriale*, the Ordinary, invariable, part of the Mass; (2) the *Antiphonale*, which contains the chants of the Divine Office, with the exception of those in use at Matins. (The *Liber Usualis*, a modern compilation, contains a wide range of chants taken from the above two books and adds Matins in full for the Feasts of Christmas, Easter, Whitsuntide, Corpus Christi, and the Assumption. The texts of all three books are in Latin only.)

NOTATION

The notation of Western chant has a long history and has taken many different forms, but we can only deal briefly with it here. The neumatic MSS. of the ninth century have special cheironomic signs derived from the accent marks of the Greek and Latin grammarians, and dots grouped by superposition and conjunction. The Greek word 'neume', which means a nod or a sign, is also used to describe a group of notes, two or more sung to one syllable, and the neumatic signs indicate the rise or fall of melody.

The grammarians regarded the acute (´) and grave (`) accents, a raising or a lowering of the voice, as melodic. The raising and lowering of pitch, and the general direction of the melodies, could be sufficiently shown, but the intervals between the notes could not; and so these staffless neumes, for the singers who had to learn the liturgical repertory by heart, were a combination of musical shorthand and *aide-mémoire*, and also 'a very sensitive and supple means of recording the innumerable *finesses* of ancient singing'.

It is possible, of course, that the choirmaster imagined a note of set pitch from which intervals could be calculated, and certainly diastematic, or staff, notation was preceded by the arranging of the notes on different levels according to the variation of the intervals. In some cases the clumsy device of alphabetic notation was used: letters placed above the neumes spelling out the notes. The tracing of a horizontal line, on the

MSS, at first dry-drawn then in red, representing F, was a great advance: to this, for greater precision, another line in yellow, representing C, was added, then two more. Clef-signs, C or F, were, finally, placed on this four-line stave.

As will be seen from Pl.4b the diastematic neumes give a more accurate graph of the rise and fall of the melody than the cheironomic ones (Pl.7). In about 1200 appeared the square-shaped neumes in use today.

The student who wishes to learn how to read the neumatic notation in the modern service books can find all the information required in the preface, in English, to the *Liber Usualis*, or in two useful little volumes, *Plainsong for Schools*. An hour's study with one or other of these books and a gramophone record of the chant will make reading of what looks difficult on paper a simple task.

It is worth while, also, to visit a museum which displays old MSS. and examine the exquisite script and illuminations of the antiphoners from which the monks, grouped round the huge and weighty volumes placed in the middle of the Sanctuary, used to sing.

The monks (or scribes) in the scriptoria of the monasteries had under them (Dom Gougaud writes in his book *Christianity in Celtic Lands*) 'a whole band of subaltern copyists, to whom their task seemed sometimes irksome and monotonous; they readily took into their confidence the parchment on which they toiled. The *marginalia* and colophons of manuscripts give us intimate details concerning the life of these workers with pen and brush.' Here are some of the comments quoted by Dom Gougaud. 'New vellum and bad ink to say nothing else.' 'A blessing on the soul of Fergus, Amen. I am very cold.' 'Oh! my hand.' 'Nightfall and time for supper.' To these I add a plaintive comment made by an unmusical scribe: 'The tedious plainsong grates my tender ears.' It is possible that, as silence had to be observed at work, some of these marginal comments were a way of conducting conversation.

I have, reluctantly, decided to use modern notation (with one exception, Ex. 13) for the musical illustrations in this account, but it must be emphasized that the picture they give of the melodies is a very imperfect one, for there are groups of neumes that indicate methods of performance, and these cannot be accurately transcribed.

MODES

The eight church or ecclesiastical modes, it need hardly be said, postdate Gregorian chant, and the idea of classifying the melodies under this or that mode is no older than the eighth or ninth century. It is more than possible that some of the melodies suffered in being forced into modal strait-jackets. The subject is complex, the system often inconsistent. Some melodies are in more than one mode, there are modulations, and transpositions to conceal chromaticisms, and so forth. The bare bones of the system are, however, easy to understand.

The modes can be reduced from eight to four, and it is preferable to give them the names by which they were first known, rather than to use the misleading Greek names that are so often employed in text books. The modes are concerned only with the diatonic scale with B flat as the one permitted accidental. They are grouped as follows:

	Final (or key note)	Range	Dominant
1. Protus authenticus	d	d – d	a
2. Protus plagalis	d	A – a	f
3. Deuterus authenticus	e	e – e′	c′
4. Deuterus plagalis	e	B – b	a
5. Tritus authenticus	f	f – f′	c′
6. Tritus plagalis	f	c – c′	a
7. Tetrardus authenticus	g	g – g′	d′
8. Tetrardus plagalis	g	d – d′	c′

It will be seen that the plagal mode starts in each case a fourth below the authentic and that the dominant is not invariably the fifth note above the final of the authentic mode. Thus mode 3, starting on e, has c and not b as its dominant. The reason for this is that b could not be used as a dominant without involving the tritone – the *diabolus in musica*, as it first became known in the fifteenth century – as for example f – b, three whole tones forming the augmented fourth. Now the plagal dominants are found a third lower than the authentic ones, so these also had to conform. As the dominant of mode 3 is c, not b, the plagal dominant has to change from g to a. This procedure shows the artificiality of the system.

The eight psalm tones (which are, of course, recitation formulas not modes) are allied to but do not in every way conform to the modes. Their reciting notes are based on the dominants,[1] but they do not follow the theory that a mode must end on its final for reasons that will be dealt with when we come to the section on psalmody in the Divine Office.

RHYTHM

Rhythm in Gregorian chant is a much debated question that generates, as a rule, more heat than light. In the late nineteenth century the monks of Solesmes Abbey undertook, in face of much opposition, the restoration of Gregorian chant based on manuscripts of the ninth, tenth, and eleventh centuries (facsimiles of which they published in the great series *Paléographie musicale*) and produced, in 1904, the first volume (*Graduale*) of the *Editio Vaticana*, which is today the only official edition of the chant, and which supplanted the corrupt Medicean and Ratisbon versions. The leaders in this great work were Dom Guéranger (1805–75), Dom Pothier (1835–1923), and Dom Mocquereau (1849–1930).

Controversy centred not round this work but round the rhythmic theories set forth in detail in the two volumes of Dom Mocquereau's book *Le Nombre musical grégorien ou rhythmique grégorienne* (1908) and expressed in the Solesmes editions of the service books with rhythmic signs. No indication was given as to which of the signs were derived from the manuscripts and which were added by the editors, a fact that many musicologists were not slow to notice and criticize. All that can be said here is that there is no authority in the manuscripts for the use of the *ictus*, a word meaning, in prosody, a

1. The reciting note of the third psalm tone, however, has been lowered to b, its primitive state, in the 1939 edition of the *Antiphonale Monasticum.*

stress or accent (indicated by a vertical stroke above or below a note) but not interpreted as such by Solesmes. They describe it as a footfall of the rhythm, marking off the groups of two and three notes into which they divide the melodies. In addition the Solesmes method insists on the equality of all the notes (their approximate value is a quaver): they can be doubled in length (shown by a dot), but not sub-divided. Solesmes' opponents appear only to agree, with any unanimity, that the original chant rhythm mingled variously long and short sounds and yielded to the 'corrupt' idea of equal note values only in the eleventh century. They produce a large body of evidence for their views from St Gregory's day up to Aribo's *De Musica*, a treatise which dates from the latter part of the eleventh century.

It may be thought strange that though the supporters of these mensural theories have been in the field ever since Dom Mocquereau's book appeared they have produced no editions of the chant by which the application of their theories may be judged.

If, however, as according to Solesmes the notes are taken to be all equal, then one must paraphrase George Orwell and add that some are more equal than others. This can be heard, indeed, in the singing of the Solesmes monks themselves, and could hardly be otherwise if a mechanical interpretation was to be avoided. It must also never be forgotten that plainsong is music, and, however free the rhythm is, it still follows basic musical laws. Thus a choir should 'sing on the phrase', towards the cadence points, with due attention to proper enunciation and accentuation of words, and flexibly, and without previous intensive dissection of the melodies. For the rest, if there ever was a generally accepted and absolutely uniform way of singing the chant, one would imagine that some unequivocal evidence would have emerged to substantiate it. Such evidence as there is has been assembled in an important book, recently published, by J. W. A. Vollaerts, s.J., *Rhythmic Proportions in Early Medieval Ecclesiastical Chant*, and the conclusions to be drawn from it are certainly striking. But the author admits that it is useless to consult the medieval authors for particulars of their rhythmic system since not one of them gives a full or methodical exposition which includes details. Only general rhythmic principles can be looked for.

Nevertheless, if it can be proved beyond doubt that the authentic rhythm of Gregorian chant consisted of proportional long and short sounds, then its restoration would mean the preparation of a whole range of new service books – a task of daunting magnitude and nothing less than a musical revolution in its sphere.

It is worth bearing in mind, however, that, as Gustave Reese says in his book *Music in the Middle Ages*, the decline from the 'authentic' rhythm which began before the end of the tenth century did not necessarily lead to anything less valid, if judged solely from the artistic point of view. This is sufficiently proved by the praise lavished by many musicians on the singing, and the recordings, of the Solesmes Choir. There is no valid comparison to be made here with harmonized music which could not be sung in notes of equal value without radically altering its character, whereas the metricalizing of the chant is more in the nature of a variation, as was the embellishment of Palestrina's vocal lines by the singers of his day. The point at issue is, which is the theme?

The matter is now under special investigation, and one can only wait patiently to see what final conclusions are drawn by the research workers and what attitude will be taken to their findings by the Sacred Congregation of Rites, under whose authority the whole question comes.

3. The Roman Rite: Gregorian Melody

'GREGORIAN MUSIC', as Dom David Knowles has said, 'is wide in its range of emotional expression, majestic, spiritual, and austere beyond all other forms of the art, exquisitely spontaneous and pure in its melody, and extremely subtle and sophisticated in its technical perfection.' These words describe the chant in its golden age, that is, the period from the fifth to the eighth centuries.

It is characteristic of the melodies to rise quickly to a high point and then gently to descend not in a straight line, 'but with small to and fro motions like a falling leaf', to points of cadence. The course of the melodies is unpredictable: there is no mathematical balance (as for example in Palestrina's music, of upward and downward motions.

The melodies show a fundamental use of step-wise movement: melodic rises or falls of a second and a third are very common, of a fourth less so, those of a fifth rare and of a sixth even more so. A rise (never a fall) of a seventh is exceptional. The range of the melodies extends from a fourth to as much, exceptionally, as an eleventh. They can be classified into three types: (a) syllabic: or one note to a syllable; (b) neumatic: two notes up to about four or five to a syllable; (c) melismatic: long florid phrases sung to one syllable. This last kind of writing occurs principally in the *Gradual*, *Alleluia*, *Tract*, and *Offertory*, and the great Responsories – 'virtuoso' chants in which soloists were able to display their skill for the greater glory of God or, regrettably, on occasion for their own glory.

The whole burden of expression is borne in the chant by a single melodic line with no vertical harmonic implications. Monotony is avoided by the use of 'contrary motion, repetitions, imitations, melodic echoes, musical rhymes, and (in a word) all that is necessary to make the Gregorian chant pleasing and artistic so long as it remains within the bounds of what is sufficiently restrained for use in worship.'[1]

1. Dom Gatard, O.S.B., *Plainchant*.

Before examining the melodies in detail, their forms, their dependence on and treatment of the texts, their expressive qualities and occasional use of word-painting, we must have a clear idea of the settings in which they are found: that is, of the structure of the Mass and of the Divine Office, so far as the portions of the texts intoned or sung are concerned.

THE ROMAN MASS

The chants of the Mass are contained in the Roman *Graduale*, which is divided into (1) the *Proper of the Time*, (2) the *Proper of the Saints*, and (3) the *Common of the Saints*. The first of these divisions, the Christmas, Easter, and Pentecost cycles, includes all Sundays from the first in Advent to the last Sunday after Pentecost, the ferial and Ember days of Advent and Lent, and of the period after Easter and Pentecost, and the Saints' days falling between 26 December and 13 January. The second, the *Proper of the Saints*, includes feasts with their own material, and the third, the *Common of the Saints*, is a collection of texts and chants that are shared by many feasts. After these comes a section containing Votive Masses. All these four sections are concerned only with the variable parts of the Mass. The invariable parts, the Ordinary of the Mass, are contained in the *Kyriale*. The last sections of the *Graduale* contain the *Mass for the Dead*, reciting tones for Collects, Epistle, Gospel, Preface, etc.

The Mass[1]

The Preparation

1. *Introit*
2. Kyrie
3. Gloria (omitted during Lent and Advent)
4. *Collects*
5. *Epistle*
6. *Gradual – Alleluia* (or two *Alleluias* and no *Gradual*, or *Tract* after *Gradual* and no *Alleluia*, or *Sequence* after *Alleluia*, according to the season or feast)

1. Italics in the following list signify the variable parts of the Mass, Roman type the fixed and invariable parts.

7. *Gospel*
8. Credo (omitted on Feasts of minor rank)

The Offering
9. *Offertory*

The Sacrifice
10. The Canon, which begins after the *Preface*, and Sanctus-Benedictus, and leads into the great Eucharistic prayer, ending with the doxology '*Per ipsum et cum ipso et in ipso*', etc.

The Communion
11. Pater noster
12. Agnus Dei
13. *Communion*

The Post-Communion and Conclusion
14. *Closing prayers*
15. Dismissal (*Ite Missa est*, or, at certain seasons, *Benedicamus Domino*).

Mass for the Dead, or Requiem Mass, omits Gloria and Credo and has a *Gradual*, *Tract*, and *Sequence*.

Liturgical Recitatives

The simplest chants, within the limited musical capacity of the majority of priests, are the liturgical recitatives, or tones, for the reading of prayers, Epistle, and Gospel. The chants for the *Preface* and *Pater noster* are more elaborate.

On ferial[1] and simple feast days the prayers may be intoned on a single note, on greater feasts a slightly ornamented tone is used. There are solemn and ferial tones for the *Preface* and *Pater noster*.

The example below of one of the Gospel tones will show how beautifully text and music are fitted together. The greeting and

1. Feria: a weekday in the Church calendar on which no feast occurs, even though the original meaning of the Latin word is 'festival day'. There are ferias of different ranks; thus all those of Holy Week are 'greater' ferias.

response are sung *recto tono* (on one note), the voice of the
deacon announcing the Gospel and the congregational response
fall a third to indicate punctuation, and so also at two other
points in the Gospel itself. A question mark is indicated by the
voice falling a semitone on the reciting note, followed by a rise
up to it, and the end of the Gospel by a little group of notes on
the first syllable of 'regnum tuum'.

(The continuation of the Holy Gospel according to Matthew. Glory to
thee O God. Jesus said to his disciples: you are the salt of the earth. If
the salt lost savour, wherewith should it be salted? . . . this man shall
be called great in the kingdom of heaven.)

How musical declamation developed is well shown by versions 3a, b, and c of the first words of *Pater noster* (Our Father

who art in heaven); Ex. 3d is the start of the solemn tone in use today.

One need only sing over these recitatives to discover how naturally the music fits the words. The Latin accents in the *Pater noster* fall indifferently on both higher and lower notes than those preceding them. There is no 'law' in this matter: but one can say (as many of the melodies to be quoted later on will show) that the accented syllable of the Latin word, often called the 'tonic' accent, is frequently put into high melodic relief, often with beautiful effect.[1]

When the Latin language, originally quantitative, became accentual in the fourth century, its tonic accent was regarded as melodic and light rather than intensive. Accent-hammering in singing the chant makes typewriter music of it and destroys its suppleness and its spiritual beauty. The singing of the chant, in general, should suggest the rise and fall of good Latin oratory, making allowance for the fact that music has a constant desire to escape from verbal bondage and become autonomous. Singers – and the Gregorian composers were in the main choir-monks – naturally wanted to have something more than musical oratory on which to exercise their art. Hence we get highly ornamental passages in chant, following the instinct that led the officiant to ornament the end phrase of a prayer or reading from the Bible, and in some cases to underline the meaning of a particular word, or to express himself in the realization of the last joyful vowel of the *Alleluia*. As in *Lieder* there are words that dominate phrases and these carry what is known as the phraseological accent.

The Chants of the Proper

Antiphonal Chants. These are the Introit, Offertory, and Communion. All three are also processional chants. The *Liber Pontificalis* (sixth century) tells us that Pope Celestine (432)

1. As has been well said, this accent 'shines down' on the group of notes given to its remaining syllables. The word is thus 'spot-lit', but not infrequently a word of secondary importance receives similar treatment, and here the music takes precedence over the text which yet remains, as a whole, the primary inspiration.

'ordered that the 150 psalms of David should be sung before the sacrifice antiphonally by all, which until then had not been done, as only the Epistle of the blessed Paul was read (that is intoned) aloud and the holy Gospel.'

By the time of St Gregory the choir (with perhaps the clergy responding) had taken over the singing of antiphon and psalm, with the result that both became much more elaborate: this becomes an all too familiar story in the history of plainsong.

The *Introit* is a processional chant because it was sung as the pontiff entered the church on his way to the altar, supported by the archdeacon and deacon, and preceded by the subdeacon censing him with the thurible and seven acolytes carrying seven lighted candlesticks. The number of verses sung depended on the pontiff – the old manuscripts only give the first verse – who gave the signal to the cantor for the *Gloria Patri* to be intoned. The antiphon was again repeated (as also between the verses of the psalm) and finally after *Sicut erat*. The custom, followed today, of singing only one verse of the psalm dates back to the time when the Introit was sung in ordinary churches, and so with far less elaborate ceremonial. Of the 149 different Introit texts found in the tenth-century Codex 339 of St Gall, at least 143 are from the Bible and as many as 102 of these are taken from the Psalms.

The *Offertory* and *Communion* are processional chants in the sense that the first of these was sung while the people came up to the altar to make their offerings, the second when they came up to take Holy Communion. St Augustine speaks of 'the practice of singing at the altar hymns drawn from the book of psalms both before the offering and when that which had been offered was being distributed to the people'.

From a psalm sung antiphonally (in the original sense of the word) by the two halves of a choir, the *Offertory* chant developed, by the seventh century, into an integrated composition of antiphon and psalm verses, the former sung by the choir, the latter much ornamented by soloists.

When the people ceased to bring their offerings to the altar the verses, as in the Communion chant, were omitted, leaving the antiphon we find in the modern *Gradual*. In the Mass for the Dead the Offertory and Communion chants still retain a verse, with the second half of the antiphon (that is the portion after the asterisk) being repeated after it.[1] The following is the Communion chant:

(Eternal light shine upon them Lord with thy Saints for ever, for thou art merciful. ℣. Lord, grant them eternal rest; and let perpetual light shine upon them; with thy Saints for ever, for thou art merciful.)

Responsorial Chants. In a responsorial chant the congregation responded to the soloist with a verse of the psalm he had just sung himself, or with some brief interjection such as *Amen* or *Alleluia*. Psalms were sung in this way between the readings from scripture, of which there were at first three, one from the Old Testament and two from the New Testament. In the sixth century the scriptural readings were reduced to two (Epistle and Gospel) between which the *Gradual* psalm and the *Alleluia* were sung. The *Gradual* is thought to take its name from the steps that led up to the ambo, or little pulpit, from which the deacon sang. Thus 'the cantor goes up into the ambo with a chant book and sings the responsory.' The rubric, it will be noticed, speaks of a 'cantor' not a deacon. St Gregory, observ-

1. A very interesting collection of Offertories with verses still in use in the twelfth and thirteenth centuries will be found in Carolus Ott's *Offertoriale sive versus Offertorium* (Desclée, 1935).

ing the overweening vanity of the deacon soloists, had in a decree of 5 July 595 forbidden them, for the good of their souls, to undertake this task. Some beautiful mosaics in the church of SS. Cosmas and Damian, Rome, show these young gentlemen, their long hair flowing over their silken dalmatics, looking very pleased with themselves. It should be noted that there is no liturgical action during the singing of *Gradual* and *Alleluia* (or *Tract*): everyone sat down and listened to a performance intended to be offered for the greater glory of God. The *Gradual*, by this time, retained only one of its verses. It was, with the *Tract*, a melismatic chant, owing much in its elaboration to the chant of the Eastern Churches.

The *Alleluia* should not be considered as part of the *Gradual*, as it sometimes is, but as a separate chant. The two are musically unconnected. The vocalization on the final vowel of Alleluia, called the *jubilus*, is described by St Augustine, in a famous passage, as 'a song of joy without words'. Cassiodorus, an older contemporary of St Gregory, tells us 'the tongue of the singer rejoices in it; joyfully the community repeat it; and like something good of which one can never have enough, it is renewed in ever varying neumes.'

There are ninety-five *Alleluia* chants in Codex 339 of St Gall. Seventy of the verses are from the Psalms, and fourteen from other parts of the Bible. It is not known when, precisely, verses were added to the *Alleluias*, but there is no trace in the MSS. of this chant without a verse.

The Tract. The *Tract*, sung in the penitential season between Septuagesima and Easter when the *Alleluia* is silenced, was purely a solo chant (though sung today by cantor and choir) without responses. Peter Wagner writes in his *Introduction to the Gregorian Melodies* 'the Tract melodies are extremely old and venerable monuments of the chant of the Latin Church, and they preserve the melodic forms of solo-psalmody of the Mass in the shape in which they were used, up to the fourth and fifth centuries in Italy, when the solo-singers began to deck their art with richer *melismata* than before, and by this innovation brought on the abbreviation of the psalm.' A large part of Psalm XC is sung in the Tract for the first

Sunday of Lent and a considerable part of Psalm XXI in the Palm Sunday *Tract*.[1]

In the other Tracts only a few verses of the psalm are sung. A remarkable feature of this chant is that its melodies are all in either Mode 2 or Mode 8.

The Sequence. The new creative impulse that arose in the eighth century to add to Gregorian chant, which I shall allude to again in describing the 'farced' Kyries of the Ordinary of the Mass, had its most important and lasting results in that form of trope that came to be known as the *Sequence*, 'that which follows on'. It was an addition to the *Alleluia*, either of melody or text, or of both, and may have had its prototype, some scholars think, in the pre-Gregorian *Alleluia*. Sequence composition was at any rate in full swing in the course of the eighth century.

In the preface to his *Liber Ymnorum* (later entitled *Liber Sequentarium*) Notker Balbulus ('the stammerer') a monk of St Gall – where he was made librarian in 890 – describes the difficulty he had in learning by heart the very long melodies of the *Alleluia*, and how delighted he was when a refugee priest from Jumièges (near Rouen), which had been destroyed by the Normans, came to the Abbey bringing an antiphonal with him which contained verses set to the *jubilus*. He had no great opinion of the verses themselves, but applauded the idea of making the melodies easier to memorize. Notker set to work to put words to the melodies himself, but when he showed the results to his master Yso, the latter, congratulating him more on his industry than his skill, corrected his efforts and said, 'every note of the melody ought to have a separate syllable.' This verdict shows that Yso was quoting a rule already known to him, and that Notker certainly did not invent the syllabic sequence. The Irish scholar and monk was so delighted with Notker's further efforts that he urged him to compile a volume of sequences.

1. The Psalms are cited throughout according to the Vulgate numbering; e.g., the Psalms here numbered XC and XXI are XCI and XXII in the A.V. and the Book of Common Prayer.

If, as Dr Wellesz says, 'it could be proved that Notker really was the first hymnographer to set words to the *entire Alleluia-jubilus* melody, we should not only have to admire in him the great poet he certainly was, but would also have to consider him as a great innovator in the rising poetic genre.'

We shall return to the poetical and musical scheme of the Sequences, considered as independent compositions, when speaking of Gregorian craftsmanship. The Council of Trent removed all but four Sequences from the Roman Missal, the four left being *Victimae Paschali* (Easter poem by Wipo of Burgundy – d. *c.* 1048), *Veni Sancte Spiritus* (Whitsuntide poem by Stephen Langton – d. 1228), *Lauda Sion Salvatorem* (*Corpus Christi* poem by St Thomas Aquinas – d. 1274), and *Dies irae* (Requiem Mass; poem attributed to Thomas of Celano, but probably by another thirteenth-century Franciscan). The *Stabat Mater* (Seven Sorrows of Our Lady: authorship of poem variously attributed to Pope Innocent II, St Bonaventure – d. 1274 – and Jacopone da Todi – d. 1306) was not admitted into the Mass until 1727.

Chants of the Ordinary of the Mass

The Chants of the Ordinary of the Mass were not originally set out in the order in which they occur, as we find them in the modern *Gradual* (except the *Credo*), but were written down in a separate book with the melodies of each category grouped together. The Solesmes edition of the *Gradual* (but not the Vatican edition) assigns dates to each piece, covering the period from the tenth to the sixteenth centuries. These dates often vary from piece to piece: thus in the latest composed setting, the popular *Missa de Angelis*, the following dates are given: *Kyrie*, fifteenth to sixteenth centuries; *Gloria*, sixteenth century; *Sanctus*, eleventh to twelfth centuries; *Agnus Dei*, fifteenth century. These are, of course, manuscript dates; but some of the melodies of the Ordinary clearly show their primitive origin, though the majority are post-Gregorian and, as their nature suggests, were composed at a time when the *schola* had taken over the singing of the Ordinary. The primitive chants are the *Kyries* of Masses XVI–XVIII; the *Gloria* of Mass XV (a Mass for Simple Feasts, which as Dom Gregory Murray says, 'is little more than a variant of the fourth-mode psalm tone . . . it bears a strong family likeness to the Preface, the *Pater noster*, and the other chants of the celebrant'); the *Sanctus* and *Agnus Dei* of Mass XVIII and the Requiem Mass (in which *miserere nobis* is replaced by *dona eis requiem*, and *dona nobis pacem* by *dona eis requiem sempiternam*).

Agnus Dei is sung, as an invocation, at the end of the Litany of the Saints on Holy Saturday – which shows the liturgy of the Mass in the earliest state now retained – the melody being the same as in the Mass XVIII mentioned above.

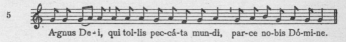

Agnus De-i, qui tol-lis pec-cá-ta mun-di, par-ce no-bis Dó-mi-ne.

(Lamb of God, who takes away the sins of the world, spare us, Lord.)

Kyrie. *Kyrie eleison* is sung at the start of the Litany of the Saints on Holy Saturday (and of course wherever else it is used) and again to the Paschal melody (Mass I), after the Litany is finished, signifying the start of the Mass of the Easter Vigil.[1]

No one knows when the *Kyrie* was first used in the Roman Mass, but it certainly formed part of the Liturgy by the early sixth century and may have done so well before. In a letter written in 598, to John, Bishop of Syracuse, St Gregory, refuting a charge of being too ready to imitate the customs of Constantinople, says 'the *Kyrie eleison* we neither have said nor do say as it is said by the Greeks: for among the Greeks all say it together; but with us it is said by the clergy and the people reply, and also *Christe eleison* is added an equal number of times, which is never said at all among the Greeks.' The fixed number of times each petition should be sung – three each, as now – is first recorded in 831 or 832, by the liturgical

1. The reformed rites of Holy Week, including the restoration of the Solemn Easter vigil, were put into force by general decree authorized by Pius XII, *Maxima Redemptionis Nostrae Mysteria* (16 November 1955), and can be found in *The Holy Week Manual* (Burns & Oates, 1956).

scholar Amalarius of Metz, who had been sent to Rome by the Emperor Louis to report on liturgical practice and other matters, and found the ninefold *Kyrie* in use there.

The great outburst of creative activity (which extended to all the arts), that produced quantities of new and adapted chants in the form of tropes and sequences, appears to have begun on a large scale in the course of the eighth century, but may go back considerably earlier.

The Greek word *tropos* means melody, but with regard to the liturgy it signifies the addition of melody or text only, or both, to an already existing chant with the result that a florid melody might be extended, or be provided as it stood, with words. The oldest tropes in existence are thought to be the work of Tuotilo, monk of St Gall, poet, player on wind and string instruments, architect, and sculptor.

The best known form of the trope is the *Sequence*, which has been dealt with in the preceding section.

Tropes and sequences were optional additions to the liturgy, tolerated only by authority, for the venerated corpus of Gregorian chant could in no way be officially tampered with.

It was a very common practice to 'farce' (or 'stuff') the *Kyrie*, and we are reminded of this in reading the sub-titles that still appear in the *Kyriale* section of the *Gradual* and give their names to the various Masses. Thus Mass IV has the sub-title '*Cunctipotens genitor, Deus*'. The word Kyrie was omitted and the interpolated text began: 'Cunctipotens genitor, Deus omnicreator, eleison', the words being fitted to the *Kyrie* melody.

(All-powerful Father, Lord creator of all things, have mercy on us.)

This process, as the example above shows, rendered the neumatic melody syllabic. Almost all parts of the liturgy were 'troped' in one way or another; and though liturgists may disapprove of these outcrops, they bear witness to the inevitable desire to break new ground. They are the first independent compositions by known authors.

Gloria and Credo. An entry in *Ordo Romanus* I, describing the ceremonial of a papal Mass in St Gregory's time, makes it appear possible that the people sang the *Gloria,* as well as the *Kyrie*:

When they have finished (the *Kyrie*) the pontiff turns towards the people and begins *Gloria in excelsis* (if it be in season) and immediately turns back again towards the east till it is finished. Then turning again towards the people he says *Pax vobis:* and once more turning to the east, he says *Oremus* and the prayer follows.

By the ninth century the *Schola Cantorum* had taken over the singing of the *Gloria.* A comparison of the simple *Gloria* of Mass XII, which rarely exceeds the compass of a fifth (in the phrase before the *Amen*), with the 'cantus ad libitum' *Gloria* III will show how far the latter is outside the scope of any but a skilled group of singers.

(In the Glory of God the Father.)

The first clear evidence of the singing of the *Gloria,* originally a Greek morning hymn, in the Mass of Christmas night, is found in a sermon by Pope St Leo I. By the twelfth century it was no longer reserved to bishops, with priests being allowed to sing it only on Easter Sunday, but could be used also by the latter at all the appointed times.

The Roman Church was the last to introduce the *Credo* into the Mass. Berno, Abbot of Reichenau, when in Rome (in February 1017) for the coronation of the Emperor, Henry II, inquired why it was not sung; he was told that the Roman Church, free, as others were not, of heretical taints, had no need to affirm its faith. The Emperor, however, finally succeeded in persuading Pope Benedict VIII to have the *Credo* sung at Mass, but it is still reserved to Masses of higher rank.

There are six settings in the *Kyriale* of which the latest composed, No. III (seventeenth-century), is the most popular and one of the few chants in which congregations today (at any rate in some churches) manage to break their prevailing silence and join in. It is most inspiring to hear the *Credo* sung by a vast throng of people of all nations in the Square before the Basilica of St Peter's on some great occasion.

Sanctus–Benedictus. The singing of the *Sanctus*, 'the angelical hymn', was, according to Ordo Romanus I, a regular feature of the Mass in the time of St Gregory and was probably sung by the people up to the sixth and seventh centuries, after which it was taken over by the clergy and finally appropriated by the choir.

In the old manuscripts, as in the modern *Gradual*, the *Sanctus* and *Benedictus* appear as one chant and their separation – one sung before the consecration and the other after the elevation of the Chalice – is wholly due to the length of time the celebrant was often kept waiting for the consecration by polyphonic settings of the chant.

The words of the *Benedictus*, taken from Psalm CXVII, are those with which the people greeted Our Lord as he rode triumphantly into Jerusalem on Palm Sunday, *Hosanna in excelsis* being their own spontaneous cry of praise. (It is now permitted to sing *Sanctus–Benedictus* as one chant in plainsong, and of course also in figured music when the setting is brief – as for example in William Byrd's *Mass for Three Voices*.)

Agnus Dei. The *Liber Pontificalis* tells us that Pope Sergius (687–701) ordered that 'at the time of the breaking of the Body of the Lord' *Agnus Dei, qui tollis peccata mundi, miserere nobis* should be sung by clergy and people. The text, as we have seen, is taken from the Litany. The *Agnus Dei*, in the ninth century, was sung twice, by the *schola* and then by the clergy, but in the twelfth century it was sung, as now, three times, with *dona nobis pacem* replacing *miserere nobis* at the end of the third petition. However, as Innocent III (1216) relates, the Roman *schola cantorum* maintained an ancient custom of singing *miserere nobis* at the end of each of the three petitions, and the Lateran Basilica still follows this tradition.

THE DIVINE OFFICE

St Benedict (*c.* 480–550), the 'Patriarch of Western Monasticism', speaking, in his *Rule*, of those who came late to the oratory, says '*Ergo nihil operi Dei praeponatur*' ('Let nothing be put before the work of God'). By the 'work of God' he meant the totality of the liturgy, but, in particular, the *Officium Divinum*, the Divine Office, also called the Canonical Office.

This wonderful treasury of prayer is generally little known except by visitors to great Benedictine monastic houses, who, if they rise early enough, can be present at the Night Office (Matins and Lauds) and at the day hours (Prime, Terce, Sext, None, Vespers) and at the monks' night prayer, the office of Compline, when the whole community gathers together at the completion of the day (*ad completorium*) after which the 'great silence' falls on the house until early the next morning, that is, at whatever hour Matins and Lauds are said.

Psalmody is the foundation of prayer and praise in the Office, and the hours themselves centre round the words from Psalm CXVIII: 164, 'Seven times a day I have given praise to thee', and from the same psalm, 'I rose at midnight to give praise to thee.'

The monk, from the beginning of his monastic life, had to try to memorize the whole psalter, and to learn by heart, also, the short lessons and the most common liturgical formulas.

Those who had every night to read the Scripture or the Fathers from manuscripts which were full of abbreviations, perhaps defaced by use or faded, by the dim light of a smoky lamp and without the help of spectacles, generally required special preparation. If the reader failed to make himself understood his hearers could not turn to their books, as we can, for breviaries were not invented and manuscripts were rare.[1]

There is considerable divergence of opinion among liturgical scholars in regard to the origins of the Office, but according to one writer all the evidence is that Vespers, Matins, and Lauds grew out of the vigil which was *the* public liturgy of the church at which everyone assisted. This therefore was an ecclesiastical, not a monastic office.

There seems to have been a double tradition from the time that certain pious persons took a larger burden of prayer upon themselves and eventually formed themselves into religious communities. The letters of the Spanish Abbess Etheria show the two types of service 'closely united but not yet entirely fused into one'. Tertullian (*c.* 160 – *c.* 220), African Church Father (and the first Christian theologian to write in Latin), speaks of regular vigils which he calls *Nocturnae convocationes* (lit. 'Nightly callings together'), a service in preparation (like the Paschal Vigil) for the Holy Eucharist. The term 'nocturns', as we shall see, was retained for the first part of the night-office, later called *Matins*, the second part, *Matutinae Laudes* (morning praises),[2] being then called simply *Lauds*. The two types of office (ecclesiastical and monastic), Benedict Steuart writes, 'were not only distinguished by the different number of services in each but by the difference in the *intention* for which such acts of worship were offered; the public service of prayer and praise offered by the Church was based upon that of the Jewish liturgy from which it was derived.' The Church, therefore, gave thanks, as did the Jews, for God's gift of light to man, the sun in the morning and man's power to produce light in the evening, but read mystical and spiritual meanings into the creation of light and the coming of darkness. Thus the last two stanzas of one of the beautiful hymns by the Spanish poet, Aurelius Prudentius Clemens (348–431), *Nox et tenebrae*

---

1. David Knowles, *The Monastic Order in England*.
2. Lauds received its name from the frequent occurrence of psalms beginning *Lauda* or *Laudate* in the monastic office at this hour.

et nubila (Lauds of Wednesday), vividly compares the dawn with the coming of Christ –

Night and darkness and clouds, all the world's confusion and disorder, be gone – light is piercing through; the sky is becoming bright: Christ is coming.

At Prime the hymn *Jam lucis orto sidere* ('Now that the sun has risen') by an unknown author, and written some time between the fifth and eighth centuries, prays for help in the day's work, as also do the hymns at Terce and Sext. They speak of 'the burning heat of noon' and allude to 'the successive change of the light of day and a prayer for light in the evening'. These last three hymns are possibly by St Ambrose, the father of Latin hymnody, and, if not, are at least by one author only.

In the hymns at Vespers fear of darkness is prevalent. The Sunday hymn *Lucis creator optime*, sometimes attributed to St Gregory, praises the creator of light and goes on to speak of 'night with all its fears' now falling. This fear is again expressed in the Compline hymn *Te lucis ante terminum* (*c.* 600) which prays that 'no ill dreams or nightly fears and fantasies' (*noctium phantasmata*) may come near.

In his Rule, St Benedict makes provision in all the hours for what he calls an *Ambrosianum* (that is a hymn, not otherwise specified, borrowed from St Ambrose and the liturgy of Milan – though the term may not have been used exclusively in that sense). The Roman Church's reserved attitude towards hymns, which were not finally admitted into the Secular Office until the twelfth century, stems from prejudice against putting other than Biblical words into the liturgy and even more from the use of the form by heretics to further their errors. The classic instance of this practice is Bardesanes (154–222), a native of Edessa and the father of Syrian hymnology, whose unorthodox doctrines were diffused through his immensely popular hymns. St Ephrem, the Syrian ecclesiastical writer, who settled at Edessa in 363, composed cycles of hymns which included some combating Bardesanes and other heretics of the age.

The long line of writers of Latin hymns includes St Ambrose (340–97), Sedulius (ninth century), Venantius

Fortunatus (*c.* 535–*c.* 600), Peter Abelard (1079–1142), and St Thomas Aquinas (1225–74). *Vexilla Regis prodeunt* ('The royal banners forward go') which Fortunatus wrote for the coming of a fragment of the Holy Rood to Poitiers became, 500 years later, the marching song of the Crusaders. Fortunatus also wrote *Verbum supernum prodiens*, sung at Lauds on the Feast of Corpus Christi, and Thomas Aquinas *Pange lingua gloriosi corporis mysterium*, used as a processional hymn for that Feast. *Pange lingua gloriosi proelium certaminis* is a Passiontide hymn by Fortunatus. The Pentecostal hymn *Veni creator spiritus*, by an unknown author of the ninth century, was in use at ordinations by the eleventh century and *Te Deum*, a prose hymn probably by St Nicetas of Remesiana (335–415), endowed with a majesty and freedom that no other hymn of the Latin Church possesses, is sung at the end of Matins on all Sundays (except those of Advent and Lent) and on feast days, and on occasions of great rejoicing. All these are well known outside their proper setting in the Divine Office; and the same is true of many of the responsories of the great days of Holy Week (Maundy Thursday, Good Friday, and Holy Saturday) which are best known in polyphonic settings by Victoria and Ingegneri, as for example, *O vos omnes* and *Tenebrae factae sunt*. We shall now see what place psalmody, hymns, and responsories take in the structure of the Roman Office.[1]

Matins

Invitatory (Psalm XCIV – *Venite exultemus Domino* – with refrain varying according to the season or feast)
Hymn

First Nocturn

Three psalms with their antiphons sung before and after the psalms
Versicle and Response. Pater noster. Absolution.[2] Blessing
Three Lessons from Scripture each of them followed by a long Responsory

1. The Office said by secular priests.
2. So called as one of the prayers said under this heading is of a penitential character.

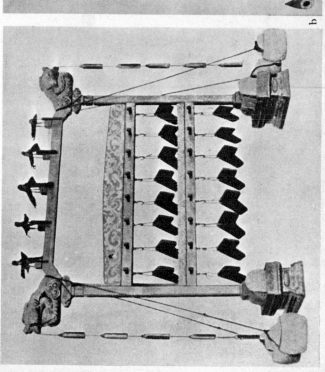

(a) Chinese stone chime, (b) Chinese reed mouth organ, (c) Chinese musical notation

I

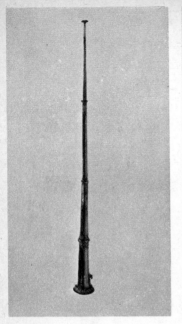

(a) Tibetan monastery trumpet

(b) Tibetan monastery oboe

(c) Tibetan skull drum and horn

(a) Monks singing from a noted Missal

(b) Choir (the Director is King David)

The antiphon *Tecum principium* in four versions:
  (a) Sarum Antiphoner, thirteenth century
  (b) Mozarabic Antiphoner, eleventh century
  (c) Roman Antiphoner, seventeenth century
  (d) German Antiphoner, twelfth century

Antiphona.

T Ecum princí- pium in die

vir- tútis tuæ : in splendó-ribus sanctórum,

ex útero ante lucí- ferum génui- te.

Psalmus
Dixit Do-
minus.

Euouae.i. Ant. Redemptiónem misit

c

Tecum principium in die virtutas tuæ in spl

doribus scorum ex utero ante luciferum

genuie Dixit dns Sv.... Redemptionem

d

5

Nuns in choir

Rhythmic notation from a manuscript at St Gall

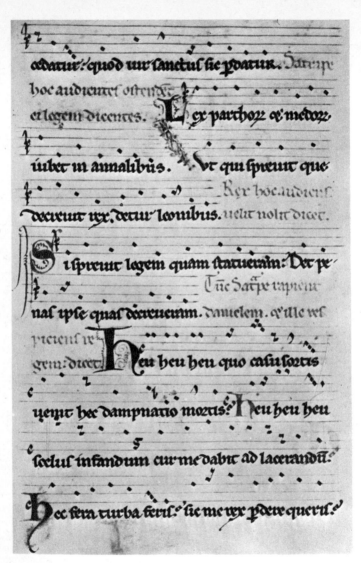

Part of *The Play of Daniel*, twelfth century

8

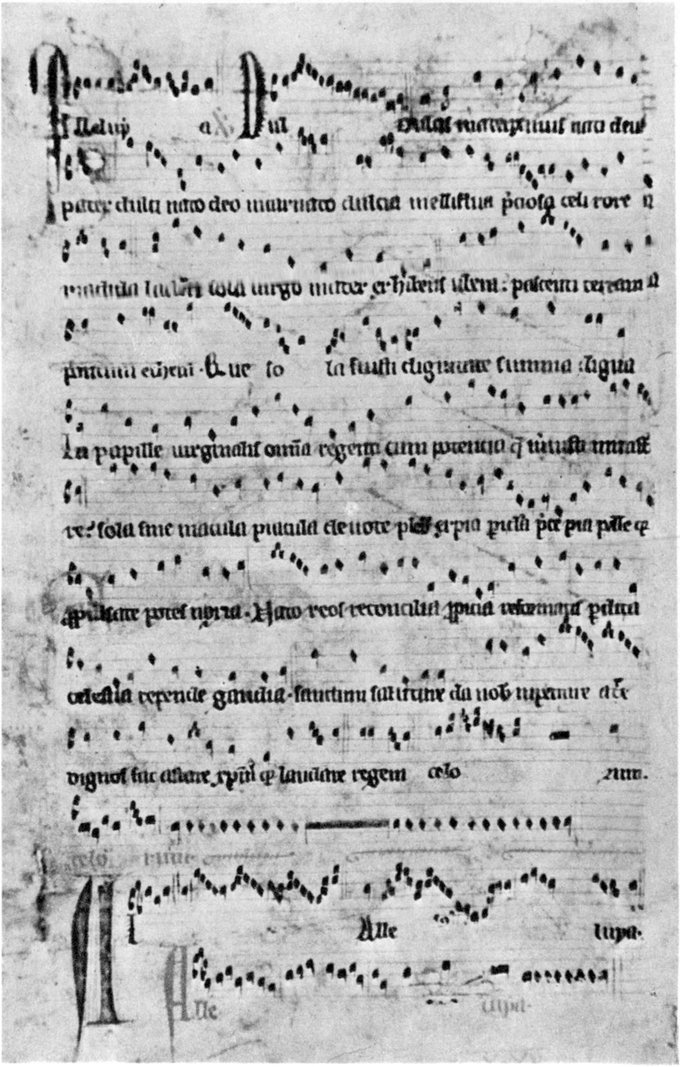

A polyphonic *Alleluia*, thirteenth century

(a) Two-part setting of *Victimae paschali laudes*, thirteenth century

(b) Jongleurs and minstrels

(a *left*) Medieval musician and cancer
(b *above*) Monks singing from a choirbook

11

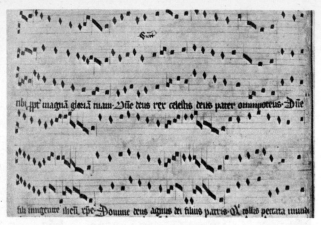

(a) Three-part *Gloria* in score notation, fourteenth century

(b) Aleyn's motet *Fons citharizancium*, fourteenth century

Gran piant' agli ochi, by Francesco Landini, fourteenth century

Music at a medieval banquet

King David and Minstrels

Medieval musicians

The first two Responsories are sung with one repeat of a section of their text after the verse; the third Responsory makes the same repeat but adds the first half of the lesser doxology and a further repeat. The following is the text of the Responsory at the end of the first Nocturn of Matins of Christmas Day and will make the procedure clear:

Quem vidistis, * pastores? dicite, annuntiate nobis, in terris quis apparuit? * Natum vidimus, et choros angelorum collaudantes Dominum. ℣. Dicite, quidnam vidistis? et annuntiate Christi nativitatem.* Natum. . . Gloria Patri. . .* Natum. . .
(O ye shepherds, speak, and tell us what ye have seen: who is appeared in the earth? We saw the new-born Child, and angels singing praise to the Lord. ℣. Speak; what have ye seen? And tell us of the Birth of Christ.

(The first asterisk in the Latin text marks the end of the *incipit*, or intonation sung by the cantor before the choir enters, the other three the points at which the choir makes the repeats. The verse and first half of the *Gloria Patri* are sung by the cantors.)

Second and Third Nocturns
These follow the same scheme as the above, with lessons taken from sermons by the Fathers of the Church or lives of the Saints, etc., in the Second Nocturn and from the New Testament in the Third Nocturn. When the *Te Deum* is sung after the ninth lesson the double-repeat Responsory is transferred to the end of the eighth lesson.[1]

Lauds
This hour has four psalms and a canticle from the Old Testament (Song of the Three Children, Song of Jeremiah, etc.) sung between the third and fifth psalms. All have antiphons. Capitulum (a brief passage from Scripture)

1. The pattern of the Responsory varies and can be markedly different from the normal scheme given above. Ferial offices only have one Nocturn.

Hymn
Versicle and Response
Canticle of Zacharias (*Benedictus*) with antiphon

Prime

Hymn. Three or four psalms under one antiphon
Capitulum
Short Responsory
   The form of this differs from the long Responsory; the following is the text for Christmas Day:

R. *Christe Fili Dei vivi* * *Miserere nobis.*
℣. *Qui natus es de Maria Virgine* * *Miserere nobis.* ℣. *Gloria Patri.*
R. *Christe Fili Dei vivi* * *Miserere nobis.*

The choir repeats the whole response after the cantors, sings the second portion of the Verse and the whole response after the *Gloria* (Christ, Son of the living God, have mercy on us, who was born of the Virgin, have mercy on us).
Versicle and response and various prayers.

Terce, Sext, None

Hymn
Three psalms under one antiphon
Capitulum
Short Responsory, Versicle, and Response

Vespers

The same pattern as at Lauds (often with the same antiphons), but with five psalms and no Old Testament Canticle. *Magnificat*, with antiphon, as the New Testament Canticle.

Compline

After the opening blessing, and a short reading from Scripture, general confession with absolution, three psalms under one antiphon, hymn, chapter, short responsory, versicle, and response. The Song of Simeon (*Nunc Dimittis*) with antiphon. One of the four antiphons of Our Lady (*Alma Redemptoris Mater; Ave Regina coelorum; Regina coeli laetare; Salve Regina*) is sung, according to the season, after Compline, and, on occasion, after Lauds and Vespers.

The completed Office, monastic or secular, is built on foundations that go back to the early ages when men and women fled from the corrupt life of the great cities – as St Antony of Egypt did from Alexandria – into the desert and there organized themselves into coenobitic communities. St Benedict, who, in a later age, himself fled from Rome to lead a hermit's life in a cave at Subiaco – and later founded the great monastery at Monte Cassino, now happily restored after its destruction in the Second World War – gave his monks a Rule that superseded all others in the West: and indeed 'from the eighth to the twelfth centuries Benedictine monachism was the only form of religious life known to the West, and the fountain-head of the liturgical tradition that flourishes in the Benedictine monasteries of today, where the *Opus Dei* is still the most important work of the monks.'[1]

It is fitting that the restoration of Gregorian chant should have been entrusted to this great Order and that they should have convinced the world that it was not a formless, rhythmless kind of barbaric ululation.

THE GREGORIAN COMPOSERS

It is convenient to speak of the anonymous authors of Gregorian chant as composers, although they would not have recognized the word; they were craftsmen inheriting, in the course of centuries, melodic formulas or actual melodies that they regarded with great reverence, working always within determined liturgical areas and subject to liturgical laws, producing, in fact, functional music that was and is the most practical kind of church music – for it never delays liturgical action – and the most satisfying aesthetically and spiritually – because of its perfect adaptation of the means to the end. It is, indeed, perfect prayer-song.

1. Knowles, op. cit.

The various forms of plainsong have been mentioned already in these pages, but now we must examine some of them more closely.

Antiphonal psalmody

The essence of antiphonal psalmody lies in the alternate singing of two groups, as opposed to one group responding to a soloist (one or two cantors) in responsorial psalmody. In antiphonal psalmody a refrain came to be sung before the psalm and after each verse or pair of verses. These refrains (after the period of mere exclamations) were first of all taken from the psalm itself, as in the one complete form of early antiphonal singing left in the Mass, the Antiphon and Canticle sung during the distribution of the candles on the Feast of the Purification of the B.V.M. It will be seen that the text of the antiphon is taken from the fourth verse of the *Nunc Dimittis*.

(A light to lighten the gentiles, and for the glory of thy people Israel. Now lettest thou thy servant depart, O Lord, according to thy word, in peace.)

The provision of an original text, that is one not taken from the psalm to be sung, but from elsewhere in Scripture, and the repetition of the antiphon only at the end of the psalm were later developments. The antiphon, in general, can be regarded as a practical way of giving the pitch, indicating the mode of the psalm tone, and, liturgically, as providing a leading idea, to be kept in mind during the singing of the psalm. An examination of the antiphons of Lauds and Vespers of Christmas or

Easter will give a good idea of the way in which the dominant note of the feast is carried through each of these 'hours'.

The psalmody of the Office occupied several hours of the night and day. To ensure a smooth transition to the antiphon the eight psalm tones[1] were provided with a number of different endings. These are indicated, in the Antiphonary, alongside the number of the mode of the antiphon. In each case the vowels *E u o u a e* are put after the *Gloria Patri* and represent the ending chosen fitted to sa E c U l O r U m A in E u. In the example, the antiphon is marked Seventh Mode, ending 7.c. The antiphon ends with the final of the mode; the psalm tone ending is chosen so as to fit on smoothly to the first note of the antiphon, for this may begin on any note of the mode.

The example below shows the intonation (*incipit*), reciting note (*tuba*), middle cadence (*meditatio*), reciting note, and end cadence (*terminatio*):

The antiphons of the Office, unlike those in the Mass, are usually of a simple character as they were intended for the ordinary choir monks, not the *schola*; but they tend to be more elaborate on great Feast days. In the canticles of the New Testament the intonation is repeated all the way through.

Responsorial Psalmody

Gradual.[2] The Gradual Responsory as sung today has lost its

1. There is a ninth psalm tone, with two reciting notes, called the *Tonus peregrinus* – the 'stranger' tone.

2. From Low Sunday to the Sunday after the Ascension the *Gradual* is omitted and replaced by another *Alleluia*.

character. When the cantors have sung the verse, the opening
section should be repeated. This would certainly lengthen the
Gradual, but the omission may make nonsense of the text, as
for example in the Feast of John the Baptist when the verse
ends '(the Lord) touched my mouth and said to me' – but what
He said (the words sung at the start of the *Gradual*) is not repeated. The *Gradual* remains, therefore, an A B form, instead
of A B A, and is truncated for reasons of convenience, not because of any ban by the Sacred Congregation of Rites.

Alleluia. The *Alleluia* is a three-part form (except in Easter
week when the Sequence *Victimae paschali laudes* immediately
follows its verse), and repeats sometimes the whole of the
Alleluia melody after the asterisk in the verse, or more usually
the *jubilus* complete or shortened: but the verse may have a
completely independent melody throughout.

(*Alleluia.* ℣ A faithful man will burgeon like the lily, will blossom in
the Lord's sight for ever. Alleluia.)

Kyrie. Sanctus. Agnus Dei. The nine-fold *Kyrie eleison* invites
and receives varied treatment in the settings of the Ordinary
of the Mass. The simplest form is A (first three Kyries) B
(Christes) A 1 (second three Kyries). In every case the artistic
instinct of composers led them to make some variation of the
melody in the final *Kyrie.*

11

Ky-ri - e * e lé - i - son. Chri-ste e - lé - i - son.
Ky-ri - e e - lé-i-son. Ky-ri - e e - léi - son.

There may be a varied strain for the last three Kyries so that
the formula is A B C (e.g. Mass II in the *Kyriale*), or the
formula may be applied to the first and last Kyries and the
Christes, or we may find this formula A B A^1, C D C^1,
D E D^1 (Ex. 2).

The 'dismissal' sentence at the end of Mass (*Ite missa est* or
Benedicamus Domino) is usually set to the melody of the first
Kyrie of the Mass used.

In the *Sanctus, Hosanna in excelsis* is usually given the same
melodic phrase when repeated after *Benedictus.* The *Agnus
Dei* may have the same melody for each of the three petitions
or follow the *Kyrie* forms noted above.

Hymns and Sequences

The Office hymns have, of course, a strophic form, but vary in
their metre. The majority of them are in the iambic dimeters.
St Ambrose used this metre, following Syrian custom, for the
hymns he wrote for his people when they were guarding their
Church at Milan against the Arians led by the Empress
Justina, so that they should, having these and psalms to sing,
not 'pine away in the tediousness of sorrow'. When the siege
ended the custom of hymn singing was retained and imitated
'by almost all of Thy congregations throughout the rest of the
world'.

St Augustine, whose report is quoted above, defined the iambic foot as 'a short and a long of three beats', but the hymns certainly by Ambrose in the Roman Breviary, *Aeterne rerum conditor* (Sunday, Lauds), *Splendor paternae gloriae* (Monday, Lauds), *Aeterna Christi munera* (Common of many Martyrs), are put into notes of equal value in the present-day Antiphonary. If the melody of, let us say, *Aeterna Christi munera* is sung according to the metre of the text it would, in modern notation, be printed as below:

12

Ae - tér - na Chri - sti mú - ne - ra - et már - ty - rum vi -
-cto - ri - as, lau - des fe - ren - tes de - bi - tas, lae-
-tis ca - vá - mus mén - ti - bus.

(With joy of heart let us sing a hymn as our tribute of praise to Christ's eternal gifts and the Martyrs' victories.) Trans. Joseph Connelly, *The Hymns of the Roman Liturgy*.

Accent was already replacing quantity in the time of St Ambrose, and so the composers of hymns thereafter were free to ignore the metre, and did so. It has been suggested that the original melodies of St Ambrose's hymns were adapted Italian folk-songs, which might account for their enormous popularity. He was, indeed, charged with 'bewitching' the people with them.

It has been said that 'the popular poetry of the Romans seems to have been founded on accent from the beginning . . . one must seek for the origins of liturgical poetry in popular rhyme founded on accent, even though the models of these compositions (the hymns in the Office) were, in general, of classical metre.'

The eighth-century hymn *Ut queant laxis*, for the Feast of St John the Baptist, suggested the modern system of solmization (tonic sol-fa) to Guido of Arezzo (b. *c.* 995). It so happens that each half-line of the melody begins on the next ascending note, and in the first verse these melodic rises coincide, all but the last, with the sol-fa syllables

> *Ut* queant laxis *Re*sonare fibris
> *Mi*ra gestorum *Fa*muli tuorum
> *So*lve polluti *La*bii reatum,
> Sancte Johannes.

The Sequence texts, of course, owed nothing in their origin to classical models, for they had to adapt themselves to the melodies of the *Alleluia*, one note to one syllable; but in the independent compositions which (when the poet expanded, compressed, or modified the melody) they became, the metrical texts follow, most usually, trochaic rhythm.

In the late eleventh century 'the words are in regular verse form; there is a marked tendency to alternate accented and unaccented syllables as well as to equalize the length of the lines, and the ends of the lines are distinguished by rhyme.' The earlier sequence was not so regular in form. The text of *Victimae Paschali Laudes* (first half of the eleventh century) is a good example of the type.

The other Sequences retained in the *Gradual*, with the exception of *Stabat Mater*, all share in one remarkable feature. After a certain number of phrases the melody 'is thrown up a fifth in the scale; not repeated exactly, but definitely continued at the higher pitch'.

The melody of *Victimae Paschali Laudes* covers a compass of an eleventh. This is, of course, paralleled in some *Graduals* – e.g. *Jubilate Deo universa terra* (Epiphany) – but these show a gradual rise to the highest point, not an abrupt change of register as here. And so while the lower phrases of the Sequence would lie comfortably for basses, the higher ones would not, and *vice versa* for tenors.

'This contrast between final and dominant is new,' as Dr

Vi - cti-mae pa-schá-li láu-des * im-mo-lent Chri-sti - á - ni.

(Christians, to the paschal victim offer sacrifice and praise. The sheep are ransomed by the Lamb; and Christ, the undefiled, hath sinners to his Father reconciled. Death with life contended; Combat strangely ended. Life's own Champion slain, yet lives to reign. Tell us, Mary, say what thou didst see on the way? The tomb the Living did enclose; shroud with grave-clothes resting. Christ, my hope, is truly risen from the dead we know. Victorious King, thy mercy show. Amen. Alleluia.) *Ex. 13 reproduced by permission of Messrs Desclée.*

Frere said, 'worked out systematically and made quite formal and normal'. 'It was', as Dom Anselm Hughes writes in the introduction to *Anglo-French Sequelae*, 'a very short step from a repetition of a melody at the fifth above by a different set of voices to the simultaneous performance of that melody by the two sets of voices, at the interval of a fifth.' But that point, involving polyphony, takes me out of my territory.

4. The Roman Rite: At Work on the Chant

IN one of his articles in the *Sunday Times* Ernest Newman wrote: 'Sibelius, like every other composer, unconsciously casts his ideas into a dozen or so type-formulas and type-procedures that recur, in whatever veiled forms, in everything he writes.'

The Gregorian craftsmen, but consciously and as a body, worked much in the same sort of way. There was a common stock of revered melodic formulas on which they drew, and of type procedures for making use of them. They did not seek to be original or directly to express themselves as individuals but worked for a common purpose – the enrichment of the liturgy *ad majorem Dei gloriam*. They could not, however, escape being individuals and we can only guess at what human touches have gone into the adapted texts and melodies or what visitations of inspiration into the newly composed melodies.

Their work falls into three classes: (a) original, or free melodies; (b) melody-types adapted to a number of different texts; (c) centonized melodies made out of traditional formulas.

ORIGINAL MELODIES

The original melodies are the most numerous of all; they are the basic chants of the Mass and Office, forming a treasure house to which later composers resorted when music was required for new feasts rather than add anything of their own to their highly revered heritage. The original melodies, of course, drew on the common stock of formulas, especially in the incipits and final cadences: these are, as Abbot Ferretti says, the framework of the picture. He analyses, in his book *Aestetica Gregoriana*, an example of an original melody, the magnificent and often quoted Offertory, *Jubilate Deo universa terra* (second Sunday after Epiphany), which begins with a very familiar formula, rises to a sublime climax with the second *jubilate*, and at *Deo universa terra* repeats and develops the theme first associated with those words. The phrases at *nomini*, *omnes* and *Venite, audite, et*, should also be noticed.

TYPE MELODIES

An original melody is used, in this kind of composition, as a type or model to be adapted to a new text. Gevaert reduces the antiphon melodies, which number over 1,200, to forty-seven types and Dom Mocquereau in a study of the intonation of an antiphon of the first mode type, *Tu es pastor ovium*, calls attention to no less than seventy-five variations on this antiphon in a single MS. The same process, on a much smaller scale, is used in the *Gradual*, and the reader, as an example of it, should compare the two Offertories in the 4th mode, *Afferentur regi virgines* (the type) and *Exultabunt sancti* (the adaptation), or the

14

(a) Tu es pa-stor ó-vi-um prin-ceps A-po-sto-ló-rum:
ti-bi trá-di-tae sunt cla - ves re-gni cae-ló-rum.

(b) Ful-cí-te me fló-ri-bus, sti-pá-te me ma-lis
qui-a a-mó-re lán-gue-o.

(c) Pu-éll-ae sal-tan-ti im-pe-rá-vit ma — ter:
ni-hil á-li-ud pe-tas ni-si ca-put Jo-án-nes.

((a) Thou art shepherd of the sheep, the Prince of the Apostles, to thee have been given the keys of the Kingdom of Heaven. (b) Stay me with flowers, sustain me with fruits, for I am faint with love. (c) To the girl as she danced her mother commanded: 'Do thou ask nothing but the head of John'.)

two *Graduals* of the 2nd mode, *Justus ut palma* (the type) and
Angelis suis (the adaptation).

Greater liberty was, naturally, possible in adapting antiphons
than in adapting Mass chants. Abbot Ferretti shows by means
of a chart how the type-antiphon *Omnes de Saba* was adapted to
twenty-one other antiphons by addition or omission of certain
notes according to the necessities of the new texts. I give
above the type melody *Tu es pastor ovium* and two examples of
adaptation.

CENTONIZED MELODIES

Centone is an Italian word for a patchwork or quilt, and is
applied in an analogous sense to text and music in antiphons
and responsories, introits and graduals, in the Gregorian
repertory that use this technique. As one example of liturgical
text centonization, Ferretti quotes the Communion antiphon
of the Mass of Ash Wednesday with a text drawn from Psalm
I: the conflation of material, made up of the words italicized in
the psalm, is done with great skill.

Original Psalm	*Communion* (centonized text)
V 1. Beatus vir *qui* non abiit	
V 2. Sed *in lege Domini*	Qui meditabitur in
Voluntas eius, et in lege eius	lege Domini die ac nocte,
meditabitur die ac nocte	dabit fructum suum in
V 3. Et erit tamquam lignum quod	tempore suo.
plantatum est secus decursus	
aquarum, quod *fructum*	
suum dabit in tempore suo.	

To show how these melodies were built up Ferretti gives a
table of five formulas of intonation, and twelve central formulas,
and applies them to thirty-two verses of text with a figure over
each phrase giving the formulas used. He then tabulates and
applies thirty-seven more of them in the same way.

It is only possible to give a few and familiar examples of
these fragments of melodic mosaic at the disposal of the
centonizer.

De - us Gá - bri - el hó - di - e vír - gam i - ste

WORD-PAINTING, EXPRESSION, AND DRAMA

The Gregorian composers were men with human emotions subject to liturgical considerations. It would be intolerable if the psalms, let us say in the long night Office, were sung according to their varying sentiments, a *Jubilate* joyfully or a *De profundis* sadly. Nothing could be permitted to disturb the even flow of the chanting: the words sufficiently conveyed their meaning and in a corporate action there is no room for *personal* expression; the feast round which Mass and Office were centred was borne in mind, and what was felt was felt interiorly. Nevertheless, outside psalmody, the choir, singing as a body, would not sing on one monotonous level of tone; they would inescapably respond as a body to a heightening of emotion in text and music as expressed in certain pieces. They would respond to the poignant words added to the *Dies irae* – 'Pie

Pi - e Jé - su Dó - mi - ne, do - na e - is ré - qui - em.

O clé - mens, O pí - a, O dúl - cis

Vír - go Ma - rí - a

O Jé - su dúl - cis. O Jé - su pí - e.

O Jé - su fí - li Ma - rí - ae.

((a) Lord of mercy, Jesus blest, grant them everlasting rest. (b) O clement, O loving, O sweet Virgin Mary. (c) O sweet Jesus, O loving Jesus, O Jesus son of Mary.)

Jesu Domine, dona eis requiem' – and to the tenderness of the closing words of the *Salve Regina* – '*O clemens, O pia, O dulcis Virgo Maria*' – or, in the *Ave Verum* – '*O dulcis, O pie, O Jesu fili Mariae*'.

With regard to word-painting it is true that in one chant such words as *ascendit* or *descendit* may be pictorially set but disregarded, in this sense, in another. Nevertheless one cannot ignore the representational settings of these words.

17

((a) He has ascended. (b) Jesus went down [with them] (c) Until [God] arose.)

Joy and sorrow are unmistakably illustrated in many chants. There is the great soaring phrase at '*Surge et illuminare*' in the *Gradual* of the Epiphany Mass, *Omnes de Saba*.

18

(Arise and shine, Jerusalem.)

What poignancy there is in the lamenting phrases of the Offertory in the Mass for the 20th Sunday after Pentecost, *Super flumina Babylonis* (Ex. 19).

And how heavily burdened with sorrow is the eighth Responsory, *O vos omnes*, in Matins of Holy Saturday; how charmingly the singing of the turtle-dove is illustrated in the

(While we remembered thee, O Sion.)

verse of the *Alleluia* in the feast of the Apparition of the B.V.M.
Such instances could be multiplied.

What, for drama, could be more striking than the sudden
cry of *Adjuva nos, Deus salutaris noster*, coming, after a low-
pitched section, in the Tract first heard on Ash Wednesday;
or the great cry from the Cross in the Good Friday responsory
Tenebrae factae sunt.

((a) Help us, O God, our Salvation. (b) My God, why hast thou
forsaken me?)

Sometimes a whole drama in miniature is presented to us, as
in the Communion Antiphon in the Mass of the Third Sunday
after Epiphany, the miracle at Cana. The phrase in Ex. 21 is
twice repeated, emphasizing the goodness of the wine.

(The Lord said, 'Fill the water jars with water, and take them to the president of the feast.' When the president had tasted the water made wine he saith to the bridegroom 'Thou hast kept the good wine till now'. This was the first sign which Jesus did before his disciples.)

Dom Gajard's notes in the booklet issued with the Decca records of chants sung by the monks of Solesmes show what the chant means to a monk who has sung it, day in and day out, for years. Each of the modes has a special ethos for him, each piece of chant its spiritual–emotional effect. His comments may be considered rhapsodic, but as showing the effect of the chant on a choir monk they should not be ignored in considering the above points.

PERFORMANCE

St Bernard of Clairvaux (1090–1153), in a direction to his monks, stated the ideals they should bear in mind in their singing.

Let the chant be full of gravity; let it be neither worldly, nor too rude and poor . . . let it be sweet, yet without levity, and, while it please the ear let it move the heart. It should alleviate sadness, and calm the angry spirit. It should not contradict the sense of the words, but rather enhance it. For it is no slight loss of spiritual grace to be distracted from the profit of the sense by the beauty of the chant, and to have our attention drawn to a mere vocal display, when we ought to be thinking of what is sung.

Monasteries, naturally, differed in their loyalty to these ideals. Professor Hamilton Thompson writes in his pamphlet *Song-Schools in the Middle Ages*:

We know that in the fourteenth century at the college of Cotterstock, in the valley of the Nene, near Oundle, Matins, Vespers and the other hours, were solemnly sung in choir daily, with Mass of the day and of our Lady at the high altar, and this distinctly and audibly, with good psalmody and suitable pauses in the middle of each verse of the psalms.

About a century earlier, on the other hand, the Dean and Chapter of Salisbury remarked that 'disorderly gestures, movements, and leapings were signs of a levity of mind inconsistent with that dignity which Vicars Choral should preserve', and blamed 'their perpetual restlessness in choir, running hither and thither, going out and returning without any obvious reason' – a reminder that medieval notions of reverence in church differed greatly from ours today.

The Cistercian monk Caesarius of Heisterbach ascribed the discord and confusion that occasionally took place in the best regulated churches 'to the intervention of demons who were constantly striving to attack monks on their weak side . . . and endeavouring by confusing the singers to interrupt such psalms as *Domine quid multiplicati sunt*'; and when a silly young monk, almost at the bottom of the choir, annoyed by a psalm being pitched low raised the key by a fifth and, in spite of the efforts of the sub-prior to stop him, successfully overtopped the rest – being imitated in this by some of his fellow monks – his indiscipline was attributed to one of those same demons!

The Benedictine Order today retains the custom of requiring

any monk who makes a mistake in the liturgy to come out and kneel, before all, on the lowest step of the altar until the Superior, by rapping on his stall, gives a sign that the defaulter has done sufficient penance. (If this system were adopted in some Italian opera houses, whole operas might be sung kneeling!)

5. Sarum, Gallican, Mozarabic, and Ambrosian Rites

THE Gallican and Mozarabic rites are held by most scholars to be essentially Western in character, the Eastern elements in them, as in Roman ritual, being simply the results of later local contacts with the East. The Sarum rite is 'a local medieval modification of the Roman rite in use at the cathedral church of Salisbury. By 1427 it was in use in nearly the whole of England, Wales, and Ireland, and in 1543 the Canterbury Convocation imposed the Sarum Breviary on the whole province.' Some of its chants are sung today in the Anglican church. The Gallican rite was suppressed by Charles the Great who, in 789, on receiving a gift of the Gregorian Sacramentary from Pope Hadrian I, ordered the Frankish singers of his court at Aachen: 'go back to the source of St Gregory, for manifestly you have corrupted the Church's chant.' We have seen that, in spite of this order, the chant returned to Rome with many Gallican elements in it: and, in general, the Franks were reluctant to adopt the Roman Mass, which seemed to them too dry and forthright. Charles himself appears, with the aid of Alcuin, the famous liturgiologist from York, to have done some revising of the Roman chant on his own account. After his death the work was continued by Amalarius of Metz (d. c. 850), Walafrid Strabo (d. 879), and Hrabanus Maurus (d. 865). Metz, in fact, became a centre of Roman liturgical life in Gaul. No complete manuscript of the Gallican chant has been preserved.

The Mozarabic rite survived until the eleventh century and even after its suppression by Popes Alexander II and Gregory VII, in some Moorish provinces, up to the fourteenth and fifteenth centuries. It was then allowed to be celebrated in a chapel of Toledo Cathedral and six parishes in the city, and is still in use today.

The Spanish liturgy of the sixth and seventh centuries enshrines elements of the highest antiquity, including a setting of the *Pater noster* that may date from the fourth century, but unfortunately the Mozarabic musicians and cantors of Toledo did not take the trouble to transcribe the chant into diastematic notation, so that though 'almost the entire cycle of the music used by the Visigothic or Mozarabic church has been preserved, the key to the reading of it, except in a few instances, is lost.'[1]

The Ambrosian chant (sometimes called Milanese) has since the fourth century been jealously preserved and is in full use today in the cathedral and diocese of Milan and in parts of the diocese of Lugano. Its earliest manuscripts, of which there are only three, date back no further than the twelfth century, and so there are none in neumatic notation to compare with the existing ones in diastematic notation. The last of these three MSS. was discovered in the hot dry attic of the little church of San Vittore at Bedero Valtravaglia on Lake Maggiore only twenty-five years ago. It contains the chants of the summer season.

The complete Ambrosian repertory, which reached its maximum development in the twelfth century and 'stands like a gigantic Romanesque cathedral', has three distinct layers that fused into a unity: the original Ambrosian layer derived from the Synagogue and early Eastern liturgies, and which was mixed with indigenous and popular elements to form a first unity; later Byzantine influences; and large Gregorian infiltrations. But to separate one from another is most difficult, at times impossible.

If there are some Ambrosian chants simpler than any in the Roman repertory there is a larger number far more ornate than any it can show, as for example the Hallelujahs. After the verse the first phrase of the *Hallelujah* is, though not invariably, repeated and the *jubilus* extended to double its length or more, a development, in fact, of the original motive. Thus the second *jubilus* of the *Hallelujahs*, *Puer natus est nobis*, for Christmas has over 200 notes. Some of the Responsories are also highly melismatic.

Certainly Ambrosian chant has not the sobriety or the

1. I have (with his permission) drawn freely, in this section, on a broadcast talk on the Ambrosian Chant given by Father Rembert Weakland, on 22 May 1957 in the Third Programme of the B.B.C.

symmetry of the Roman chant and it inclines more to the dramatic, as these two settings of *Christus resurgens*, the first Roman, the other Ambrosian, will show.

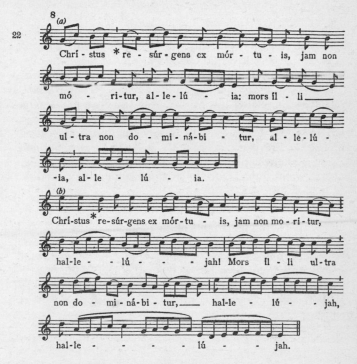

(Christ, now that He has risen from the dead, cannot die any more. Alleluia: death has no more power over Him, Alleluia, alleluia.)

The theorists of the Middle Ages paid no attention to Ambrosian chant, so it has no system of modes, no systematized psalm tones. Father Weakland writes:

One must accept Ambrosian chant for its own aesthetic and artistic musical expression. Our ears must become more accustomed to its roughness, its musical caprices, its sudden changes, and its peculiar exuberance. Perhaps our concept of medieval music has become too refined and too 'classical' so that we miss the charm in the freeness and fantasy of the Ambrosian chant.

It may be of interest to give a ground plan of the proper chants of the Ambrosian Mass and show the correspondences to and differences from the Roman Mass.

Ingressa (Introit). Text usually taken from the psalms, but with no verse added and no *Gloria Patri*

Psalmellus. Sung after the Prophecy (O.T.). A responsory, with one verse, corresponding to the *Gradual*

Hallelujah. Sung after the Epistle, with usually a psalm verse (In Lent a *Cantus*, corresponding to the *Tract*)

Antiphona Post Evangelium. Corresponding to the *Offertory*

Offertorium. Previously allied to the preceding chant, but now sung after the preparation of the bread and wine

Confractorium. Sung before *Pater noster* and during the breaking of the Host

Transitorium. Corresponding to the Communion chant

There are only a few chants of the Ordinary of the Mass and these are grouped according to their category as follows: *Gloria* (4 settings), *Credo* (1), *Sanctus* (4). *Kyrie eleison* is not sung as a separate chant but at the end of the *Gloria* (3 petitions). *Christe eleison* is not sung, nor is *Agnus Dei. Asperges me* and *Vidi aquam* (*Tempore Paschali*) are sung before Mass as in the Roman rite.

6. Byzantine and Russian Rites

SUNDRY allusions have been made in the course of this section to the debt owed by the West to the East in liturgy and chant, and it must again be stressed here. The visitor to Rome will find a marked Byzantine influence in, for example, the mosaics in the church of SS. Cosmas and Damian at Rome, and in the Byzantine church of S. Vitale at Ravenna; and when he has his first sight of St Mark's basilica at Venice he may well wonder if this fantastic church has flown there, overnight, on a magic carpet. Anton Baumstark, in his book *Comparative Liturgy*, gives an impressive list of poetical pieces that have passed from the Orthodox Rites into the Western, as for example the antiphon *Adorna thalamum tuum* sung at Candlemas, and the antiphon to the *Magnificat* of the Second Vespers of the Nativity of Our Lady.

Such things can be observed and read about; but to make direct contact with Byzantine liturgy and chant is a much more difficult task for us in the West.

The ancient liturgies of Antioch and Alexandria are the parents of all the Eastern rites, of which the Byzantine is by far the most wide spread. The Greek city of Byzantium had a Christian community at least from the second century, and Constantinople, which Constantine made his capital on the site of Byzantium, was from its inauguration a Christian city whose bishop, styled of the New Rome, took rank with those of Alexandria, Antioch, and Rome. The great basilica of St Sophia (the Holy Wisdom, that is the Person of Christ) was built between 532 and 537 and consecrated in 538.

The head of the Orthodox Church was the Emperor, and it is with the coronation of the Roman Emperor Justinian I[1] in 527 that the history of the Byzantine liturgy begins. He wanted the splendours of St Sophia to be copied by all the principal churches of the Empire. 'The morning and evening

1. He and his wife, Theodora, are pictured in the mosaics in S. Vitale, Ravenna.

services were enriched with hymns, which were introduced in steadily increasing number and gradually the music assumed a dominating role in the liturgy.'

The Byzantine liturgy differs notably from the Roman liturgy in laying great emphasis on hymnody and also in its dramatic presentation of the Mass. Those who have attended Mass in the Orthodox Church or in one of the Uniate Churches of the Byzantine rite (churches in communion with Rome) will have found it strange to see a screen (the *iconostasis*) separating the Sanctuary from the Nave. This screen, covered with icons, has three doors, the Royal Door in the centre leading to the altar, that on the right hand to the table on which the solemn preparation of the Eucharistic elements takes place, that on the left to the sacristy. Through these doors the sacred ministers pass to and fro, the high points being the Little Entrance (the procession with the Gospels Book) and the Great Entrance (the solemn procession just before the Offertory, carrying the bread and wine to the altar).

Hymns are sung during both these entrances as well as between the lessons in the 'Mass of the Catechumens'.

Only three texts are used in the celebration of Mass, the Liturgies of St Basil and St John Chrysostom, and (in Lent) the Pre-Sanctified; and it is in the Divine Office that the Proper of the season and the feasts of Our Lord, Our Lady, the Apostles, and the Saints have their place.

The accumulation of hymns in the 'Hours' was so large by the eleventh century that a halt had to be called to any further additions, though embellishments continued to be added to the melodies.

The Byzantine hymn 'is the poetical expression of Orthodox theology, translated, through music, to the sphere of religious emotion', and therefore text and music are intimately linked together. The poetical forms are (a) *Troparion*, originally a monostrophic prayer sung after the last three or six verses of a psalm, and later enlarged into a hymn connected with the event or saint commemorated in the Office for the day; (b) *Kontakion*, a poetical homily of eighteen, or more, stanzas all structurally alike. The single stanza is called *Troparion*, and all are composed to a model stanza called *Heirmos*. There are short and independent introductory stanzas, with a refrain at the end of each of the succeeding stanzas. The choir sang the refrain, a soloist the *Kontakia*. At the end of the seventh century, the last period of Byzantine hymnography, the *Kanon* was introduced into the Morning Office (Lauds in the West). It is 'a complex poetical form, made up of nine Odes and structurally similar to a short *Kontakion* but different in context'. Instead of the poetical homily of the *Kontakion*, 'the nine Odes of the *Kanon* are modelled on the pattern of the nine Canticles from the Scriptures and have the character of hymns of praise.'

Byzantine notation uses two systems of musical signs, one (ecphonetic) regulating the solemn reading of the Lessons, the other (neumatic) fixing the flow and execution of the melodies of various poetical texts. The melodies themselves 'are built up from a number of melodic formulae which are linked together by short transitional passages, somewhat after the manner of Gregorian centonized and type melodies, both methods deriving from a ruling principle of composition in Oriental music.' Dr Wellesz in his book on *Byzantine Music and Hymnography* analyses the structure of Byzantine hymns almost as thoroughly as Abbot Ferretti the structure of various Gregorian melody types. The old treasury of hymn melodies was regarded by composers as an echo of the divine beauty, as prototypes of the songs of the angels. They could be, and were, embellished but not, as in the West, replaced by free compositions. The melodies of the Canons, composed at the time of the struggle between the image-worshippers and the image-breakers (Iconoclasts), were syllabic from the start and so remained to the end of the empire. This was so because the words of the hundred or more stanzas of the Canon had to be heard and understood by the congregation.

There are eight Byzantine modes, four authentic and four plagal, and each of them is characterized by a syllabic formula connected with a formula-tone, which was intoned with each chant. Thus they are not scale-formations, but belong rather to the category of melody types. Apart from the four examples of Byzantine chant recorded in *The History of Music in Sound* and printed, words and music, with some comments, in the second volume of the pamphlets issued with the discs (*Early Medieval Music*), there are no recordings of the chant available in this country. One cannot gain much idea of the beauties of Byzantine music from the printed page, but Dr Wellesz's book, on which I have drawn freely in this chapter, contains a number of musical illustrations, all, however, with Greek text only. We must hope, therefore, that an opportunity to come into closer contact with this music and that of the other Eastern rites, Coptic, Armenian, and Syrian, will present itself.

It may be useful, at the end of this regrettably brief sketch of Byzantine chant, to give some idea of the order of the Mass and any correspondence it has with the Roman rite.

GENERAL ORDER OF THE MASS RITES IN THE EASTERN LITURGIES

The Mass of the Catechumens or the Preparatory Synaxis
1. Preparatory prayers
2. Opening chants (corresponding to the Roman *Introit*)
3. Little Entry, or Entry of the Gospels
4. Trisagion (see p. 149)
5. Lessons (a) from the Old Testament, (b) from the Epistles, the Acts, or the Apocalypse, (c) from the Gospels. These are separated from one another by the *Prokeimena* (verses corresponding to the Roman *Gradual*) and by *Alleluias*
6. Prayers after the Gospel and dismissal of the Cathechumens

The Mass of the Faithful
A. Before the *Anaphora*
1. Prayers for the faithful
2. The Great Entry or procession for the transference of the *oblata*, that is the bread and wine to be consecrated
3. The Offertory
4. The Kiss of Peace
5. The Creed

B. The *Anaphora* (the *Canon* in the Roman rite)

1. The great eucharistic prayer, or prayer of thanksgiving
   (a) the Prologue (corresponding to the Latin Preface),
   (b) the *Sanctus*, (c) and (d) the commemoration of Our
   Lord's life and the Last Supper
2. The Consecration
3. The great prayer of intercession (in which comes the *Pater
   noster*, with a paraphrase of its final clause)
4. Elevation, Fraction, and Communion

Father Sévérien Salaville, from whose book *An Introduction
to the Study of the Eastern Liturgies* I have reproduced the plan
given above, sums up the seven categories that constitute a
principle of unity in the abundance of languages and rites
which make up the Eastern liturgies as follows:

a wealth of theological teaching; devotional spirit; richness in
ascetical doctrine; a frequent and special use of Holy Scripture;
importance assigned to patristic elements; the lyrical beauty of
hymnology; and, finally, a variety, a splendour, and a popularity
which give these liturgies a clear superiority over the corresponding Western rites.

Dr Wellesz believes the music of the Byzantine Church to

Free translation:
'Tis the day of Resurrection
Earth, tell it out abroad!
The Passover of gladness,
The Passover of God!
From death to life eternal,
From earth unto the sky,
Our Christ has brought us over
With hymns of victory.

J. M. NEALE

be no less great than that of the Western Church and its hymns certainly surpass their Western counterparts 'in power of passionate expression and dramatic force'. The example above *Anastaseos imera*, is taken from the first Ode of the *Kanon* for Easter Day by St John Damascene. The Greek Orthodox Church calls it the Golden Kanon, or the queen of Kanons. Words and music fit together beautifully.

It was not until A.D. 988 that Byzantine chant was imported into Russia – together with Christian ritual – and it becomes fully legible only in the manuscripts of the fifteenth century. Alfred Swan writes in his account of Russian chant in the *New Oxford History of Music* (Vol. 2): 'The Russians, a people with a very strong aptitude for music, possessing their own rich folk music, could not endure an alien chant for long, even in church', and so they developed a national liturgical song. We think of Russian chant as homophonic, and though the Russian church did not adopt part-singing until the seventeenth century it was probably in use before then. The whole subject needs a great deal of further study as up to now the 'bulk of the chant is untranscribed and the source material has not yet been examined.'

Italian influence is strong in the church music of the earliest known composers such as Bortniansky (1751–1827) but Tchaikovsky, Grechaninov, and Rakhmaninov have all composed beautiful settings of the liturgy of St John Chrysostom which, sung by a genuine Russian choir, make an unforgettable impression of solemnity and timelessness.

LITURGICAL DRAMA

The earliest recorded play of the medieval Church developed out of a prose trope attached to the Mass of Easter. It is found in its simplest version in tenth-century manuscripts from the monasteries of St Gall and Limoges.

Interrogatio: Quem quaeritis in sepulchro, Christicolae?
*Responsio: Jesum Nazarenum crucifixum, O caelicolae. Non est
    hic, surrexit sicut praedixerat. Ite, nuntiate quia surrexit de
    sepulchro.*

(*Question:* Whom do you seek in the sepulchre, servants of
    Christ?
Answer: Jesus of Nazareth who was crucified, celestial ones
    [Angels]. He is not here, he is risen as he foretold; go,
    announce that he is risen from the sepulchre.)

The *Introit* to the Easter Mass, *Resurrexi*, then followed. Approach to a dramatized form of this trope – that is with an attempt by the speakers at impersonation of the characters they represent – but still followed by the *Introit*, is not found until the fifteenth century; but true dramatization and independence from the Mass only came about with the placing of the trope at the end of Matins in the Canonical Office. 'In this new position it achieved a generous amount of literary freedom, and developed into an authentic Easter play, the *Visitatio Sepulchri*'.[1]

The way was open for other Easter plays – the Journey to Emmaus, the Ascension, Pentecost, and the Passion Play – and for plays associated with the Nativity and other Biblical and legendary subjects. The music to these plays 'was sometimes adapted, but usually specially composed by anonymous creators.' The plays are really music dramas, and though the earliest examples were probably unaccompanied the mention in some texts of the organ, and solo instruments such as harp and drum, indicated – though we have no actual knowledge of

1. *New Oxford History of Music.* 'Liturgical Drama'. W. L. Smoldon.

what was done – that there was instrumental accompaniment. One tune, in some of the plays, is attached to a particular character (as in the St Nicholas play *The Son of Getron*), and in many of the plays plainsong antiphons were used, or the sequence *Victimae Paschali*.

The twelfth-century *Daniel*[1] play, which has been performed successfully today, called for a large number of characters and contains nearly fifty melodies, one of which, demanding surely instrumental accompaniment, is reproduced here:

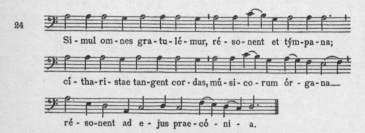

24

Si - mul om - nes gra - tu - lé - mur, ré - so - nent et tým-pa-na;

cí - tha - ri - stae tan-gent cor - das, mú - si - co - rum ór - ga - na—

ré - so-nent ad e - jus prae-có - ni - a.

(Let us all with one accord wish him joy; let the drums sound; let the harp players touch their strings; let the instruments of music sound in his praise.)

The plays, with the introduction of secular as well as clerical performers, moved inevitably from the sanctuary of the church to the porch, and so out into the market-place, and eventually into the theatre.

1. Text, music, and commentary are published by the Oxford University Press (ed. Noah Greenberg) and by the Plainsong & Mediaeval Music Society (ed. W. L. Smoldon). An LP disc has been recorded by the New York Pro Musica, available on American Decca (mono, DL 9402; stereo, DL 79402) and on English Brunswick (mono, AXTL 1086; stereo SXA 4001).

III · ARS ANTIQUA

Denis Stevens

1. The Birth of Organized Polyphony

In his autobiography, Sir Osbert Sitwell tells us that among the numerous and variegated subjects on which his father made copious notes, there was 'the origin of part-singing – a subject which did not greatly interest him, apart from the fact that it *had* an origin'. Part-singing and part-writing are the very stuff of which our Western music is made; they have served innumerable musics for just over a thousand years, beginning with the expert combination of two voices and advancing to the complex polyphony of forty. By way of reaction, there subsequently began the age of monody, which (in spite of its name) was basically a composition for two lines of melody, and so a return in both texture and ethics to the primal state.

Present-day scholars are in general agreement that polyphony, like many other good things in life, came from the East. Indeed, it even exists in primitive society, though the great Eastern and middle-Eastern civilizations shaped and refined it, so that its matter and manner might be perpetuated in written symbols. These symbols were in some respects the great gift to music of the Carolingian renaissance, for the ninth and tenth centuries were above all centuries of the book – the richly illuminated manuscript, nearly always liturgical, on the one hand; and the humbler yet more widespread codex crammed with poetry, copies of Latin classics, and ecclesiastical histories on the other. The art of writing, of calligraphy, became wedded indissolubly to the art of music. Thus the polyphony of earlier times and distant nations, however well organized into parallel melodies, tunes-upon-drones, or thematic imitation, lacked the means to perpetuate itself unequivocally. It was the task of Western nations to transform multiple sounds into symbols.

The prime task, however, was to show clearly the relative pitch of notes in a single melodic line, for once this could be achieved, two or more lines could be invented and notated at will. Much of the credit for introducing a clear and workable method of pitch-notation goes to a Franco-Flemish monk named Hucbald (840–930), whose longevity was no less remarkable than his logic. He modified most skilfully the Greek letter-notation which had been handed on to posterity by the Roman philosopher and statesman Boethius (d. 524), reducing nearly 300 different signs to a manageable fifteen. In his book, *De Institutione Harmonica*, Hucbald writes the word 'Alleluia' with conventional but vague symbols above each syllable. 'The first note', he says, 'seems to be higher: you can sing it wherever you like. The second you can see is lower, but when you try to join it to the first you cannot decide whether the interval is one, two, or three tones. Unless you hear it sung you cannot tell what the composer intended.'

He then adds his letter-notation and so fixes the pitch of each note, while retaining the conventional symbols (called neumes) because they show certain expressive characteristics of the chant. Thus Hucbald's system embraces the old and the new, and taught the singer accuracy of pitch and variety of expression. It also taught him the rudiments of harmony, or consonance, defined as 'two notes, entirely distinct in pitch, which are sounded together'. Elsewhere Hucbald gives a longer definition: 'Consonance is the calculated and harmonious mixture of two notes which occurs only when these two notes, produced from different sources, are combined into one musical unity, such as when a boy and a man sing together. This is usually called *organizatio*.' From that time on, *organizatio* became the accepted term for musical composition, while *organista* referred to the composer.

No polyphony by Hucbald has survived, but he was acknowledged to be an excellent musician. Evidence of this survives in his Gloria trope *Quem vere pia laus*, and in his three Offices for St Andrew, St Theodoric, and St Peter. The structure of the last-mentioned anticipates the Baroque practice of writing sets of preludes in all possible keys: Hucbald sets the antiphons for Matins to each of the eight modes in turn, coming back to the first mode at the ninth and last antiphon. He was long thought to be the author of a small musical handbook and its commentary (*Musica Enchiriadis* and *Scholia Enchiriadis*) but the attribution is now considered to be without foundation.

Nevertheless, these volumes owe something to Hucbald's initiative and invention, and they provide us with the first written examples of counterpoint to a plainsong.

It is important to remember that composers of the early Middle Ages were not permitted to write counterpoint to any plainsong they chose. The Church gave careful instructions as to what sections of the Mass and Office might be elaborated by additional voice-parts. Generally speaking, the greater the feast, the greater the amount of elaboration allowed; though an additional factor of considerable significance was the nature of the plainsong itself. Certain kinds of responsorial chant, whose various sections are allocated to chorus and soloist(s) in alternation, might have only the solo portions set. Similarly, in singing psalms, only the antiphon to the psalm was given an 'organized' setting. In hymns and sequences, only the alternate verses might be set, while in chants for the Ordinary of the Mass there was a tendency to compose music only for the tropes, and not for the basic texts. These tropes were thus musico-poetical insertions into the texts hallowed by custom and rule, and the composer (as we have seen with Hucbald) was not infrequently poet and musician combined.

Musica Enchiriadis was not a standard handbook. Different copies contained different appendices on the art of composing, so that it comes as no surprise to find in a Paris copy of the treatise one of the earliest examples of harmonized music. The notation, consisting of zig-zag lines connected by tiny circles, has been compared by some scholars to an engineer's design for a bridge; but it might equally well be said to resemble the temperature chart of a hospitalized musicologist. For years this strange design kept its secret, until eventually it was discovered that the melody was that of the sequence for Trinity Sunday, *Benedicta sit beata Trinitas*. Further investigation reveals that only alternate verses or parts of verses are set in harmonized form, so that the sequence must have been performed in accordance with generally accepted rubrics, alternating between soloist and choir, or between two sides of the choir.

The *Scholia Enchiriadis* was written in dialogue fashion, as

for master and pupil, like so many theoretical works of the
Middle Ages and the Renaissance. It too includes musical
examples, but all are based on the same text and melody: *Nos
qui vivimus, benedicimus Domino*. This is the antiphon to
Psalm CXIII (*In exitu Israel*) sung at Vespers on Sundays, and
thus permitted to undergo contrapuntal elaboration. The
examples demonstrate the effectiveness and grandeur of various kinds of doubling, at two, three, or four levels, and in
fourths, fifths, or octaves. This scheme does no more than repeat the original melody at intervals corresponding to the
harmonic series, but the effect of this, when taken at the steady
and solemn pace recommended by theorists, and in a large
building such as an abbey or cathedral, is magnificently
sonorous. It looks so simple and mechanical on paper; but we
must beware of judging music from the written page only, as
Berlioz did with Palestrina, much to the latter's disadvantage.

Hand in hand with the encouragement of harmonized music
went the teaching of notation, and this was a task considered
not beneath the dignity of a venerable abbot. Cluny, the abbey
which in less than two centuries caused well over a thousand
other abbeys and priories to follow its lead in liturgical and
spiritual matters, was famed for its musical training. Odo of
Saint-Maur, who studied there, wrote a musical handbook
setting out his method for teaching choirboys to attain perfect
sight-singing in less than a week. He used an instrument called
the monochord, a simple contrivance with a string stretched
over a sounding-box and supported by a movable bridge. The
letter-notation was inscribed beneath the string, so that when
the bridge was moved to a certain spot, and the string plucked,
a sound would emerge to give the singer his note. Odo says:

When any antiphon is marked with the same letters, the boys
learn it better and more easily from the string than if they heard
it sung, and after a few months' training, they are able to discard
the string and sing by sight alone – without hesitating – music
they have never heard.

Not that the choirboy's lot was an easy one. He had to pay
strict attention to his master, for there was an immense amount

to be learnt in the field of chant, quite aside from the newly-growing art of polyphony. An eleventh-century custumal, or book of regulations, for the Cluniac monastery of Saint Bénigne at Dijon (later the cathedral), tells us that 'at nocturns, if the boys commit any fault in the psalmody or other singing, either by sleeping or such like transgressions, let there be no sort of delay, but let them be stripped forthwith of frock and cowl, and beaten in their shirt only, with pliant and smooth osier rods provided for that special purpose.' The standard of music remained high, not only in Dijon, but wherever the Cluniac rule managed to penetrate. It was, in a sense, a rule for the élite and the wealthy, and its insistence on high standards bore artistic fruit of ripe quality.

There were already signs of a breakaway from the strict doubling of voice-parts in the sequence *Benedicta sit*, and this desire for freedom of linear movement may be found in certain of the two-part compositions in the Winchester troper (which unfortunately cannot be transcribed with complete certainty) and in the Cornish manuscript containing the polyphonic verse *Ut tuo propitiatus* designed to be sung after the responsory *Sancte Dei pretiose*, for the Feast of St Stephen. This feast, traditionally assigned to the day after Christmas, was an important one in the Anglo–French liturgical calendars, and towards the end of the twelfth century Pérotin was to write his famous setting of the gradual for St Stephen's Day, *Sederunt principes*. The Winchester troper includes harmonized plainchants for almost every section of the Mass apart from the Credo, which – as the symbol of Christian faith – was almost immune from contrapuntal elaboration. This same troper also includes responsories, proving that the practice of elaborating plainsong had spread from the Mass to the Office. Indeed, it is possible that this cycle of responsories prompted a similar but later cycle by Léonin, the predecessor of Pérotin at Notre Dame Cathedral in Paris.

Further evidence of the widespread practice of 'organizing' plainsong may be found in accounts of hymn-singing, such as that describing the dedication of Ramsey Abbey in November 991. In spite of rules and regulations, harmonized music filtered surreptitiously into every aspect of Church worship. Tropes had gained a firm hold, adding a baroque touch to the comparative purity of the original chant; soon the baroque was to yield to a debased though in some ways delightful rococo, whereby the tropes themselves were troped. Among the Winchester pieces, for example, there is a Gloria into which nine extra clauses have been incorporated, the last being *Regnum tuum solidum permanebit in aeternum.* Between the third and fourth words a long phrase of over twenty words has been inserted, each syllable placed beneath a note in the melodic flourish on *per* [*manebit*]. Decay was clearly setting in, yet it took another three centuries before the troping of tropes was finally abandoned.

By the time Winchester's famed scriptorium had finished the troper, continental developments in the notating and teaching of music had taken great strides forward. The advocacy, if not the invention, of the staff system of notation is usually attributed to a French-born Benedictine who spent the greater part of his life in Italy: Guido of Arezzo. In the prologue to his antiphoner he explains the ease and logic of his system, and offers genuine proof to the reader. 'Should anyone doubt that I am telling the truth,' says Guido, 'let him come, make a trial, and hear what small boys can do under our direction, boys who have until now been beaten for their gross ignorance of the psalms.' Guido was eventually invited to Rome, where he expounded his theory and practice to Pope John XIX with considerable success. The slow and tedious method of teaching by means of the monochord now gave way to a more rapid and accurate system, the excellence of which is proved beyond all doubt by its survival until the present day.

The number and variety of musical instruments used in religious services of the Middle Ages must have been remarkable. But these small instrumental groups were by no means standardized, for they were dependent more often than not on purely local resources. Some idea of the instruments available can be gained from early illuminated manuscripts, and from carvings preserved on Romanesque and early Gothic churches, this plastic evidence being corroborated by the names given to popular sequence melodies: *Musa* (= bagpipe), *Cithara, Fistula* (= reedpipe), *Lyra, Organicis, Symphonia, Tuba, Tympanum*. Chief of all instruments was the organ, which had been perfected in the East and brought to Europe from Byzantium. As early as the tenth century, organs could be found in abbeys and cathedrals in Compiègne, Erfurt, Magdeburg, Halberstadt, Winchester, Abingdon, and Malmesbury, to mention but a few. Vivid descriptions of some of these instruments survive, and from these descriptions it is clear that certain organs were enormous both in size and tone. The Winchester organ had 26 bellows and 400 pipes; three players were needed, and since each could manage only one gigantic 'key' it is possible that this fact points to an early use of three-part harmony. This would almost certainly be of the parallel variety discussed in *Scholia Enchiriadis*. The organists therefore imitated vocal techniques as far as they were able, either by using more than one player (or organ-striker, as they were called), or by building the organ in such a way that each key admitted air to pipes sounding at different pitches. The principle thus followed was comparable to the mixture stops used in later organs, but with this one important difference: the upper ranks of pipes in medieval organs were of the same strength as the fundamental, not weaker as they tend to be today. An eleventh-century Hebrew manuscript, now in Paris, goes into great detail over the matters of scaling and tuning organ pipes, and from this information it is obvious that medieval organs had a very special timbre and temperament.

Organum was the generic word for any kind of musical instrument, and it was also the particular word for organ. The issue became confused somewhat when the art of combining melodies, rightly called diaphony, also shared the term organum, though not perhaps without good reason. The installation of an organ in a church might well have encouraged the singing of parallel organum through its ability to accompany the singing in simpler psalmodic formulas, and the casual listener needed no excuse to call this aggregate of vocal and instrumental sound 'organum'. He was not primarily concerned with which came first historically, organ or voices: he merely wished to find a portmanteau word which would express a musical phenomenon of rapidly increasing currency and importance. Thus it came about that the interaction of two basic musical types, vocal and instrumental, remained for centuries in an etymological mist. As a further analogy, the case of melismatic organum may be cited. This kind of singing, in which florid melodic passages were heard over a long-held note, clearly derived from the sounds produced by an instrument of the bagpipe family. Once this drone principle had been accepted in places of worship, it was an easy matter to perform such music with the aid of an organ, the instrument *par excellence* for long, powerful, held notes.

Some of the first and most characteristic examples of this type of composition, called melismatic organum, are found among the musical remains of the great libraries at St James, Compostela (now Santiago), and St Martial, Limoges. These two great centres of religious and cultural activity were interlinked by the unending procession of pilgrims from northern Europe to the shrine of St James, and it was only natural that they should share to some extent the same musical style and ideal. True, they also found a place in their liturgies for the older, note-against-note organum, but they broke new ground chiefly in their experiments with florid chant over a relatively slow-moving plainsong theme. Florid and imaginative designs may be seen in another famous product of Limoges – the enamel work, *cloisonné* and *champlevé*, held to be among the greatest glories of Romanesque art. It is unfortunate that less is known about the music than about the enamel, for in spite of the fabulous collection of manuscripts (sold to France's National Library in 1730, when the abbey was short of funds) very little music has been published.

The St Martial polyphonic repertory is rich in settings of chants for the Mass and Office. A typical example of florid writing is found in the troped gradual *Viderunt* for Christmas Day, and the extent of the inserted phrases may be seen from the following translation of the text, in which the trope appears in italics:

All the ends of the earth have seen *Emanuel, the only-begotten Son of the Father, offered for the fall and the salvation of Israel, man created in time, word in the beginning, born in the palace of the city which he had founded,* the salvation of our God. Be joyful in the Lord all ye lands.

The opening of this piece is only moderately florid, but when the first word of the trope is reached, the upper voice rises to a climax and slowly descends for more than an octave, over a held note in the lower part. At the next lengthy florid passage, something remarkable and impressive happens – the lower voice, not to be outdone by the upper in ornament and flexibility, joins in this infectious jubilation until the section comes to be repeated. The same music now recurs, but with different text. In the next new section the two parts again move in consort, but not in jubilation, for here the words of the text follow each other closely, until the last two syllables are reached. Of these two, the last but one keeps both voices on the move, and the final syllable bears a falling, then somewhat rising, flourish over a simple cadence.

A more regular pattern is to be seen in certain of the sequences. In *Sancti spiritus assit nobis gratia*, for Whit Sunday, the upper voice moves in a continuous and flowing line above the steadily progressing melody of the sequence. The flourishes or melismas are of subtly differing lengths, but the harmonic effect is one of great beauty, for the more active upper voice, besides providing a wealth of ornament, also manages to help define the outline of the sequence melody. Similarly, the purpose of the cupola in Romanesque architecture was at the same time decorative and functional. Much of the music composed for Compostela exhibits the same characteristics, and doubtless derives from a common origin. The Kyrie trope *Cunctipotens genitor* might almost have been written by the same composer as *Sancti spiritus*, so closely do the styles match in their élan and fluidity. But just as neighbourliness and religious affiliations tend to bring about unity of style, so the opposite may sometimes be seen to provoke differences, for away to the north of Scotland, where a comprehensive book of organa was once copied, certain pieces contemporary with the

St Martial and Compostela pieces strike out on independent lines. There are examples of imitation and sequential melodic passages in certain of these earliest compositions in the St Andrews manuscript, and it is by no means rare to find an added third voice joining in at cadences, thus affording an early glimpse of the desire for a full sonority in medieval English music.

Various explanations of polyphonic phenomena among primitive peoples have been offered by ethno-musicologists of note, and recurrences among eastern and western nations have been commented upon without any definite conclusions being reached. It is indeed difficult to find the link between Chinese recruits who sing first in discordant notes, then in fifths, and finally in octaves; and French village congregations who sing in fifths all the time. Yet, at least on paper, there are similarities between the songs of Russian prisoners, whose plight apparently reduces them to singing in perfect fifths, and the songs of medieval monks. A case may even be made out for links between melismatic organum and eastern dance-songs, for polyphony has always been known in the East: the tribes of Chang-Naga, Badike, Xosa, Lhota-Naga, and Lepanto can provide adequate proof of this. The contribution of the West was to perfect, over a long and difficult period of time, the manner of notating these combined melodies so that they might be reproduced with reasonable accuracy in other towns and times.

2. *Organum*

FOR many years it was generally supposed that the great cathedrals and abbeys of the Gothic era were anonymous creations by a host of skilled and semi-skilled craftsmen, and although this cult of anonymity has been almost completely banished through the researches of art historians, it still remains valid for the majority of musicians, who, if asked the names of some of the greatest among twelfth-century composers, could probably get little further than Léonin and Pérotin. Before the time of these two great luminaries of the Notre Dame school, there was a certain Master Albert of Paris, who is credited with the composition of a brief three-part vocal work in a Spanish manuscript; and contemporary with them or after them were Frenchmen such as Jean Probus, Robert de Sabillon, and Thomas de Saint Julien, and Englishmen 'who sang most exquisitely' – Master John Filius Dei, Makeblite of Winchester, and Blakesmit, one of the courtiers of Henry III. It is true that these men rarely signed their works, or so it appears from the few complete manuscripts that have survived, but there were theorists and commentators who left details of certain masterpieces of the age and their respective composers. An English monk from Bury St Edmunds took copious notes on a lecture course in music which he attended at the Sorbonne, and when he returned home, he wisely kept his notes and thus enabled later scholars to piece together something of the puzzle that medieval music must have seemed to be, even during the last century or so.

During the latter half of the twelfth century, there were many composers at work in many corners of Europe, and the styles that coexisted (often with fascinating results and subtle influences) were also many and various. Besides the Parisian composers, there were important schools of musical activity at Chartres, Limoges, Compostela, St Gall, Cividale, Padua, Winchester, and Worcester, to mention only a few of the most important. Composers were just as prone to nationalist influences in those days as in more recent centuries, and though the differentiation of styles is not easy for a modern observer or listener to grasp, it was certainly apparent to most medieval musicians of standing. Our monk from Bury mentions, for example, various unique features in Italian polyphony, especially in Lombardy; he also calls attention to one of his colleagues in Paris, 'a certain Englishman who had a homespun method of notation and also to some extent of teaching'. That peculiarity of English notation is recognized by modern scholars, who call it 'English mensural notation'; and those same scholars might also agree that there is a certain peculiarity about English methods of teaching music.

Different, though related, musical styles were in use at one and the same time, just as there were divergencies in the application of commonly accepted architectural features. Abbeys of the Cistercian monks were considerably less ornate than those of the Benedictines, and it is logical to think of their music, too, as being less prone to elaboration for its own sake. Whereas the Benedictine houses, and especially the richer Cluniac ones, went forward with the development of new styles, the Cistercians kept in the main to the earliest and simplest form of organum. These two styles, the old and severe, and the modern and ornate, were practised side by side for many years, continuing in the service of the liturgy, yet at the same time throwing out ideas to the secular world.

As happens so often in musical history, there was a thrust northwards across Europe, about the middle of the twelfth century, so that the music composed and sung in Spain and southern France gradually warmed up the music-making of northern communities, as if by some kind of cultural gulf-stream. The immediate result of this may be found in the kind of organum developed at Notre Dame, Paris, by Léonin. Based on the finest products of the St Martial school, Léonin's compositions improved on them in sheer beauty of melodic phrases, in carefully organized yet flexible rhythms, and in an altogether more magnificent sweep in line and contour. Whereas the ornamental flourishes of the southern composers are relatively short, even to the point of being epigrammatic,

Léonin's melismata move freely and convincingly from one concord to another, with rise and cadence perfectly planned and expertly matched. Between 1150 and 1175, he provided two-part organa for all of the responsorial chants on major feasts; responsories and their verses for Vespers and Matins, graduals and alleluias for High Mass. His vast plan has been subsequently rivalled only by the somewhat smaller cycle of three-part organa by Pérotin, and by the great publications of Isaak in the sixteenth century and Byrd in the seventeenth.

One of Léonin's major contributions to the art of organum was his masterly use of flexible and variable rhythms, in spite of the cramping features of first and second mode patterns. These usually consist of regularly alternating long and short notes, and are transcribed nowadays in what looks like a pastoral ⅜ metre (see Ex. 25, *Tamquam sponsus*, Léonin). But

25
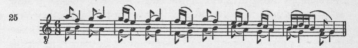

Léonin's music is far from being academically regular, for though he conforms to the basic rhythmical pattern, he breaks up both long and short notes into lesser values, called *copulae* (links) by theorists of the day. The *copulae*, which are not so very far removed, musically, from the melodic variations of 'divisions' of the Baroque composers, were for many years little more than thorns in the flesh of modern musicologists, who were baffled by the insistence of medieval theorists on the fact that copula was 'between discant and organum'. Looking horizontally through a medieval score (for the music was, at that time, largely written in score form) it would indeed be difficult to find anything 'between' a section in organum and a section in discant: the one merges into the other with hardly more than a rudimentary bar-line to keep them distinct. The theorists who used the word 'between' meant that copula partook of the nature of both organum and discant, and that since it could be classified strictly as neither one nor the other, it was betwixt and between them in *genre* and character. This is quite logical, for organum sets several notes against one, and discant exploits note-against-note movement. *Copula* has the general homophonic character of discant, both parts moving in the same basic rhythm, but if each of the tenor notes is considered as a miniature organum, with two notes (literally a 'link') above it, the theorists' definition becomes clear.

Léonin's music was already widely accepted throughout Europe when a younger and bolder musician came upon the scene. He is known to us, like his predecessor, only through a familiar diminutive name – Pérotin. Just as Léonin is a familiar form of address for Leo, so the original name of Pérotin must be Pierre. The problem now becomes one of identification, for there were at least five men named Pierre, during the late twelfth and early thirteenth centuries, attached to Notre Dame. The ecclesiastics of superior grade must be eliminated, for it is hardly likely that even the good singers among them were called the equivalent of Joe and Charlie in public. There is however one Pierre, a precentor who flourished during the last few decades of the twelfth century, who may well have made so great a contribution to the art of music. He was a deacon, not a priest, and may therefore have been referred to by nickname with comparative impunity.

Once again it is the English monk who tells us about these changes in musical style, and the men who wrought them:

Léonin was the best composer of organum. He wrote the Great Book of Organa, for Mass and Office, to enlarge the divine service. This book was used until the time of the great Pérotin, who shortened it and rewrote many sections in a better way. Pérotin was the best composer of discant – he was even better than Léonin – and he wrote the best four-part organa, such as *Viderunt* and *Sederunt*, with the most ample embellishments of harmonic art.

He goes on to describe how the four-part organa were kept in one volume, the three-part organa in another, and so on throughout all the available musical styles and textures. Unfortunately the many references to this *Great* Book of Organa, divided into several *volumes*, have given the impression that its physical size and weight must have been enormous.

On the contrary, the actual music books were small. Some

of them have come down to us, and are now preserved in various libraries in Florence, Madrid, and Wolfenbüttel, to mention only three of the most important. The size of each page is not much larger than the open book you are now reading, so that two or three singers at the most could have looked over one of these 'great' books of organa. The adjective applies of course to the magnitude and variety of the contents, to its quality rather than its actual size. It was indeed a great achievement to compose harmonized music for so many parts of the divine service, and it is certain that the Parisian copyists were kept constantly at work providing beautifully limned and bound reproductions of the mother-volume, for use in cathedrals and abbeys in the four corners of Christendom.

The two four-part organa mentioned by the monk of Bury are referred to in ordinances of the Bishop of Paris, who wished to celebrate the Feast of the Circumcision (Octave of Christmas) in 1198, and the Feast of St Stephen in 1199, with especial splendour and solemnity. Pérotin had reached the height of his powers before the end of the twelfth century. Possibly a pupil of Léonin, he had improved on his master's work, experimenting with three-part and then four-part writing, and over and above this he had perfected a new kind of composition known as *conductus*.

3. Conductus and Clausula

CONDUCTUS differed from organum in several important respects. Its most distinguishing feature, from a purely musical point of view, was the similarity of rhythm in all the parts, whether there were two, three, or four of them. It was essential to have a simple rhythmic structure, with regularly recurring stresses, for the principal use of the conductus was, as its name implies, in conducting priests and deacons from the altar to the choir-steps and back again. The verses of responsorial chants were often sung at the steps (*gradus*, hence Gradual) and the procession therefore took some time, especially in a large building. Complicated and changing rhythms would obviously have put the procession off its stride, so the conductus was invented as a practical solution to a liturgical problem.

A secondary feature was the lack of plainsong. Whereas the composer of organum and its dependant discant was bound to use a plainsong basis, the composer of conductus had either to compose his melody or borrow it. Oddly enough, some conductus settings borrow short sections from the music which Pérotin and his followers wrote for insertion into the old organa. Thus it comes about that plainsong does appear in conductus, but only incidentally, and in comparatively small fragments. One other important aspect of the conductus was its text, which was invariably written out beneath the lowest voice only, but since all voices proceeded in the same rhythm, it was quite easy for those singing the upper voice-parts to memorize the words of the text and apply them to the notes as they went along.

A medieval German theorist described the procedure for writing a conductus as follows:

First, choose the loveliest melody you can think of, then write a descant to it in the manner already shown. If you wish to add a third part, look carefully at the melody and the descant, so that the third part will not be discordant with them both together.

In other words, if the new part – at any given point in the composition – made discord with the melody, and harmony with the accompanying part (or *vice versa*) the result would be perfectly correct. As long as any two parts were concordant, all was well. This widely followed harmonic practice, although it was modified as time went on, and changed somewhat according to the country in which the composer was working, accounts for much of the spicy flavour of medieval music.

Quite two-thirds of the known conductus repertoire is clearly liturgical. The music was written for special feast-days and accordingly many of the verbal texts comment on the readings, from lives of saints, heard at Matins. Conducti written for Christmas, Lent, Easter, and Whitsun were often embellished by the addition of florid and textless preludes and postludes. These may have been assigned to instruments, though it is far more likely that they were sung to the requisite vowel-sound, just as the long-drawn-out organa were. There is no doubt that the medieval singers possessed a technique of vocalizing far in advance of anything known today. When well and fluently performed, the conductus must have been a particularly satisfying experience for singer and listener alike, for it began with a musical flourish, setting the pace of the procession, continued with a syllabic section referring to the feast or saint being commemorated, and concluded with another flourish. Not surprisingly, it soon began to be used for occasions of state and special ceremonies held within the precincts of the church though not in the church itself. Chapter meetings and similarly solemn gatherings must frequently have been enlivened by performances of these new, quasi-secular conducti, which will be dealt with in detail at a later stage.

The borrowing and reshaping of musical materials has been one of the most constant of phenomena in the history of music. As mentioned earlier, writers of conducti often borrowed from other sources, and similarly writers of organa took over existing settings and added a voice-part to increase both interest and sonority. One might profitably compare all this with the later *Minnesingers* (see p. 257) who took over melodies from the earlier *trouvères*, or with fifteenth-century composers of cyclic

Masses who 'parodied' previous settings either by way of homage or to save time. The sixteenth century abounds in arrangements and adaptations of all kinds, while the succeeding Baroque era culminated in two great figures who were adept at borrowing: Bach from Vivaldi, and Handel from Telemann. In each case, the borrowings were justified by the improvements effected, and precisely the same is true of medieval composers.

For example, the first syllabic section of a conductus *Si membrana esset celum* ends with a florid passage, for all three voices, on the word 'celum'. The melody in the lowest voice of this passage corresponds note for note with a Kyrie trope *Celum creans*. Clearly the composer was reminded by the one word 'celum' of a Kyrie trope which began with just this word, and so, as if to point up the reference, he quoted the entire melody. Thus a pre-existing trope is here used to 'trope' a conductus. A very similar instance of word-suggestion is to be found in a two-part conductus *Deus creator omnium*, whose last two lines read

> regnante sine termino
> benedicamus domino.

The melody on which the last two words are based corresponds exactly with one of the best-known *Benedicamus Domino* chants so that the end of the conductus is in fact a miniature piece of liturgical organum. An even more subtle example is the conductus *Columbe simplicitas*, which has a *Benedicamus Domino* at the end, not as an integral part of the text (as in *Deus creator omnium*) but as an optional addition. It is certainly based on plainsong, but not on a *Benedicamus* plainsong; instead of this, its support comes from the florid passage on the syllable 'ne' of 'Domine', the third word of the verse *Adjuva me Domine* from the St Stephen's Day gradual *Sederunt principes*. This florid passage, together with many others of the same type, was kept in the Great Book of Organa until needed as a substitute for the corresponding passage in (for example) Léonin's *Sederunt principes*. Medieval writers referred to these substitute sections as *clausulae* or *puncta*.

Léonin's organa can be compared to a well-spaced plot of

sturdy trees, which are grafted, grow to great height and girth, and shoot forth branches bearing fruit in every field of music. It is instructing as well as fascinating to trace the development of different musical forms and styles from the root of one organum. The starting point is, of course, plainsong, and the example chosen is the *Alleluia, Nativitas gloriosae virginis* sung at Mass of the Nativity of the Blessed Virgin. Léonin's two-part organum, in its original version, would have been performed in the following manner. Passages sung in plainsong by a unison chorus are shown in roman type; organum by italics; discant by capitals.

alleluia alleluia-a-a-a *nativitas* GLORIO-*o-o-o-se* VIRGINis *marie-e-e* EX SEMINE-E-E-E *abrahe orta de* TRI-*i-i-i-bu* JU-*u-u-u-da* clara ex stirpe david. [*alleluia*-a-a-a.]

Léonin's method of stressing the beginning of important words by subtle changes in musical texture is easily apparent. Organum and discant sections are contrasted throughout. (The repeated vowels are shown in groups of three for purely diagrammatic reasons: the actual sections vary considerably in length.) It will be noticed how often a new word is begun in discant and concluded in organum, though at one significant point – 'ex semine' – the discant is continued until the very end of the last vowel. The importance of this will be seen when the emergence of the motet is discussed. In another manuscript there is a later version of this organum. Some of the notes are different, others correspond very closely. At the end, instead of repeating the first 'Alleluia' in organum, a newly-composed 'Alleluia' has been provided, using of course the same plainsong.

The next important stage came with Pérotin's reworkings of this plainsong. He composed a three-part setting which is known in four slightly differing versions, and he introduced many more discant sections than Léonin did in his version, thus reducing its length and adding more contrast:

alle-E-E-E-LU-*ia* Alleluia-a-a-a NA-TI-VI-*i-i-i-tas* GLORIO-*o-o-o-se* VIRGINIS MARIE-E-E-E EX SEMINE-E-E-E-*e-e-e* *abrahe orta de* TRIBU JUDA-A-A-*a-a-a* clara ex stirpe david. [*alle*-E-E-E-LU-*ia-a-a-a*.]

Another three-part setting of this *Alleluia* is found in a Worcester manuscript. It differs completely from the Pérotin versions, except at the point where discant begins on EX SEMINE. Here the Worcester composer takes over Pérotin's clausula note for note, but instead of allowing his singers to vocalize on the final E, he uses one of the two sets of words commonly associated with motets based on Pérotin's clausula. These words thus trope the organum, and are shown here in brackets:

. . EX SEMINE ABRAHE [DIVINO MODERAMINE
   IGNE PIO NUMINE PRODUCIS DOMINE
   HOMINIS SALUTEM PAUPERTATE NUDA
   VIRGINIS NATIVITATE DE TRIBU IUDA
   IAM PROPINAS OVUM PER NATALE NOVUM
   PISCEM PANEM DABIS PARTU SINE SEMINE] ORTA DE . . .

It was thought at one time that this 'motet-embedded-in-organum' was an almost unique example of an unusual method of composition, but it is now known that the practice was fairly common, though not perhaps standard in the same way as was the substitution of untexted clausulae.

Less important from a purely musical viewpoint was the practice of adding alternative sets of words to an entire organum, a process generally known as *contrafactum*. It was inevitable that compositions enjoying a high degree of popularity should be pressed into use for liturgical occasions other than those for which they were originally intended. Thus both Léonin's and Pérotin's music has been provided, in certain manuscripts, with alternative texts: one of these is *Optimam partem* (Alleluia Verse, St Mary Magdalene), another is *Diffusa est gratia* (Alleluia Verse, Virgin & Martyr). All Saints' Day is represented by the addition of a new text, the Alleluia *Judicabunt sancti*, while the continuing influence of Compostela may be seen in the special Alleluia *Sanctissime Jacobe*, for the Feast of St James. In general these new texts entail no musical changes. Sometimes they are even written below the proper text so that the singers will have both versions at hand.

While the main object of the clausula was to shorten and beautify an existing organum, its subsidiary effect was to offer the singer a kaleidoscopic variety of combinations within one basic framework. One gradual or alleluia might contain half a dozen places where substitute clausulae could be inserted, and for explanatory purposes they may be called *a b c d e f*. Many of these existed in different forms, for varying groups of voices, so that the total number of available pieces would be, for instance, four of *a*, two of *b*, two of *c*, and so on. The singers might then decide to use *a1*, *b2*, *c1*, *d3*, *e1*, and *f4*, or perhaps *a3*, *b1*, *c2*, *d3*, *e1*, and *f2*. The number of possible combinations was prodigious. In the case of our Alleluia *Nativitas* there are five known points at which substitute clausulae are available for insertion: the first 'Alleluia', the syllable 'tivi' (from 'Nativitas'), the words 'Marie' and 'ex semine', and finally the syllables 'Abra' from 'Abrahe'.

4. Development of the Motet

IT has already been hinted, in discussing the Alleluia *Nativitas* of the Worcester manuscript, that the early form of the motet was nothing more complex than words added to a clausula. The clausula is a harmonic addition, therefore trope, to plainsong; and so the motet is a verbal addition, or trope, to the clausula. This extension was both inevitable and logical, but it remains difficult to prove at what stage the words were added. Was it in the early stage of clausula formation, or did it occur later, when the music had gradually spread throughout Europe? Since Latin was a common language, it is only possible to state a definite origin for a piece of music when its text refers to a local saint, or when the internal evidence of the manuscript is strong enough to dispose of all doubts. Nevertheless, there is no doubt of the activity and interactivity of monastic poets and composers, who may (like the troubadours and *trouvères*) have frequently combined both functions.

Before investigating the history of the motet, it is as well to consider the broader aspects of its career, which oddly enough suggest a circular motion rather than a single, straightforward line of development. Since the motet was predominantly a style, and not a form, its metamorphoses can be more easily understood simply as different musico-textual variants of one basic idea. Assuming that the motet resulted, in its earliest stage, from the addition of words to a clausula, it would (in its simplest form) consist of a lower part, called the *tenor*, and an upper part, *motetus* (*mot* = word). Since the tenor was always part of the original organum, it would have two or three words, or perhaps only one word, or even just one or two syllables attached to it. Our example from Pérotin provides evidence of all these classes: 'ex semine' (two words), 'Marie' (one word), and 'tivi' (two syllables). These verbal tags were sufficient for medieval singers to identify the source of the clausula, though nowadays some of them seem rather obscure, especially odd fragments like 'Go' (virgo), 'Reg' (regnum), and 'Doce' (docebit).

This tenor may have been sung by a group of singers whose task was to accompany the soloists, or it may have been played by the organist. The singers who thus sang alongside the more florid upper parts were often called *paraphonistae*, and the organists *organatores*. Composers were referred to as *organistae*. As a purely vocal phenomenon, the effect of performing a clausula with text in the upper part would be to suggest polytextuality, for while the motetus declaimed a complete Latin text, usually bearing on the subject of the organum at that point the lower voice (or tenor) would pronounce the requisite tagword or words. Once uttered, however, this tag would be prolonged by vocalizing on the appropriate vowel sound, so that the combination of a rapidly declaimed upper part and a steadily vocalized lower part cannot be described as polytextual, whatever it may look like in the manuscripts; it can only *suggest* polytextuality.

Yet it remains true, by and large, that one of the most important features of the early motet was its polytextuality, and this becomes clear as soon as a third part enters the picture. This third part, or *triplum*, usually had its own text, so that both music and words were different from those of the motetus. Since clausulae could be for two, three, or four voices, it follows that above the tenor (which had its own tag) a writer might add one, two, or three different and distinct texts, thus converting the clausula into a motet, a double motet, or a triple motet respectively.

The motet grew away from the clausula, and began to assume relative independence, when composers first thought of stripping away the upper parts and using the remaining one, the tenor, as the basis of an entirely new composition. Some of these new works, of which many hundreds were written in the thirteenth century, still remained essentially liturgical, for their texts were a gloss on the subject of the tenor, and the tenor itself was sung or played once only. With the addition of secular Latin and French texts, and a tendency to lengthen the work by repeating the tenor melody two or more times, the breakaway was complete. Yet at this very point in the development of the motet, the circular movement alluded to above began to manifest itself. The general preoccupation with the composition of motets meant that both clausulae and conductus were almost forgotten, so that when singers needed new substitute clausulae they had no alternative but to reverse the process by omitting the motet texts and performing the music as a vocalized clausula.

This is what nearly happened in the Worcester version of Alleluia *Nativitas*. The Worcester composer realized that the music of Pérotin's 'ex semine' clausula and that of the 'ex semine' motets was very similar: the main differences were very superficial ones, such as the special kind of notation to go with the syllabic texts of *Abrahe divino moderamine* and *Rosa prodit spine fructus olee*, and the slightly different ending which brought the motet, as opposed to the clausula, to a rounded and satisfactory conclusion. What he did therefore was to consider stripping away the texts to provide a clausula for his organum, but instead of removing both texts he decided to retain one: *Abrahe divino*. This text, although written below the three staves of music, fits only the two upper voices. They move in similar rhythm, and sing the same text; thus the effect is that of a conductus, sung over a pre-existent tenor.

With this close interaction of forms and styles, and the linking of organum and discant, conductus and clausula, motet and conductus, it can be seen how amazingly interdependent are these types of medieval music. However clearly one may try to separate them and divide them into rigid categories, the various types seem to cling together as if unwilling to be classed as parallel and independent phenomena. In this strong tendency towards interrelation, something of the subtlety and variety of the medieval mind may be seen, some practical reflection, perhaps, of the doctrine of the Trinity or the harmony of numbers.

The growth of the tree that was Léonin's organum has been traced as far as some of its lower branches, as far as the later expansions of Pérotin, the contrafacta, the clausulae, and the motets. In the higher branches, we meet a new style which was destined to hasten the establishment of the secular motet: the contrafacta, or new texts, that were neither Latin nor liturgical.

They were, in fact, French, though naturally enough the nationalist tendencies discussed earlier brought forth a few examples of English, Walloon, German, and Provençal texts. The style of the Worcester conductus-motet is found again in a work based on identical music. The two upper voices, instead of singing *Abrahe divino*, now sing a love-song *Se iai ame*, so composed that its syllables fit the music without any undue contortion. Below, as a constant reminder of the sacred origin of this music, is the tenor 'ex semine'. Another poet has provided a different love-song, still for the same music, in a French manuscript of the early thirteenth century, and this time the text is *Hyer mein trespensis*, underlaid to the lower of the two vocal parts only. The uppermost voice has been removed entirely, so that the result is in effect a song for one voice with a simple accompaniment for harp, viol, or wind instrument. This reduced form of the music enjoyed great vogue towards the end of the century, as may be seen by the removal of the upper voice of *Se iai ame*, and even of *Abrahe divino*. There was a similar move towards solo song in the renaissance, when passages from Masses were rearranged for one voice with lute accompaniment.

The distinction between the liturgical motet and its secular counterpart may not always have been a hard and fast one. There are ample proofs of the disfavour shown by eminent churchmen when confronted with gaily discanting musicians, mingling French and Latin texts just as they wished. Even before the hey-day of the motet, John of Salisbury had written concerning 'organized' music:

Could you but hear one of these enervating performances executed with all the devices of the art, you might think it a chorus of Sirens, not of men; and you would be astounded by the singers' facility, with which indeed neither that of the parrot or nightingale, nor of whatever else there may be that is more remarkable in this kind, can compare. For this facility is displayed in long passages running up and down, in dividing or in repeating notes, in repeating phrases, and in clashing together of voices, while in all this the high or even the highest notes of the scale are so mingled with the lower and lowest, that the ears are almost deprived of their power to distinguish.

Ailred's satirical reference to the *hocket* (a kind of speeded-up antiphonal effect, perhaps referred to by John of Salisbury when he mentions 'dividing or repeating notes') is no more complimentary than the foregoing; it is taken from Prynne's translation of the relevant passage in *Speculum Charitatis*:

Sometimes thou mayst see a man with an open mouth, not to sing, but as it were to breathe out his last gasp, by shutting in his breath, and by a certain ridiculous interception of his voice to threaten silence, and now again to imitate the agonies of a dying man, or the ecstasies of such as suffer.

This is clearly a forewarning of the time when Pope John XXII issued his decree from Avignon, forbidding all but the simplest kind of harmonization of liturgical chant. This decree, dated 1322, specifically deplores singers who 'truncate the melodies with hockets, deprave them with discants, and even trope the upper parts with secular songs.'

This is almost certainly a broad hint that clausulae were first troped with Latin texts, and then with French ones, these latter texts (nearly always secular in character) being actually sung in church by unscrupulous and unreliable singers. Many years after the decree, Notre Dame de Paris still observed it faithfully, 'at least in regard to the men singers' who were not apparently to be trusted as implicitly as the boys. Yet throughout the thirteenth century, polyphony flourished in every corner of Europe, and in spite of the loss of vast quantities of the musical material used, there is plentiful evidence of its quality, besides documentary indications of a widespread interest in whatever form it happened to take. Even the comparative reserve of Cistercian Tintern, whose ruins were later immortalized by Wordsworth, admitted singing in three and four parts. At St Paul's in London, towards the end of the century, there was a massive collection of polyphonic tropers and books of organa. In some cases the titles of the actual pieces are mentioned, and they ring a familiar bell: *Viderunt, O mira Christi pietas, Virgo generosa*. Among the most prized possessions of Edward I's chapel royal were two books of organa beginning *Viderunt* and *Alleluia* respectively, and there is no doubt that these '*discantuum volumina*' (which the Tudors would have called 'pricksong books') stemmed from the greatest masters of the Parisian school.

The cyclic motion of the motet's career can be seen also, with admirable clarity, in its texts. First came the Latin words; then one Latin text was replaced by a French one (often a contrafactum), then French texts entirely usurped the Latin ones, until at last there came a strong tendency to translate recently-composed French texts back into Latin. Fashions changed as rapidly in the thirteenth century as in any other, and music was as prone to alteration as costume or architecture. Nevertheless, the liturgy exerted its authoritative hold for some considerable time, so that motets of the early and middle parts of the century often have texts that paraphrase the tenor's verbal tag. The magnificent four-part *Mors* employs as its tenor the one word 'mors' from the Alleluia *Christus resurgens*, and the accompanying melisma is stated twice, the second time being subtly different in that rests are inserted from time to time, lengthening the tenor artificially and letting more light into the closely-wrought harmonic texture. Above the tenor are three vocal parts, each with its own text. But each text begins with the word 'mors': *Mors a primi patris vicio*; *Mors que stimulo*; *Mors morsu nata venenato*, and one of them even ends with 'mors', the other two parts blending with a similar final vowel. This is a motet in which the tenor is completely troped in each of the upper voice-parts, and thus it would still be possible to make use of the music in the original Alleluia *Christus resurgens*.

Other examples of this textual trope or gloss are works based on the tenors *Benedicta*, *Veritatem*, and *Per omnia secula*. *Benedicta*, from the gradual *Benedicta et venerabilis* (Vigil of the Assumption, and at other times) has *Benedicta Marie virginis* in the upper voice and *Beate virginis* in the lower. It will be noticed that both texts begin with the syllable 'Be', and of course both are in praise of the Virgin. Similarly, *Veritatem* in one motet bears the text *In veritate comperi* immediately above it, and in the topmost voice *In salvatoris nomine*. Again, both texts begin with an identical syllable. The tenor is from the gradual *Propter veritatem*, also for the Feast of the Assumption. For the third example (*Per omnia secula*) we have a tenor based on one of the common tones of the Mass, 'Per omnia secula seculorum'. The two upper texts agree as far as the sixth syllable: *Per omnia secula seculorum, Maria*; *Per omnia seculorum secula, Virgo regia.*

One of the main reasons why so many texts were in honour of the Virgin Mary was the rapid and widespread growth of Marian cults. Another was the necessity for combining a memorial or commemoration of the Virgin with services for other feasts or saints' days. Thus a motet could be constructed from a melisma or group of notes taken from any gradual or alleluia, and the upper texts provided with poems in honour of the Virgin, bringing about a dual-purpose work.

Side by side with the composition of new motets built on old tenors goes the constant revising and reworking of earlier material. Replacing or translating texts was one matter; replacing music quite another, since the whole aspect and sound of the composition, together with its texture, rhythm, and character, would change at the same time. Quite frequently in the course of the thirteenth century there appear favourite double motets to which as many as three different, and alternative, upper parts have been written. A state of affairs such as this goes far to confirm the theory that music changed with its environment; that basically the same piece of music would sound different if heard at Santiago, Avignon, Paris, London, and Worcester within a few months. However powerful the central repository of style and ideas (and there is no doubt that for a long time this was Paris) the local and peripheral musicians contributed very considerably towards the modification and even improvement of the current harmonic practices.

Fragments of manuscripts in Italy, Germany, and Spain (as opposed to the larger and more complete sources copied in France and then brought to those countries) prove the enthusiasm and patience of lesser musicians who may have had no chance to study at the fount and origin of all that was best in music. In England too there was much experiment, though even the most advanced examples of this can be clearly connected with the great European mainstream of liturgical polyphony. The English fondness for a ground bass, or (more correctly) tenor, was probably inspired by the remarkable *Amor potest/Ad amorem* in the Montpellier manuscript, and other works displaying a similar technique. In Worcester, this ubiquitous tenor-repetition took on many forms, from short phrases like those sung by the lowest pair of voices in the Summer Canon, to long ones that anticipate the far more complex rhythms and isorhythms of the succeeding age.

English composers used the word *pes* to describe this kind of repeated tenor, usually based on a simple symmetrical scheme not derived from plainsong, though devised by an organist. Viewed alone, these tenors seem little more than harmonic doodles, the result of an idle half-hour. Consider the *pes* of *Prolis eterne genitor | Psallat mater gratie*: it consists only of the five notes between middle C and the F a fifth below. The player sounds a C, repeats it, and goes down the scale to G, then a cadence A G; now comes a matching phrase, this time starting at the bottom note, F, and so up the scale to B, then once more the cadence A G. What a pleasant musical rhyme, thinks the composer. So he finishes the *pes* by repeating A (on a long note) and G (see Ex. 26). All this can be played by a novice, on a piano, with one finger. Yet it is the sole basis and structural support of a three-part motet of no mean length; this nine-bar phrase is repeated eleven times in all.

26

Two matching phrases also appear in the resplendent four-part *O quam glorifica | O quam beata | O quam felix*, where (once again) the total range of the tenor is very small. This time it covers just a major sixth. Less than half of that already small range is covered by the tenor of *Virgo regalis*, for only three notes are used, F, G, and A. The pattern of the *pes* is simply F G F G A F G G F, repeated nine times below two voice-parts which exchange both their music and text at regular intervals, corresponding to the length of the *pes*. Voice 1 vocalizes, voice

2 sings; then voice 1 takes up the music and text that voice 2 has just sung, and voice 2 vocalizes on the cast-off music of voice 1. To the ear, of course, the effect is simply that of a repeat, though to be sure with a slight change of tone-colour since no two human voices can be exactly matched. This kind of voice-exchange was a classical feature of the motet, and flourished for well over a century, without however outliving the hocket.

The Worcester repertory contains many polyphonic settings of Mass tropes. These, unlike the original tropes, had no connexion with Alleluia melodies, any more than the motets were connected with organa (except in a few rare instances). There are tropes to the Kyrie and Sanctus, besides two examples of Gloria tropes that have themselves been troped. *Regnum tuum solidum* is interrupted at precisely that word for yet another interpolation, beginning *O rex glorie*. Similarly the first section of the *Spiritus et alme* trope (for Masses of the B.V.M.) becomes instead '*Spiritus* procedens a patre, venis mundi regnans per aera *orphanorum paraclite*'. (The trope to the trope has been left in roman type.) Yet, amongst all this over-refinement and super-subtlety, there are many fine and powerful pieces, still singable and enjoyable: *Alleluia psallat*, *Fulget celestis curia*, and the remarkable four-part motet on Thomas à Becket, *Thomas gemma Cantuarie*. Before the thirteenth century drew to its close, Anglo-Saxon angularities had begun to be smoothed down by a mellifluous and disarmingly simple method of composition based on successions of six-three chords (or, as they are often called, chords of the first inversion) with an occasional fifth-plus-octave formation at important cadence points.

A well-known Worcester example of this style is the motet *Beata viscera*, and its wide popularity and rapid growth were due in no small measure to the ease with which it could be composed, or rather improvised. All that was needed was a melody; above, below, or around it other singers would add parallel parts, following in the main all the contours of the original. These other singers performed according to set rules which could be applied to any pre-existent melody, whether liturgical or secular; and the result was a kind of medieval *Gebrauchsmusik*, or utilitarian music, which is variously known as 'English discant' (when the tune is in the lowest part) and '*fauxbourdon*' (when the tune is in the treble). Quite frequently, however, it held the middle part, so that works of this kind belong by strict definition to neither category, though in terms of pure sound they come very close to both. Similarly, the familiar architectural pattern of double-lancet and trefoil is found not in one position, but sometimes on ground level in a cloister wall, sometimes on high in some lofty clerestory. The mind of the medieval artist and musician can never be called narrow.

SECULAR POLYPHONY

In the same way that liturgical forms influenced one another, borrowed and paid back, and engendered new forms and styles, so the secular art forms of the Middle Ages interacted upon each other to a remarkable degree. It was a common occurrence to build a love-song or pastoral ditty from a basic plainsong type, or even on a particular tune; and it was equally common (as the thirteenth century drew to its close) to use secular songs as the tenors of motets, whatever their function or character. But, just as easily, a dance-theme could become a song, or a song-tune material for a dance. The commonwealth of musical currency was such that the greatest composer, the lowliest singer, the most high-born troubadour, and the humblest jongleur all shared certain formulas or clichés, and it was this very act of sharing that enabled ideas on a larger scale to be transplanted without withering, or to be grafted without ill effect.

Sometimes modern theories concerning this transplanting of musical elements seem to have been carried too far. It is, for example, commonly supposed that the tail-pieces (*caudae*) of many conductus settings, whether liturgical or political, were used as 'suites of dances' by medieval minstrels. It is true that a certain lilting rhythm was common to many liturgical forms, and that if the wordless sections of a three-part composition are played by instruments at a sufficiently rapid pace, a dance-like measure will result. But there is no proof that this happened, whereas there is proof through formal affinities that the *estampie*, a well-known medieval dance, was indebted to the liturgical sequence for its paired *puncta* or phrases. There is one important difference, however, even in this ostensibly clear derivation: the sequence and the *estampie* share the idea of paired verses, but in the *estampie* the first- and second-time endings are different to the extent of perhaps half a dozen notes, and of course the actual cadence. Moreover the two different endings appear consistently in each pair, rather like a kind of refrain.

Most of the court dances (*danses royales*) conform to this pattern, and so too, in the main, does a well-known English dance which sheds its monophonic character in the last few bars for a duet passage below a repeated note in the treble. This short passage, though in three-part harmony, may not have required more than two players, since the repeated note could well have been an open string, assuming that the viol was the instrument intended. With two players, the piece could have been performed in antiphonal manner, so that the first player always gave out the first statement of the tune, the second player repeating it with the *clos* ending. Medieval minstrels often went about in pairs or in groups of three or four, and they were usually conversant with the technique of more than one instrument. Their repertoire would consist largely of *estampies* and the shorter though allied forms, *nota* and *ductia*, which are often mentioned in medieval literature, just as the instruments are portrayed in carvings and illuminations. There are examples of two-part dances that might well qualify for the title of *ductia*, and these too display the expected pattern of melodically matching phrases, as well as extending the composition by repeating the three pairs of phrases with new material in the top part. The resulting pattern is not dissimilar from the idea and principle of variations over a ground bass, which worked so well for the Worcester school of composers.

Besides their stock of dances, both courtly and bourgeois, the minstrels certainly knew by heart some of the tenor tunes

that composers had used time and time again for motets with
secular words. As Johannes de Grocheo said: 'On the viol all
musical forms are precisely distinguished. . . . A good artist
plays on the viol every cantus and cantilena and every musical
form in general.' With few exceptions, the tenors are best
suited to performance on stringed instruments, not excluding
the vielle (or hurdy-gurdy) whose powers of sustaining tones
equalled the organ. This is an entirely different situation from
that which prevailed in later centuries, when tenors became
more angular and arpeggic, postulating performance by wind
instruments. Nevertheless, there are some peculiar tenors in
thirteenth-century motets that may require two or three hand-
bells to give the best effect. That for *Dieus! comment puet li
cuers | Vo vair oel* consists of only two notes, C and D. Also
uniquely represented in the Montpellier manuscript is *Amor
potest | Ad amorem*, already mentioned for the interest of its
'ground tenor', which consists of only three notes, F, E, and G.
In its formidable insistence on these three notes and an almost
unbroken dactylic rhythm it out-medievalizes even Carl
Orff.

Often the tenors themselves had French titles, and the tunes
that are enshrined in these tenors can sometimes be reconstructed to the extent that the song and its form become once
more tangible realities, instead of mere shadows of lost compositions. Some melodies are revealed as *virelais* (refrain-songs
for soloist and chorus): *Entre Copin et Bourgois | Je me cuidoie
tenir* is built on *Bele Ysabelos*, and similarly *Nouvele amour |
Haute amor* rests upon *Hé! dame jolie*, though the original form
of this latter example is less clear than the former. *Hé, resveille-
toi, Robin* (often cited in medieval literature) serves as tenor to
the double motet *En mai quand rosier | L'autre jour*, and was
later borrowed by Adam de la Halle as a refrain in his *Jeu de
Robin et Marion*. An unusual example of a tenor having been
composed of a series of refrain fragments occurs in *Qui amours
veut maintenir | Li dous pensers*, whose tenor *Cis a cui je sui amie*
contains no less than nine such refrains. Equally unique,
though for a different reason, is the Parisian street-cry *Frese
nouvelle!* which does excellent duty as tenor to a couple of texts

(*On parole de batre | A Paris soir et matin*) glorifying the gastro-
nomical pleasures of the great city.

Yet other tenors are based on sections lifted wholesale from
estampies, and they are generally given the name of the composer: *Chose Tassin* (a minstrel named Tassynus, in the service
of Philippe le Bel) and *Chose Loyset*. These themes, as may be
expected, have a markedly instrumental flavour, some of them
even foreshadowing the trumpet-like themes which were to
become so popular with later composers of tenors (see Ex. 27).

27
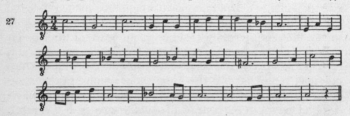

French songs were used by English composers, too, for the
very good reason that French was the language spoken at court,
and was also used by certain administrative departments of
state.

In the discussion of conductus, its links with clausulae and
other styles were stressed. There is still another feature, however, which links certain conducti to pre-existent monophonic
rondeaux, or secular songs of the refrain type. The well-known
tune *A l'entrada del tens clar*, *Eya*, reappears as the lowest voice
of *Veris ad imperia*, *Eya*, the Latin contrafactum having taken
over the acclamation as well as the melody. Yet another conductus, *Legis in volumine*, quotes the beginning of all three
voices of *Veris* before digressing and going its own way. Two
songs by the *trouvère* Blondel de Nesle have served as melodies
for conducti: *Ma joie me semont*, supplied with a new text by
Gautier de Chatillon, became the two-part *Ver pacis aperit*
(for the coronation of Philip Augustus, 1179), while *L'amour
donc sui espris* had an even more chequered career. It was rearranged as a sacred monody by Gautier de Coincy, and as a
monophonic conductus, *Suspirat spiritus*, this text being attributed to Chancellor Philippe of Paris. There are two conducti

for three voices, still using the same melody – *Procurans odium*, which extols the virtues of distraction, and *Purgator criminum*, exhorting the Jews to turn to Christ.

Bernard de Ventadorn's famous lark song, *Quan vei l'aloette mover*, underwent an even more remarkable series of vicissitudes. It was as if fame brought to a melody more in the way of change and even of mutilation than ever it might have suffered in obscurity. Yet it is true that the more versions exist, the easier it is for a modern scholar to learn about these melodies, even though the comparison of many versions may involve questions of judgement other than purely musical ones. Bernard's song was known to singers in its original *langue d'oc* text, as well as in its Old French version. To a later generation altogether, it was known by a text not even remotely connected with the lark song – *Plaine d'ire et de desconfort*. Even more strange it was given Latin words by Chancellor Philippe, and under the title *Quisquis cordis et oculi* was known and sung throughout the monasteries of Europe. There was also a French translation of the Latin text, *Li cuers se vait de l'uiel plaignant*, and a sacred contrafactum in the Mystery of St Agnes: *Seyner mil gracias ti rent*. It is hardly surprising that so many legends grew up about this song, nor is it remarkable to find Dante mentioning what can hardly be other than this same lark in the twentieth canto of his *Paradiso*.

To return to the secular, or rather para-liturgical conductus: this kind of music differed from the related type discussed earlier, for it generally lacked those florid passages at the beginning and end of the composition (and sometimes even in the middle), consisting only of carefully arranged declamatory phrases shared by all voices. The subjects of these conducti were for the most part connected with the affairs of church and state, and sometimes with a particular person, usually a dignitary of the church or a member of a royal family. The first category includes the vigorous exhortation for the Crusades, *Crucifigat omnes*, which was written towards the end of the twelfth century and is still preserved in seven European manuscripts. It also includes one of the few known four-part conducti, *Mundus vergens*, which bemoans the political struggles in early-thirteenth-century France; the two-part *Ut non ponam os*, which discourses upon the prerequisites for leadership; and the two texts mentioned in connexion with Chancellor Philippe's *Suspirat spiritus*.

Among the second category are several conducti in honour of kings and princes. *Ecclipsim patitur* is an elegy on the death of Geoffrey of Brittany (1186), while the three-part *Nemo sane spreverit* commemorates the death of Philip Augustus (1223), whose coronation in 1179 had already brought into being *Ver pacis aperit*. When Richard Cœur de Lion was crowned in 1189, the conductus *Redit aetas aurea* was sung. It is a straightforward and optimistic piece, singing of the return of the golden age and of equality, and the banishment of wickedness and vice. Almost epigrammatic in word and music, it nevertheless breaks into natural and fitting ornamentation as each verse comes to its close. Other famous commemorative conducti include those on the death of Thomas à Becket: one is monophonic (*In Rama sonat gemitus*) and concerns the archbishop's exile in France (1164–70), while the other (*Novus miles sequitur*) emphasizes his martyrdom, and is written for two voices. Unusual both in its length and in its use of melismatic sections is the conductus *O felix Bituria*, in honour of a Cistercian monk called Guillaume de Donjeon, sometime Prior of Pontigny, and later Archbishop of Bourges in 1200. His canonization in 1218 was almost certainly the occasion for which the conductus was written.

In the British Isles, polyphony flourished from the very earliest times. The late-twelfth-century descriptions of Wales, Ireland, and Scotland by Gerald the Welshman prove how vigorous a tradition there was in both vocal and instrumental polyphony:

Among these people I find a commendable diligence only on musical instruments, on which they are more skilled than any nation we have seen. For among them, the execution is not slow and solemn as on the English instruments to which we are accustomed, but it is rapid and lively, though the sound is soft and pleasant. It is astonishing that, with such a rapid plucking of the fingers, the musical rhythm is preserved, and with art unimpaired in spite of everything, the melody is finished and remains agreeable, with such smooth rapidity, such unequal equality, such discordant concord, throughout the varied tunes and the many intricacies of the part music.

Gerald is here trying to describe music in words, and like countless critics and observers in the centuries after him, he has found it very difficult. Such phrases as 'unequal equality' and 'discordant concord' lose some part of their apparently paradoxical sense when we consider their possible relationship to such universally common devices as *rubato* and the clever use of suspensions, whereby even the most harsh concord may be prepared and resolved without giving offence to the ear. In a later passage, Gerald discusses instruments:

It is to be observed that Scotland and Wales – the former by virtue of trade and affinity, and the latter by propagation – strive in practice to imitate Ireland in their tunes. Ireland uses and takes delight in two instruments, the *cithara* [= lyre] and the *tympanum* [= dulcimer], Scotland in three, the cithara, tympanum, and *chorus* [= small crwth, a bowed string instrument], and Wales in the cithara, *tibia* [= pipe] and chorus. Moreover they use strings made of brass, not of leather. In the opinion of many people, Scotland has not only equalled her mistress Ireland in music, but today surpasses and excels her by far. For this reason people look upon her now as the fountain of the art.

This remark takes on a special significance when we recall the amount of insular, if not actually Scottish, music in the eleventh fascicle of the St Andrews manuscript, which has already been discussed as one of the principal sources of Notre Dame organa and of imitators of this illustrious school. Even the simplest kind of part-music, such as the hymn to St Magnus (*Nobilis*, *humilis*) written in the Orkney Islands, shows a marked predilection for thirds in succession, and this type of sound on a fuller scale was the *raison d'être* of the later English discant style. Turning again to Gerald's *Description of Wales*, striking proof is found there of the Welsh love of part-singing:

In performing music they do not sing in unison like the inhabitants of other countries, but in polyphony; so that in a

group of singers (which one very often meets with in Wales)
you will hear as many melodies as there are people, and a
distinct variety of parts, finally uniting at last in a single consonance and harmony with the sweet softness of B flat. In the
northern districts of Britain, beyond the Humber and round
about York, the inhabitants use a similar kind of singing in
harmony, but in only two different parts, one singing quietly
in a low register, and the other soothing and charming the ear
above. Neither of the two nations has acquired this facility
through skill, but by long habit, which has made it natural and
familiar. And this practice is so firmly rooted in them, that one
never hears singing in unison, but either in several parts (as in
Wales), or at least in two, as in the North; and, what is still
more wonderful, the children – even from their infancy – sing
in the same manner. As the English in general do not adopt
this mode of singing, but only the northerners, I believe that it
was from the Danes and Norwegians (by whom these parts of
the island were more frequently invaded, and for more lengthy
periods) that the inhabitants contracted their way of singing
and of speaking.

The style of *Nobilis, humilis* is that of an extremely simple
conductus. More complex examples, still of insular origin
though supplied with Middle English texts, may be seen in
such compositions as *Foweles in the frith, Edi beo thu hevene
quene*, and *Jesu Christes milde moder*. These are all for two
voices, and they all share a forward-looking attitude to the new
ideals of consonance, embracing a fuller use of thirds and sixths
rather than the consonances of fourth, fifth, and octave
favoured by composers of earlier centuries. *Foweles in the
frith* is very short, yet it sums up in a brief space the darkest
despair of mankind: lesser beasts are in their element, yet man,
capable of madness, walks in sorrow, a creature of flesh and
blood. It dates from 1260–70, as does *Edi beo thu*, a conductus
of completely different character. It seems to have been the
work of a chaplain or schoolmaster of Llanthony Priory, in
Gloucestershire, and its text – *Blessed be thou, queen of heaven* –
is a Middle-English version of lines from various well-known
Marian sequences. The first line is obviously a translation of
Benedicta es, celorum regina, but there is no attempt to use the

sequence melody. The two voices, instead of remaining in their respective positions (as in *Nobilis* and *Foweles*), cross over one another and thus produce chains of thirds by a simpler yet more subtle means. The lower of the two voices sings only three notes, F, G, and A, yet the more agile upper voice, leaping up and down through intervals of a fifth, combines with it to give a most mellifluous and delightful effect of mobile consonances and shifting tone-colours. Both this and *Jesu Christes milde moder* are of the strophic type, the former having eight verses and the latter ten.

In the case of *Jesu Christes milde moder*, the affinity with the sequence is stronger still, for the text is none other than that of a favourite Holy Week sequence, *Stabat iuxta Christi crucem*. Yet again there is a reluctance to use the sequence melody (though this is used for another Middle English version, this time for one voice only: *Stond wel moder under rode*) and a severely limited compass for the two voices. Together, they do not exceed the range of a seventh, so that the impression is one of veiled grief and pent-up emotion. Indeed, the intensity of musical expression is here in inverse proportion to the means employed.

The secular conductus, then, was a style which embraced political events such as coronations, commemorations of the deaths of kings, princes, and martyrs, general themes of a topographical or philosophical nature, and popular religion such as that encouraged by the Franciscans. Its secular nature did not, however, necessarily enable laymen to qualify as performers or interpreters. The art and science of music was kept within the confines, if not of the Church, at least of the educated classes, and such popular polyphony as was then current almost invariably borrowed its methods, as well as some of its melodic material, from the Church. The reverse, as we have seen, could and did happen on occasion; but the wealth to maintain and encourage composers and performers lay in the hands of the barons and the bishops.

5. Secular Monody

THE word monody is used here in the same sense as for the Italian monodists of the early seventeenth century. In other words, monody does not exclude an instrumental accompaniment, but rather presupposes one. It is unfortunate that most accounts of medieval song either pass by the role of instruments, or else minimize its importance and (in transcriptions of songs) leave its practical aspect to the imagination. On the other hand, one or two modern versions of troubadour melodies do provide a welcome accompaniment for string or wind instrument. It is known that plucked and bowed instruments as well as reed and flute-type wind instruments were used by medieval minstrels, and these minstrels accompanied (in both the literal and musical senses) their masters, who were the medieval counterpart of modern virtuosi of the voice.

Medieval illuminated manuscripts show the minstrels (or *jongleurs*) not only as musicians, but as versatile entertainers. Besides being adept in playing the harp and viol, they were apparently no mean acrobats, and could throw knives, juggle with spherical objects, and manage performing animals. Their musical function is clearly set forth in medieval literature. One poem tells how the minstrel tuned up, drawing attention to himself by playing several strings at once, then going on to a prelude that brought in notes of a quite different kind. In between the verses of the song, more short instrumental pieces occurred, and at the end there was a brief postlude. Obviously, once the song was under way, the minstrel's role was a subordinate one; but at the beginning he was free to command the audience's attention.

These accompaniments were not written down, and (with only a few exceptions) they have not come down to us. But neither have the right-hand parts of Baroque continuos come down to us. They were left for the player to improvise, just as one line (or even two) of a fifteenth-century *fauxbourdon* fell to the lot of the singer's imagination and training. Nobody nowadays would dream of performing *fauxbourdon* as a solo or a duet, any more than they would dare to omit the continuo realization in works from Monteverdi to Bach. Medieval song, however, is frequently performed and recorded without any hint of instruments whatever, and the distortion of its true texture is consequently violent. Although it is doubtful whether the average minstrel ever achieved more than a simple doubling, with slight elaboration, of the melody, his more skilled colleagues could easily have added a simple counterpoint, probably together with a drone note of some kind. Harmony was based on the concords of the fourth, fifth, and octave, and in later times on the third and sixth. A poem with music, by Neidhart von Reuenthal, mentions intervals of the unison and third.

Songs with Latin text existed many centuries before the flowering of troubadour and *trouvère* art-song, but the lack of carefully heighted notes precludes all but a purely fanciful transcription. This is a pity, as many of the songs illuminate historical personages, while others (the work of the wandering scholars or *goliards*) offer a lively picture of the joyous and amorous side of medieval life. In rare cases the melody of a song can be reconstructed when contrafacta exist in manuscripts with heighted neumes or solmization syllables. *O admirabile Veneris idolum*, which also occurs with the text *O Roma nobilis*, is one such instance. There seems to be no musical or historical connexion between these Latin songs and the later products of northern and southern France.

It is often stated that the origins of troubadour song are not known. Yet one of the most satisfactory derivations of the word troubadour is from *tropus*, which means a song or musical turn of phrase. In course of time, tropus or trope came (by metonymy) to mean the actual insertion of both text and melody, as has been mentioned previously in connexion with early liturgical music. It was natural that gifted laymen should imitate the fine music and singing of the clerics, and while it was probably thought indiscreet at first to remove melodies from the liturgy, it was fair play to draw upon the tropes, which were an optional accretion to the liturgy, tolerated by the Church but never officially sanctioned. It cannot therefore be an entire coincidence that all but one of the strophic poems by the earliest known troubadour, Guillaume IX (Count of Poitiers and Duke of Acquitaine), are traceable to conducti written at St Martial, Limoges, at the end of the eleventh century. Melodies from this same centre of medieval musical art also fit poems by Guillaume for which no music has been preserved.

From a geographical point of view, it is not by any means remarkable that the vast and fertile valleys of Limousin should have given birth not only to the flower of ecclesiastical poetry and polyphony, but also to the greatest creations of the troubadours. At roughly the same time Saint Séver had produced one of the finest manuscripts of all time: the Apocalypse, truly Romanesque in character yet copied from an earlier Christian source. In the field of sculpture, this same area was the cradle for an almost miraculous rebirth of monumental carving from stone, as the portals of Moissac, Souillac, Beaulieu, and Toulouse prove abundantly. At the time when the Church began to stress the worship of the Virgin Mary, composing poems and music in her honour, men of wealth and men of the world who felt themselves drawn to the art of music began a similar cult, the worship of womankind.

There were, of course, other causes for this cult besides the purely religious motive. Many of the troubadours were of noble birth, and would thus have known of knightly vows respecting the fair sex; they would have known, too, the accounts of fateful love, as told by northern writers imitating the stories of ancient Greece. Another contributory source may have been the Celtic mythology introduced by Geoffrey of Monmouth into his *Historia Regum Britanniae*. Yet not all was fiction: there were the lovers, Héloïse and Abélard, whose adventures and ultimate tragedy kept Europeans of the early twelfth century in a state of excitement and sympathy. All this was calculated to add fuel to the fire, and even though one troubadour, Marcabru of Gascony, managed to be both singer and woman-hater, the great majority of troubadours lived up to their new philosophy. Its essence was that love was a secret, even mysterious passion; that the lover, in order to win his lady's devotion, must accomplish special tasks to fulfil the promises made to her; and that the lady, in turn, must be merciful and faithful to him who has chosen her.

The troubadours wrote in *langue d'oc*, which was a literary and courtly language derived from the dialects of south-western France. As a language, it had a comparative short life, for the *chanson* was a minor verse form, and was not destined to give rise to further linguistic development. The music, on the other hand, was used time and time again for different texts, and some melodies can be traced across Europe through three or even four centuries. Similarly, one and the same text is often given different melodies, so it becomes difficult at times to discover who is the real author and composer. It is generally assumed however that the troubadours who proudly signed their songs with a gesture of the true old Roman individualism composed both words and melody.

The greatest of their number included such men as Bernard de Ventadorn, a genius in the art of combining lyric melody and fine poetry; Guiraut de Bornelh, who more than made up in technique what he lacked in inspiration; Peire Vidal, an urbane and widely-travelled parodist for whom verse was a completely natural medium; Bertrand de Born, whose visit to England was unfortunately more political than musical; Folquet de Marseille, a man of many parts who founded a university, organized a crusade, jointly founded a religious order, and ended up as a bishop. These were lively and colourful personalities, and their songs reflect, for the most part, their intense joy in living and their devotion to a difficult art.

In formal and emotional content their songs varied very considerably. The famous lark song of Bernard de Ventadorn is concerned with despairing love; so too is *Lanquand li jorn* by Jaufré Rudel, whose melodies are more often than not greatly superior to his verses. Arnaut Daniel, in a virtuoso song *Chanson do · ill mot*, links the last line of each verse to the first line of the next, by sense as well as by word. Some melodies are highly organized, while others, like *Ha! me non fai chantar* by Albertet de Sisteron, unfold in a natural, almost extempore manner. The *planh*, a kind of musical elegy, is frequently found in the works of the troubadours; some of these pieces actually name the person commemorated, as in Guiraut Riquier's *Ples de tristor*. The dawn song (*alba*) was immensely popular too, for its function as a warning to lovers made it utilitarian music *par excellence*. Guiraut de Bornelh's *Reis glorios* is a justly famous example of the alba at its most refined and best. In certain songs, the influence of the dance is strongest, and in at least one instance (*Kalenda maya* of Raimbaut de Vaqueiras) we know that a dance inspired the composition of the song.

As the best liturgical music spread northwards from Limoges, so did the best of the troubadour lyrics. They may well have been introduced to northern French courts by the granddaughter of Guillaume, Eleanor of Acquitaine, who patronized many troubadours including Bernard de Ventadorn. For many years the older northern French poets, those who wrote the *langue d'oïl*, had remained anonymous, yet as the twelfth century moved towards its close there grew up a great and gifted school of musician-poets known as *trouvères*. They wrote in Old French, and (like the troubadours) drew on such melodic stock as existed in and out of church, transforming basic types and phrases into magically potent tunes of unsurpassed beauty and proportion. Some 1,400 *trouvère* melodies have survived, and about 4,000 poems, as against 260-odd troubadour melodies and 2,600 texts.

The earliest of the *trouvères*, as might be expected, wrote lyrics in the same vein as their troubadour forerunners and contemporaries. Blondel de Nesle is known to every schoolboy through a delightful though fanciful story about his seeking out the imprisoned Richard I of England, also a writer of songs. Conon de Béthune led no less remarkable a life, for he took part in the crusade of 1204, and achieved some degree of success in the field of politics and statesmanship. Guy de Coucy was for some years castellan of the now destroyed Château de Coucy, and the author of a handful of songs in the best tradition of the *trouvère courtois*. The last, and certainly the greatest of this group was Thibaut IV King of Navarre, whose songs are of amazingly high quality, in spite of his alleged preoccupation with worldly affairs. An almost equally brilliant group of bourgeois *trouvères* included Colin Muset, Rutebeuf, and one of the greatest of them all, Adam de la Halle, who wrote numerous polyphonic *rondeaux*, *ballades*, and *virelais*, besides the charming pastoral *Le Jeu de Robin et Marion*. There were many followers and imitators, but their work became gradually more stereotyped and didactic, and consequently less inspired.

Once again we find in the music of the *trouvères* that wide range of types and themes, both poetic and musical, that gives the repertory such breadth of appeal. The love songs are there in abundance: *Cil qui d'amors me conseille*, by Gace Brulé, tells of despairing love in a suitably plaintive first-mode melody; Gautier d'Epinal, one of the earliest *trouvères*, brings freshness and vigour to the old yet perennially new theme of spring and love in his *Commencemens de dolce saison bele*. In Thibaut de Navarre's *Pour conforter ma pesance* the Crusader's curse '*Mort Mahom!*' is heard in one verse, shattering for a brief instant the complaint of the lover. The beauty of melody enshrined in *Ce fu en mai*, by Moniot d'Arras, was recognized by Hindemith, who used it in his ballet *Nobilissima Visione*. Robert de Rains, in a charming pastoral whose text makes use of an echo effect (*Bergier de ville champestre | Pestre ses aigniaus menot*) draws on another typical first-mode formula; Guillaume d'Amiens, on the other hand, tends to draw on themes with a folk-song character in his pastoral *rondeaux*.

Attempts have been made to classify this vast song repertory in various ways, either by verse-form, probable derivation of structure, or content of the texts. But tunes, like poems, have an occasional resistance to classification, and it is not unusual to see scholars perform a complete *volte-face* in the treatment of rhythmical problems, or in the acceptance or rejection of a given technical term describing a medieval song-form. Moreover, it has frequently been pointed out that singers, in all countries and at all periods of history, have reserved the right to interpret music in their own way, slowing down a little here to swell out the tone on a high note, or quickening up to heighten the effect of a decorative figure or run. There is indeed no proof that *rubato*, the playing with time-values so often attributed exclusively to romantic composers and executants, was not known and practised in the Middle Ages.

Just as the marriage of Eleanor of Acquitaine and Louis VII brought troubadour art northwards, so another royal marriage, that of Frederick Barbarossa and Beatrix of Burgundy, served to spread the influence eastwards to Germany. Beatrix retained the *trouvère* Guiot de Provins at her court, and well before the end of the twelfth century a poet named Friedrich von Husen had penned a German version of one of Guiot's songs. Although the melody does not survive, the German words fit the *trouvère* melody extremely well, and in view of this and other imitations by von Husen it seems that he may have been the principal channel for *trouvère* influence in Germany. The Germans had a previous tradition of their own, but the *trouvère* cult gradually seeped into musical circles, and it must have been hard at first to resist its appeal. The same sources that had helped to mould French song were once again active in the indirect formation of a distinctively German school of composers. Plainsong and folk melody played their traditional role, and their influence can be seen in the best of the *Minnelieder*.

As poets the Germans were far more cerebral than the French, especially in the matter of balance in planning a long work such as a *leich* – roughly the German equivalent of the *lai*, which is structurally related to the sequence. A *leich* by the great musician and poet Walther von der Vogelweide yields a symmetry in both text and music no less remarkable than that of an isorhythmic motet. In numbers of half-lines (the true unit of measurement) the following figures speak for themselves:

12+8	10+21+10	12+8	8+12+8	10+10	8+25+8	8+12
20	41	20	28	20	41	20
	81		28		81	
			190			

Numbers held a mystic power for the mind of medieval man,

and this power can be seen at work in countless ways wherever music and poetry join forces. The example from Walther is by no means isolated. Melodically some of these German songs appear delightfully simple, yet this very simplicity often hides a subtle structure only apparent to the listener who is instructed in the art. There is also a frequent flavour of the major mode, of square metres, and other modernizing influences.

Contrafacta of good quality were written by Dietmar von Eist, Ulrich von Gutenburg, and Bernger von Horheim, as well as by the Friedrich already mentioned. Besides Walther von der Vogelweide, the original minds were to be found among such singers as Neidhart von Reuenthal (whose melodically agile *Mayenzeit* is justly praised), Wolfram von Eschenbach, and Heinrich von Meissen, known as 'Frauenlob' because he gallantly upheld the word *Frau* as against *Weib* – 'lady' rather than 'woman'. In some ways Heinrich was a transitional figure, a *Minnesinger* by temperament and tradition, but looking forward to the era of the Mastersingers, who are strictly speaking outside the scope of the present study.

Besides spreading to Germany, the art of the troubadours and *trouvères* found its way into Spain via Compostela, where also French polyphony had made its mark in the field of sacred music. It was a *trouvère* (albeit of the cloth) who first took over and remodelled melodies, setting to them new verses of his own composition in honour of the Virgin. Gautier de Coincy was thus indirectly responsible for the upsurge of enthusiasm for Marian worship in Spain, and in turn for the compilation of the *Cantigas de Santa María*. These songs, written during the second half of the twelfth century by King Alfonso the Wise and his musicians, made use of the delicately melodic Galician language as a vehicle for their ideas and narratives. Their melodies probably owe something to Arabic and Hebrew models, as well as to plainsong and folk-song, for Alfonso's entourage included the best scholars and the most renowned, whether Christian, Jewish, or Moorish.

Of these many songs (there are over four hundred) one in ten is in praise of the Virgin; others recount in breezy narrative some of the miracles attributed to her, and since the characters are mostly drawn from everyday types, the *Cantigas* are in effect a musical microcosm of the Middle Ages. *A Uírgen sempr'acorrer* tells how the Virgin saved a courtier who was the victim of slander; *Muit'amar deuemos* is the story of a near-shipwreck off the coast of Brittany; *Oraçon com piedade* explains how a Moorish woman and child were saved from death when a tower collapsed, because Christians prayed for their safety.

In Italy, French art-song was admired and imitated, but little trace of it has come down to us. Instead we have the *laude spirituali*, hymns of praise sung by bands of penitents as they wandered through the country. These songs are not always of such artless simplicity that they can be assigned, even in the imagination, to a group of ambulating flagellants. Indeed, it is more than likely that they were sung when the groups stopped at some village or city for a public demonstration of their penitential sentiments. Many of the *laude* were in praise of the Virgin, though others told in simple story and touching melody of the great festivals in the Christian year – *Gloria in cielo* for Christmas, and *Alta Trinita beata* for the Holy Trinity.

The cult of the flagellants spread to Germany, where its upholders were known as *Geissler*, and the songs they sang *Geisslerlieder*. Apparently it did not penetrate to England, though English songs of the time are often imbued with melancholy and pessimism. Although Eleanor of Acquitaine (after the annulment of her marriage to Louis) came to England as the wife of Henry II, and brought with her Bernard de Ventadorn, troubadour song seems to have made little impression. The songs of St Godric, a Saxon hermit, are secular only in that they have English texts that are non-liturgical: their subjects and melodies display ecclesiastical influences. True secular lyrics are found in such songs as *Mirie it is while sumer ilast* and *Worldes blis ne last ne throwe*, both of which again show strong elements of pessimism and foreboding. Lighter in both melodic vein and sentiment is the love song *Bryd one brere* and the famous canon *Sumer is icumen in* (now dated at about 1280), which adeptly turns a single line into four-part polyphony, then adds a pair of crossing and repeating figures below, creating a glorious six-part sonority that is unique for its age and country.

IV · ARS NOVA

Gilbert Reaney

1. Historical and Cultural Background

IT is too late now to change the labels which we attach to the thirteenth and fourteenth centuries in music, namely *Ars Antiqua* and *Ars Nova*, and in fact they are convenient if not as precise as we could wish. After all, Latin was commonly used in the Middle Ages, and it is simple to contrast the two principal styles of medieval music as the old and the new. But of course there was more to the matter than that. The fact is that by the fourteenth century change was evident in both forms and style, so much so that a famous theorist and composer, Philippe de Vitry (1291–1361), was able to codify the rules of the old and the new art in a short but valuable treatise which has only been preserved in the form of lecture notes written down by students. The clear division of Vitry's teaching in this work is particularly evident in the title applied in one manuscript: *Both methods of measuring motets*. The *Ars Nova* was primarily a new method of notating motets, which were exemplified in a practical way in compositions by Vitry himself. It is important that we should be clear about the limited validity of Vitry's own definition of Ars Nova, since at the present day all fourteenth-century music except that of a clearly archaic character is termed Ars Nova music, and with reason, since it is generally quite different from that of the preceding century. However, it is the fate of stylistic labels like Ars Nova, Gothic, Baroque, etc. to be paradoxical as well as pertinent. Thus fourteenth-century polyphonic song is hardly mentioned in Vitry's treatise, while the complex late fourteenth-century compositions are only Ars Nova works in that they carry on earlier traditions of form and notational precision.

The question may be and often has been raised as to how far Italian and English music can be considered Ars Nova. The answer is probably simpler than specialists have led us to believe. Obviously Philippe de Vitry's *Ars Nova* was a treatise relevant only to a particular point in musical history and to French music as it was cultivated historically and actually *c.* 1320. Nevertheless, its clear notational principles and their application in the contemporary motet influenced French music decisively during the course of the century. In so far as English music followed those principles and employed French musical forms it can be described as Ars Nova, but the Italian *trecento* music had more independent beginnings. The phrase Ars Nova was not used contemporaneously by fourteenth-century Italian writers. However, the polyphonic songs which were cultivated in Florence and northern Italy from the 1320s onwards were new enough, as was the notation of which they made use. Curiously enough, both French and Italian music seems to have developed its notation at this period from that current at the time of Vitry's predecessor, Petrus de Cruce of Amiens. In some ways the Italian notation was more developed than the French, but its limitations and only local importance brought about its downfall. Chiefly responsible was the lack of precision to be felt in the semibreve in an age when note-forms were multiplied for the very purpose of making note-values absolutely clear. To be sure, the same difficulties must have been felt in both France and Italy about 1300, for the slowing down of note-values made it necessary to distinguish between three different rhythms all represented by the semibreve, which had formerly been the smallest note-value. These were called major, minor, and minimal semibreves, and it was the smallest type of semibreve which finally emerged as a new note, the minim, a semibreve with an ascending tail. This note-form must have had a purely theoretical importance at first, for it is said that it was invented in the College of Navarre in Paris and sanctioned and employed by Philippe de Vitry. But nevertheless, if we admit that Vitry's *Ars Nova* was completed about 1316, it was only some two years later that Marchettus of Padua published his treatise *Pomerium* describing the Italian notation, complete with minim note-form for the smallest values and with a full comparison of French and Italian rhythmic methods. There can indeed be no doubt that the Italian system was as much an Ars Nova as the French, perhaps more so for us, since we cannot trace the Italian Ars Antiqua as we can the French via Petrus de Cruce to Franco of

Cologne in theory and through the motets of the *Roman de Fauvel* and the Montpellier MS. in practice. In this respect the recent discovery of some two-part polyphonic settings for dramatic offices in Padua, dating from around 1300, is most valuable, for we were previously dependent on a single two-part sequence written about the same time for the knowledge of independent Italian polyphony before Marchettus.

In the first part of the fourteenth century, Spain evidently clung to thirteenth-century French music, to judge from the Las Huelgas codex, but particularly in the second half of the century the route via Avignon and Montpellier brought new music and poetry in quantity from the north French schools of minstrelsy. In Germany the influence of the French Ars Nova was limited, largely owing to the backward state of polyphony in that country, and was mainly restricted to German translations with very much the original music of much earlier French works. The late Ars Nova in Italy made its way via south Germany into Poland, mainly in the form of mass movements, though by this time we are well into the fifteenth century. Taking into account these peripheral regions, the Ars Nova lasted from *c.* 1310 to *c.* 1435, about which date French music came decisively under English influence and Italian polyphony came practically to a halt as far as manuscript sources are concerned.

The fourteenth century has a fascination due in large measure to its *fin-de-siècle* aspect, in which it appears as a romantic, many-faceted period of decline tempered by a cultural flowering which looks both forward and backward, combining the impersonal, cosmological aspirations of the Middle Ages with the subjective humanism of the Renaissance. Historically the decay of feudal ideals is all too apparent and the Catholic faith became the plaything of princes and prelates. Philip IV of France (1268–1314) was a tyrant who certainly strengthened the state by his marriage with Joanna of Navarre but was an indefatigable opponent of the new strong pope, Boniface VIII, whom he actually imprisoned in Rome. When Boniface died, Philip nominated the new pope and placed him at Avignon as Clement V. This began the so-called Babylonian captivity which lasted from 1305 to 1378, after which the determination to have a pope in Rome as well as the determination of the Avignon popes to remain in power led to the schism (1378–1417). Only the election of Martin V (1417–31) at the Council of Constance finally ended the division. Not only was Philip IV responsible for this whole catastrophe, but he also condemned the order of Knights Templar and had its members put to death. A succession of kings reigned between 1314 and 1328, when Philip's nephew Philip VI Valois came to the throne. His reign lasted till 1350, though his right to be king was rejected by Edward III of England. The Hundred Years' War, which was directly caused by this Anglo-French stalemate, was to last with but few interruptions from 1337 to 1453. And in Philip's own reign came the destruction of the French fleet in 1340, the débâcle of Crécy in 1346, and the plague of 1348, which wrought havoc all over Europe. John II (1350–64) anachronistically clung to the code of chivalry, but was defeated and taken prisoner with ease at Poitiers in 1356. His sons stood hostage for him when he returned to France, but when one of them broke his word, John returned to England and died there in 1364. Charles V learned from his father's mistakes and gradually regained a good deal of the ground previously lost, but Charles VI, who had bouts of madness, was forced to give way to Henry V at Agincourt. Finally, in 1420, English hegemony was assured by the peace of Troyes. It was only after the accession of Charles VII in 1422 and the siege of Orléans in 1429, with Joan of Arc as the architect of success, that the English were gradually turned out of France, but it took till 1453. The dukes of Burgundy were out-and-out defenders of chivalry, but were careful to ally themselves with the winning side, the English, and their accumulated wealth was used for the cultivation of art of every kind.

The Italians naturally suffered continually from the strife caused by the opposition between Church and State, and, owing to the fact that the country was divided up into numerous sovereign states, often representing no more than a single town, party faction was rife. It seems certain however that these overlords, like those in other countries, were extremely fond of minstrels and cultivated music. It may well have been Robert of Anjou (1309–43), king of Naples, whose father was the son of Louis VIII of France, who influenced other Italian courts in this respect. Certainly Marchettus of Padua dedicated the *Pomerium* to him, stating in the dedicatory letter that Robert loved to have a crowd of musicians round him. Philippe de Vitry, too, dedicated a motet to him. Strangely enough, musical composition does not seem to have been greatly affected by the constant changes in ownership of important towns like Padua, Verona, and Florence. Undoubtedly the major power in northern Italy in the second half of the fourteenth century was the Visconti of Milan, who controlled most of the important towns in this area except Florence by 1400. However, with the death of Gian Galeazzo Visconti in 1402, it was the turn of Venice to assume greater leadership.

In Spain the kings of Castile were constantly engaged in wars with the Moors, who were only finally driven out in 1492, but the kings of Aragon and Navarre preferred to keep out of these struggles, being more concerned with keeping up good relations with their powerful English neighbours. Gaston Phébus, count of Foix, also a member of the house of Aragon, was a valiant soldier, but tried to keep the balance between the French and English, who constantly wooed him as an ally. In Cyprus, which had been a possession of the Lusignan family since Richard Cœur de Lion handed it to Guy de Lusignan in 1192, French culture reigned supreme as it did in Aragon and Navarre. Pierre I de Lusignan (1359–69), who inspired Guillaume de Machaut's long poem *La Prise d'Alexandrie*, led an abortive crusade. In spite of his adventurous exterior, he was a despicable character and was murdered by his own subjects. King Janus (1398–1432) was even less successful as a politician and brought about the sack of Nicosia by the troops of the Sultan of Cairo in 1426.

Germany, Bohemia, Hungary, and Poland were often affected by the same political policies in the fourteenth century, since the German emperor wanted to rule them all. John of Luxembourg, a born warrior, was generally successful in his campaigns, though Guillaume de Machaut, who was his secretary from 1323 to 1346, complained of the forced marches and the severe cold of Lithuania and Poland. Wenceslas (1378–1400) proved to be a weak ruler and was deposed in 1400. Sigismund, his brother, proved a better candidate, and instigated the Council of Constance (1414–18). In Poland, Louis of Hungary became king in 1370, but was soon succeeded by the dynasty of the Jagiellos, stemming from Jagiello, duke of Lithuania, who, on the death of his wife, Hedwige, a daughter of Louis, became King Ladislas Jagiello (1399–1434). One of his sons became king of Hungary in 1440 after the death of Sigismund (1437).

The European cultural background is a colourful one, as one may expect in countries with so many influences at work. Indeed, so manifold are these influences that one may be chary of seeking them out, even when they are restricted to general medieval and Renaissance traits. Still, it is clear that in France, the centre of the Gothic spirit, medieval tendencies remained predominant, while in Italy, the home of Roman antiquity, the Renaissance first clearly comes to light as early as 1300. And a mere glance at Italian Gothic cathedrals will show how earthbound they are at the side of the soaring French masterpieces, a living proof of the essential humanity of the Italian spirit. In sculpture too a new natural quality is to be found in the faces of certain people in scenes by Nicola and Giovanni Pisano, different as their work may at first appear. The Sienese painters were clearly under Byzantine influence, but in Giotto's work, as for instance the *Pietà* in the Arena Chapel at Padua, the personal nature of the emotions on many faces is perfectly clear. Musically, such features may be compared with the tendency towards vertical harmony which manifests itself in the harmonic bass lines of Italian *caccie*, and also in the personal nature of individual compositions, which no longer need to be based on Gregorian motifs.

In France and Burgundy things were more conservative. The Gothic continued on its way, but from a classic form was derived a romanticism which manifested itself in detail work. The cathedrals were mostly built by the end of the thirteenth century and new work was concentrated on small sections. Columns became more slender and sculptured foliage more luxuriant. Painters lavished their efforts on manuscript miniatures, which were no longer stereotyped but often refined and varied. The tendency to flamboyant tracery in cathedrals is more a feature of fifteenth-century art, but it already appears in music in the fourteenth century with its plethora of note-forms and complex rhythms. But perhaps the situation is best visible in literature. While the French continued to write long verse *romans*, which deal with the fantastic amorous adventures of chivalric heroes, the Italians produced masterpieces like the *Divine Comedy* of Dante, the *Decameron* of Boccaccio, and the *Canzoniere* of Petrarch. The French, headed by the poet-musician Guillaume de Machaut, concentrated on formal elements and the externals of versification rather than on the actual material and language of poetry. When employed as a basis for music, short lyrics in this style had some purpose, as the Italians with their madrigals and *ballate* knew, but for serious works of permanent value they were useless. The Italians, however, realized that the *canzone* was too subtle to be set to music and set it free from melodic ties in the fourteenth century. Nevertheless, the nobles and princes for whom they were written eagerly absorbed the *romans*, and we learn that the famous chronicler Froissart went from the very north to the south of France to read his excessively long chivalric poem *Meliador* to Gaston Phébus. In England Chaucer evidently admired Machaut's work, and even employed the decasyllabic line for his *Canterbury Tales*.

As fourteenth-century Italian lyric poetry was derived from that of the troubadours, so Alfonso X of Castile (1221–84) sought inspiration from the same source in his songs. Eventually the Second Rhetoric of Guillaume de Machaut made its impression on fourteenth-century Catalan poetry, and such men as Andreu Febrer, Jaume Escriva, and Luis de Vila Rasa made considerable use of the *ballade* form. The French language, too, was often employed, though the musicians of the house of Aragon were often French to start with. King John I himself is known to have been a composer, and doubtless he was responsible for much of the French influence in the poetry and music of his court at Barcelona.

The linguistic factor is one to be reckoned with in fourteenth-century cultural life. Formerly Latin had been all-important, though the vernacular had been employed in secular monody, as also to a limited extent in longer literary works for which a larger audience was desired. Now, however, Latin itself began to lose its hold except in scientific writing and among intellectuals. The humanistic trend already mentioned showed itself too in the naming of composers in manuscripts, though this only occurred sporadically in the case of motets. It is characteristic of the French that at first they often disguised their names in poetry in the form of anagrams.

It will be evident that, in spite of a number of embryonic Renaissance elements, the fourteenth century was still primarily medieval. French music and art continued in the direction of greater detail in ornamentation, often at the expense of size; and Italian music, in spite of the flowering of an Ars Nova of considerable importance *c.* 1320, soon succumbed to French models and notation. Similarly, in spite of Giotto's example, it is clear that Byzantine traditions still prevailed in Italian painting till Masaccio in the early fifteenth century. Literature too showed up the medieval element in French work, the early flowering of Italian *trecento* lyric poetry and the overpowering influence of French poetry in Italy at the end of the fourteenth century. Other countries were perhaps even more susceptible to French influence, where native traditions and language enabled them to absorb it, as in Spain.

2. Sources of the Period

IN a period such as the fourteenth century the actual existing manuscripts are of first importance in defining our view of contemporary music, since for one thing they are very restricted in number. In France the first half of the century is represented by three principal sources: the *Roman de Fauvel*, the Machaut manuscripts, and the Ivrea codex. The former is an allegorical *roman* whose popularity is proved by its existence in twelve manuscripts. Fortunately one of these, a splendid folio manuscript with numerous illustrations, contains an anthology of practically every type of music popular in the early fourteenth century, including motets, conductus, *lais*, *ballades* and *rondeaux*, refrains, and various types of Gregorian chant. Some of the motets and conductus reach back over a century from the time when the MS. was written, between 1310 and 1316, while a number of pieces can be considered as extremely up-to-date works attributable to Philippe de Vitry. Like its immediate model, the *Roman de Renart*, *Fauvel* is a biting attack on the vices of the times. Fauvel the horse personifies the sins represented by the letters of his name: Flattery, Avarice, Usury, Villainy and Variability, Envy, and Lowness. By his wiles Fauvel is so successful that he even aspires to marry Fortune, the stock personification of every medieval writer, but she is annoyed and substitutes for hers the hand of Vain Glory. The offspring of Fauvel and Vain Glory become a menace to France. The *roman* must have been written originally for Philip IV, and attacks on the Templars do occur in it, but the music often employs texts which are merely general attacks on sins embodied in Fauvel (*Je vois douleur / Fauvel nous a fet present*). All the pieces are anonymous here, though we know that Gervais du Bus wrote the *roman* and Chaillou de Pesstain inserted the music.

Guillaume de Machaut stands out in the history of early French music, since his complete works are consigned to no less than six manuscripts in which the arrangement of the pieces is generally his own. These well-illustrated manuscripts

were obviously destined for important patrons, and we know
that one belonged to the Duke of Berry and another to the
Count of Foix, while Machaut himself on one occasion mentions that he has a manuscript in preparation for one of his
masters. If this preponderance of sources could produce an
unbalanced judgement of his music, and there are furthermore
numerous miscellaneous manuscripts and fragments containing
single works, an unbiased examination reveals that Machaut is
a masterly craftsman and even his poetry reveals a fluent hand.

Fortunately, the Ivrea codex gives a much better picture of
the normal musical repertoire of an important religious centre
in the mid fourteenth century, probably Avignon. This practical manuscript shows signs of use and its compositions date
back to the early fourteenth century. It is a key source for the
compositions of Philippe de Vitry, for nine of the fourteen
motets attributable to him are contained in it, but also there
are many more anonymous motets and an important collection
of separate *Kyrie*, *Gloria*, *Credo*, *Sanctus*, and *Agnus Dei*. Four
chaces testify to the finished technique of canonic writing,
while secular songs are sparingly introduced.

In the second half of the century we are indebted to a
number of Italian sources for the preservation of the main
body of late Ars Nova French music. These are still mainly
quarto manuscripts, but occasionally folio sources are to be
found, like the famous Chantilly codex, which is a masterpiece
of notational complexity. This is doubtless an Italian copy of
a French manuscript, for all the music is French, and is mainly
in the forms of the polyphonic song. A few motets are remnants of an older tradition. The Modena manuscript is similar
in character, though it also contains Italian pieces, particularly
works by the Milanese singer, Matteo da Perugia, including
some Mass pieces. The third important source, from northern
Italy, again contains secular pieces of French origin, though
its first part is composed of Italian works by important *trecento*
composers and its second of pieces from the Dufay period. A
manuscript of the early Dufay period now at Oxford contains
mostly French works, though it seems to have originated at
Venice. A number of late Ars Nova French works occur in it

together with a valuable sprinkling of very late *trecento* songs. Church music is mainly to be found in a French manuscript at Apt, obviously connected with the Avignon repertoire, though other isolated sources in France and Spain contain Mass pieces.

The perhaps even larger repertoire of the Italian Ars Nova, with a total of some seven hundred compositions, is not less interesting as it is distributed in the manuscripts. The five principal manuscripts all belong to the end of the century and only one short codex connects directly with the epoch of Marchettus. All the pieces in it are anonymous, while in general the *trecento* sources give composers' names. At the other end of the scale the largest manuscript of the group contains no fewer than 352 compositions and bears every sign of having been written as a more or less complete source-book of the principal *trecento* secular compositions. The composers represented have their portraits at the beginning of their respective sections. The manuscript as a whole may well have been written for Antonio Squarcialupi, the Florentine organist who died in 1470, for it certainly belonged to him. The other three MSS. are of a more practical nature and contain between 110 and 120 works each, with the exception of the Florence MS., which contains 151 Italian compositions. The late *trecento* is represented particularly in the Lucca codex, but, owing to its fragmentary condition, the number of works it contains is not high. Italian composers of the early fifteenth century like Matteo da Perugia and Antonio da Civitate frequently employed French texts, and sacred compositions were cultivated more often. A number of these motets and Mass pieces occur in two early fifteenth-century Bologna manuscripts.

In England a different situation prevailed. Italian *trecento* music was nearly all secular, but English part-music was mainly sacred, even the polyphonic carol which came into being about 1400. This means that most English manuscripts contain little but Mass pieces and motets, which may account for the evident destruction of English manuscripts at the time of the Reformation. The fact remains that apart from four carol manuscripts, only one full-sized manuscript exists from the early fifteenth century in England, while the rest are fragmentary. This is even true of the fourteenth-century Worcester fragments which were formerly part of one large manuscript. The one existing complete manuscript is made up mainly of Mass pieces, though there are a few motets as well. Continental influence of the Ars Nova type is frequent enough, but the English background, rough-hewn as it may be, stands out. Obviously the French language was an obstacle in England for one motet known to be written by a Frenchman stresses the fact that Latin is more congenial to the English ear than the original French. More interesting still perhaps was the recent discovery that an anonymous *Gloria* in incomplete state was the work of the Italian Zacharias. This particular piece thus has the honour of being one of the most widely diffused medieval compositions, since from Italy it travelled to south Germany and thence to Poland. However, in the case of Poland, the two most important manuscripts of the first half of the fifteenth century reveal that this Italian influence was very definite in sacred music at least, for there are not only Mass pieces by Zacharias, Ciconia, Grossin, and Engardus, but also nine pieces by Nicholas of Radom clearly modelled on the Italian compositions. Even more important than the Polish manuscripts is the Cyprus source now in Turin, which contains a very extensive collection of late Ars Nova compositions of the French type, including 103 *ballades*, 64 *rondeaux* and *virelais*, 41 motets, and several Mass movements. In Germany secular music remained mainly monodic, though there are a few transformations of French Ars Nova pieces in Oswald von Wolkenstein's manuscripts. Polyphony tended to be very archaic as a rule and had not the slightest claim to be called Ars Nova. As in England manuscript sources are fragmentary but extensive, and the notation ranges from Gothic neumes, often without a stave, to French square notation, generally of the thirteenth-century type. In Strassburg, as might be expected, manuscripts like the big one destroyed in 1870 and the Prague codex made room for French, Italian, German, and Dutch pieces. Natural as this mixture may be, it is unique in manuscripts of the period, which usually preferred the music of their own country or that of France.

3. Ars Nova in France

FRANCE was clearly the centre of musical art in the fourteenth century as it had been in the twelfth and thirteenth centuries, even if other countries were developing the art of polyphony independently. And Philippe de Vitry's teaching on the old as well as the new art of practical music, imparted in Paris, was fruitful enough to benefit and inspire music in many countries outside France. It is clear enough from his own words that he wanted to distinguish between the old notation in longs and breves and the new one in shorter values: breves, semibreves, and minims. But he also defined the position of the longer note in groups of semibreves and minims as the modern one, namely at the front. This produced the following kinds of rhythm ♪♩. ♩ ♪, ♩ ♪♩ ♪, ♫♩ ♩ ♪ instead of the old, ♪♩ ♩. ♩♩ ♪♩. ♫♩♪♩. which sound strange to us. Older musicians had been concerned by this problem as early as 1279, but they had resolved it by saying that either method was good. Vitry's dogmatic statement, however, gave a lead to four-teenth-century motet writers and the almost complete absence of the old rhythm in this type of composition is a practical testimony to his influence. However, in secular song-writing the free use of all types of semibreve and minim combinations provided a vivid contrast to the strict motet usage, and undoubtedly led to the complex syncopations of the late fourteenth century.

Another consequence of the lengthening of note-values and the use of short semibreves and minims was that it became possible to combine a number of separate parts so that the long notes were in the lower voices which carried the plainsong, and the short ones in the upper voices which had extensive new texts. Such motets were ideally suited to scholastic rhythmic schemes, and, although at first the upper voices were relatively free, the tenor (and contratenor if there was one) soon acquired the chameleon-like ability to change from one rhythmic pattern to another (actually called 'color'). The term was taken from rhetoric and meant a repetition. At first the plainsong was merely repeated several times in the tenor, but later the repetition became more subtle, so that, for instance, if the melody was performed three times, a rhythmic pattern might be given six times, i.e. twice to each performance of the melody. This practice led to complex overlapping of melodic and rhythmic patterns and even the repetition of whole sections of this type with all values divided by two or three or more. The identity of sections rhythmically was a feature soon taken on by all voices of a composition, and this isorhythm, as it has been called since about 1900, was almost invariably applied to compositions written between the middle of the fourteenth century and about 1430. It seems as if the technique was already employed at the time of Vitry, since an old motet from the Ivrea codex is completely isorhythmic and its text, concerned with the fate of the Templars, suggests a date around 1312. Nevertheless, in the first half of the century, isorhythm is only to be expected in hocketing sections and passages with rests. The hocket of course was a form on its own in the thirteenth century, and we find the technique employed in primitive cultures, but in the fourteenth century it was primarily used at the end of isorhythmic sections, especially quick ones.

If all this preoccupation with form seems more like mathematics than music, the reason is probably that for the medieval man music was a science closely related to arithmetic, and it acoustically, has to be admitted that music is based on numerical relationships. It is not surprising therefore if even practical music was regulated by mathematical principles. Certainly the actual values of notes from the minim to the maxima were considered mathematically, whether in triple or duple time, by Philippe's contemporary Johannes de Muris (c. 1290–c. 1351). He was a firm advocate of Vitry's *Ars Nova* and called his own work on the subject *Ars novae musicae*. It is actually dated 1319 in one manuscript. Philippe himself was evidently much concerned with the mathematical basis of his own principles, for he asked the celebrated Jewish mathematician Gersonides (1288–1344) to solve a problem connected with the ratios existing between the various note-values of his system.

The introduction of duple time was of prime importance in Vitry's reorganization of measured music. Before the fourteenth century triple rhythms were almost inevitable in art-music, but by Vitry's time people could no longer accept the principle that duple time was imperfect, in other words lacking a part of the perfect number three. Vitry's wholehearted acceptance of duple time made him able to propose the basic measures of the modern time-system, namely $\frac{9}{8}$, $\frac{6}{8}$, $\frac{3}{4}$, and $\frac{2}{4}$. Nevertheless, $\frac{2}{4}$ never acquired the popularity one might expect in the fourteenth century. $\frac{6}{8}$ was most important and $\frac{3}{4}$ a close runner-up. Vitry's foresight is revealed further by his introduction of time-signatures and red notes to distinguish between different types of measure since, although these were little used at first, they later acquired great importance. Indeed, we still use one of Vitry's signatures, the letter C, and our black notes are the successors to his red ones. Admittedly, not everyone accepted Vitry's innovations unreservedly, and Jacobus of Liège, writer of the monumental musical encyclopedia *Speculum musicae*, was a wholehearted defender of the old system and opponent of the new. Even Pope John XXII was moved to issue a bull, not against the theory, but against the practical results of the new art. He seems to be chiefly concerned that the due sanctity of the office and the tranquil movement of the plainsong should be maintained. In fact the new pieces are agitated by short notes and disturbed by hockets and the plainsong is made unrecognizable by the rhythmic treatment to which it is subjected. Such practices are condemned outright, and the only polyphony allowed is to be the simple addition of consonances like the octave, fifth, and fourth to the plainsong on feast days. It goes without saying that even in the new polyphonic Mass such simplicity was not considered adequate by musicians, and even in the motet little change was to be observed. In any case, the bull was promulgated as early as 1324, and it seems that only in these early days was the Ars Nova considered a menace.

THE MOTET

The reason why the motet was the principal aim of Vitry's new art was probably that it was the only polyphonic art form of importance in the early fourteenth century. Pope John's complaint that the plainsong was often obscured by upper voices singing texts in the vernacular could well have applied to late thirteenth-century motets, but Philippe de Vitry adhered mainly to Latin texts. These, however, have little connexion with the liturgy and are often concerned with specific events. Vitry has been called the creator of the free art-work, but some of the fourteen motets attributable to him are little more than confessions of faith (*Adesto sancta Trinitas* / *Firmissime fidem teneamus*). On the other hand, of those to be found in the *Roman de Fauvel*, three have political implications which link them together. Biblical allegories disguise the main theme, but the chief target is obviously Philip IV's chief counsellor, Enguerran de Marigni, who was partly responsible for the condemnation of the Templars. Philippe de Vitry had a vitriolic tongue and in his motets he overwhelmed opponents like the unidentified Hugo and poor Jehan de le Mote, the poet-musician from Hainaut, who unfortunately visited his patroness Queen Philippa of England around the time when the Hundred Years' War broke out. Another work pays homage to Clement VI of Avignon on his election in 1342, while a more personal feeling is to be found in Vitry's abjuration of court life. Nevertheless he was unable to leave the busy life of officialdom, and his friend Petrarch, whom he had undoubtedly met at Avignon, poured out his dismay on learning that Vitry had become bishop of Meaux in 1350.

Guillaume de Machaut (1300–1377) may not have been the inventor of the isorhythmic motet, but he is certainly the fourteenth-century master of it. The variety of his rhythmic arrangements is a source of wonder to the present day, though melody tends to be conventional. Certain pieces show the influence of the *Fauvel* motets, though most of Machaut's works use French texts, except in the tenors. In three cases even the tenors use secular song texts, like many late thirteenth-century motets. One feels that these French works generally belong to the experimental period of the Ars Nova motet, while four Latin works, insatiable in their demands for peace, must belong to the period of the Hundred Years' War. Probably they even refer to events after 1357, for the constant references to a duke may signify the duke of Normandy, afterwards King Charles V, whom Machaut knew between that year and 1364. One Latin work which can be dated was written for the election of Guillaume de Trie as bishop of Rheims in 1324, and this is clearly in an older style than the mature Latin works just mentioned. One Latin piece with a text clearly based on certain *Fauvel* motets of recent date looks more modern owing to its introductory prelude for the top voice only. Machaut seems to have developed these so-called introits, which are for the two top voices in four-part works and do not belong to the iso-rhythmic scheme. They form a most effective opening and are usually quite beautiful. Like Vitry, Machaut preferred the three-part motet as a rule (e.g. *Qui es promesses de Fortune se fie / Ha, Fortune*), but he wrote a few four-part works. Harking back to the thirteenth century again, he even wrote a couple of motets with one text in French and the other in Latin. Latin, as the learned language, was reserved for more serious and religious texts, while French was above all the language of courtly love poetry. Machaut's example in writing mainly French motets was not followed generally, probably because he also seems to have given up this procedure himself on behalf of the polyphonic song. In the Ivrea codex the practice of paying homage to important people is continued with Latin motets to Philip VI Valois, John II of France, and Gaston Phébus, the count of Foix. Eventually the Latin motet became almost completely associated with special events, particularly state occasions, but it also continued to serve for the adoration of the Virgin Mary in particular as well. The moralizing tendency which is so prominent in the *Fauvel* motets, and doubtless derives from the thirteenth-century conductus, became far less evident as the Ars Nova period progressed. An interesting work which looks like a motet appears in the Ivrea codex. The use of independent texts in each voice is deceptive, for the work is not isorhythmic and all three parts rarely sing at the same time. It turns out to be a very early example of the *quodlibet* or *pot-pourri*, incorporating a most valuable collection of street cries and snatches of folk-song, one or two of which were already employed as tenors in late thirteenth-century motets.

If complete isorhythm rarely appeared before the middle of the century, it was unusual for a motet to be without it later. In fact, however, the second half of the century saw the polyphonic song acquire the popularity previously possessed by the motet, and so the sources contain far less motets than secular polyphonic songs. Indeed, a number of motets which do occur in later sources must belong to the first half of the century, though some have been brought up to date by the addition of a fourth voice and the introduction of more regular isorhythm. Strangely enough, now that the four-part motet was becoming the standard form, attempts were also made to provide a voice which could take the place of tenor and contratenor together. The principle was to take the lowest notes of the combined voices as a separate bass voice, since these two parts constantly crossed. Apparently it was not always easy to find four suitable voices (or instruments, since the slide trumpet was becoming popular at the end of the century).

An unusual but very interesting type of motet cultivated from the early fourteenth century to the time of Binchois is the so-called musician motet. It is represented by only about half a dozen works but they all contain lists of practising musicians of their period. The earliest two motets, doubtless dating from before 1350, give very much the same names, including such well-known musicians as Johannes de Muris, Philippe de Vitry, Guillaume de Machaut, and Egidius de Murino, who composed a treatise on motet composition. Few of the other men are known elsewhere, though Henricus Helene is another musical theorist. Two later motets from the Chantilly codex enumerate the members of two different choirs, one English. The composer of the English work was John Alan, a member of the Chapel Royal between 1364 and 1373 and a trusted servant of Edward III.

The motet, which gives a list of English musicians in its

texts, is isorhythmic, and it has been reasonably suggested that it was written for Edward III's celebration of the battle of Poitiers (1356) in 1358, at which the king of France and the duke of Burgundy were present. It is a brilliant piece with its top voice in quick triple rhythms, the middle one slower with occasional cross-rhythms and the lowest voice in long notes, but undoubtedly written under the influence of French musical culture.

At the end of the fourteenth century, even motet composers lost the habit of anonymity. Three men are said to have startled all Paris about 1400, and we have at least one motet by each of them. Their names are Cesaris, Carmen, and Tapissier. In most of these motets isorhythm still reigns supreme, though in the last of Carmen's three motets, probably written about 1430, not only is the isorhythm very free but also the upper parts employ the same text in canon at the unison. The motet by Tapissier and one of Carmen's isorhythmic motets plead for the end of the papal schism and thus can be dated about 1417. Carmen and Tapissier were apparently mainly active as Mass and motet composers. Jean Cesaris, who was still active in 1417, is the composer of a four-part motet and eight secular pieces. Brought up in the late Ars Nova school, as we can see from the syncopations and changing rhythms of the *rondeau*, *Se par plour*, he nevertheless produces delicate *rondeaux* like *A l'aventure* with no complications at all. Both works are products of a superior mind, for Cesaris is a master of melody and harmony alike. He is fond of vocal duets, whether accompanied or not, but the opening of the four-part motet *A virtutis / Ergo beata* is particularly fine. Yet in the early fifteenth century motet writing was even less popular than before, to judge from the manuscripts, for few writers have left more than one work in ten in motet form and many have left no motets at all. It was left for Guillaume Dufay to sum up the era of the isorhythmic motet with over a dozen fine compositions.

BALLADE, RONDEAU, AND VIRELAI

Whereas the motet was a traditional form, in spite of its changed aesthetic, greater length, and increased formal ingenuity in the fourteenth century, the polyphonic song was strictly speaking a newcomer altogether. Admittedly, Adam de la Halle had written a set of three-part *rondeaux* in the latter part of the thirteenth century, but quite apart from their isolation, these charming works had little in common with most fourteenth-century *rondeaux*. They were written in conductus style, namely note against note with all three voices singing the same text. This manner was followed in Jehannot de Lescurel's only polyphonic work (*A vous, douce debonnaire*), which must have been written about 1300 since this Villon-like character was hanged for abortion, rape, and other offences in 1303. Lescurel's thirty-four songs are all contained in the Fauvel MS., and they include *ballades*, *rondeaux*, and *virelais* as well as two curious works called '*Dits* grafted on to refrains'. These are long strophic poems with different refrains to each strophe, and the only music provided is that to the refrains, some of which occur in both works. If the music of all pieces is monodic, since even the polyphonic *rondeau* employs the music of one of the monodic *rondeaux* for its middle voice, the style is fairly modern with frequent semibreve groups in the manner of Petrus de Cruce. Even more striking is the sudden appearance of the fourteenth-century *ballade*, *rondeau*, and *virelai* in more or less their mature literary forms. The *rondeau* in its eight-line form already existed in the thirteenth century as in the works of Adam de la Halle.

The *ballade* and *virelai* were not at that period fixed in form like the *rondeau* but in the one case existed as strophic *chansons* and in the other as a variant of the *rondeau*. The *ballade* became standardized in the fourteenth century with three stanzas and a recurring refrain.

Musically the most obvious formal feature is the repeat of the first half of the composition. The *virelai* did not even have a name in the work of Lescurel, and Guillaume de Machaut only calls it '*virelai* or *chanson balladée*'. Basically the *virelai* is a *rondeau* without the repeat of the first half of the refrain in the middle, but, like the *ballade*, it acquires three stanzas and has a metrical form more like the *lai*. All these lyric forms are primarily concerned with courtly love, but the *rondeau* lends itself to trick work with puns and anagrams. The first line of one of Machaut's best-known *rondeaux* gives the numbers corresponding to the letters of the alphabet to be found in his beloved's name: '*Dis et sept, V, XIII, XIV, et XV*' (Renop = Péronne).

Musically it would appear that Vitry discovered how to write *ballades*, *lais*, and simple *rondeaux*, but this may well be legendary since only one curious mythological work in *ballade* form can be attributed to him, and this must date from after 1337. Like the motet in the same manuscript, it is another attack on Jehan de le Mote and that hated country England. Strangely enough, an anonymous composer of the Chantilly codex brought the metre up to date and adapted the text of this poem to a musical setting in the late Ars Nova manner with complex rhythms and notation (*En Albion de fluns environnée*). Unfortunately, apart from about a dozen songs actually interpolated in the *Roman de Fauvel*, but in the style of Lescurel, we have to wait for Guillaume de Machaut before we find any more *ballades*, *rondeaux*, and *virelais* with music. Whether the *ballades* in Jehan Acart's *La prise amoureuse* or those in Jehan de le Mote's *Li Regret Guillaume* (1339) were sung or only recited, they certainly contributed to the regularization of the fourteenth-century form, particularly with regard to the ten-syllable line and the unvarying metric scheme. The *virelai* and the *lai*, because nearly every line is different in length from its neighbour, have a more traditional appearance and a closer relation with the music.

If it is impossible to call Machaut an innovator in most respects, he seems to have developed the polyphonic song to become the foremost musical art-form of the time. The mere fact that he at first cultivated the secular motet suggests that he did not at first see the possibilities of the solo song, but it may well have been the two-part motets of the late thirteenth century, which are little more than solo songs over a plainsong tenor, that led him in the mid-thirties to write his early two-part *ballades* with a simple instrumental tenor instead of one derived from plainsong. He soon added an instrumental contratenor to the tenor, so that the three-part work became normal till the

end of the Ars Nova period and indeed till the final demise of
the Burgundian chanson at the end of the fifteenth century.
This is true at least of the *ballade* and *rondeau*, though the
virelai, like the *lai*, remained monodic except in some half-
dozen two-part works by Machaut (for example, *De tout sui si
confortee*, and *Se je souspir*). In the second half of the century
the *ballade* was by far the most popular form, but, where the
virelai was cultivated, it was usually for three voices. Four-part
works remained a *tour de force* to be attempted only infrequently, though Machaut acquired more fluency with them as
his career advanced. The influence of the motet on the development of the polyphonic song is revealed by certain early
ballades and *rondeaux* in three parts which consisted of a
Triplum, Cantus, and Tenor. It was soon discovered that it was
far more convenient to have two more or less equally spaced
lower parts under the voice-part than to have one instrumental
part below and one above the voice. Of course occasionally
Machaut had voices in all parts, in one case as a canon at the
unison with different texts in all voices like the motet (*Sans
cuer | Amis, dolans | Dame, par vous*), but this was rare. Even
in four-part works there was usually only one voice-part,
though in one famous piece Machaut had the two upper voices
singing different texts in motet style (*Quant Theseus | Ne quier
veoir*). The reason was probably that he had been sent the first
text by a friend, to whom he paid the compliment of writing
a second text with the same refrain and metre. He also composed a remarkable four-part musical composition, but modest-
ly gave the credit to his friend for writing the original text.

It is difficult to convey the impression of these works in
print. They are more personal compared with the colourful,
brilliant frescoes of sound represented by the motets, which
thrill by their virtuosity, but this is largely due to the solo
voice and not to any subjective elements. Indeed, the long
vocalises, the syncopations, the chopped-up rhythms, and the
sudden accents on long notes sound very strange to the modern
ear, which is nevertheless charmed by the fantasy and expres-
siveness of the melody. The key-system is not ours, but neither
is it that of the ecclesiastical chant. Still, in spite of extraneous

flats and sharps, the usual impression is of major or minor, with transpositions to close keys. The *virelais* are much closer to our world, simply because they usually have only one or two notes to each syllable and do not sacrifice melodic charm for rhythmic ingenuity. The polyphonic pieces have simple tenors which we can associate with the minstrel's viol and perhaps with the improvised accompaniments of thirteenth-century song.

Machaut, like Vitry, was accustomed to the world of royal luxury and pomp, and, as a man who found favour with kings and princes like John of Luxembourg, John of Berry, Charles of Navarre, and Charles V of France, he was not afraid to publish his models of the principal types of lyric poetry and music in the allegorical love poem *Le Remède de Fortune*. This contained examples of the *ballade*, the *rondeau*, the *virelai*, the *lai*, the *complainte* (*Tels rit au main*), and the *chanson royal*. Later, in the *Voir Dit*, the true story of Machaut's love for a young girl called Péronne in verse, letters, and music, he restricted himself to *ballades* and *rondeaux*. In spite of a less didactic aim, he is more informative here. He tells us that the *ballade*, *Plourés, dames*, is not difficult and that he was very satisfied with it and that *Nes qu'on porroit* is German in style, slow in tempo, and quite suitable for performance on organs, bagpipes, or other instruments. Contrary to our first impression, he believes that music should be felt personally and says all his music is deeply felt. Elsewhere he confirms the suspicion that not only was the text of a song written before the music but also the tenors and contratenors might be written long after the original voice part.

In the second half of the century there is no great name to couple with Machaut's in the field of polyphonic song writing, but numerous less prolific writers wrote *ballades*, and these often reached undreamed-of heights of rhythmic complexity. *Rondeaux* were sometimes isorhythmic, so that the second half of the piece was an exact repetition rhythmically of the first. *Virelais* generally followed a simpler pattern and gave expression to pictorialism in the form of bird-calls (e.g. *Or sus, vous dormés trop*), battle noises, and the like. The popularity of the polyphonic song led to its use as a homage-piece like the motet, and indeed it is not surprising that it sometimes employed a Latin instead of a French text. F. Andrieu, probably the Magister Franciscus who paid homage to Machaut in a *ballade* based on one of the master's own works, actually wrote a lament on Machaut's death to a text by Eustache Deschamps (1345–1406). The two-part duet, accompanied by instrumental lower parts, seems more straightforward than many of Machaut's own *ballades*. The melody is more flowing, the tenor simple, and the chords at the words '*la mort Machaut*' quietly moving.

The cult of syncopational and notational complexity reaches its peak in the works of musicians of the court of John I of Aragon such as Jacob de Sentluch and Rodericus. Vaillant, Solage (see his *En l'amoureux vergier*), and Grimace followed more directly in Machaut's path, while Suzoy, Galiot, Guido, and Cuvelier fall into the same category as Jacob de Sentluch. Jacob de Sentluch, or Jacomi as he was called at the court of Barcelona, or again Jacob de Senleches as he is called in the most important manuscript of his music, has left only six compositions, but all are fine works and extremely varied musically. The three-part *virelai, En ce gracieux tamps joli*, is a spring song with cuckoo calls alternating between the two upper parts. The harmonic texture is clear, but the cantus is full of syncopations. In this piece however they are well controlled and help to give expression to the falling melodic line. The *ballade, En attendant esperance*, is a real masterpiece, for the many syncopations and varied rhythms result in an expansive vocal line of passionate intensity, which is heightened by the completely different rhythms in the lower instrumental voices.

Nothing is known of the life of Johannes Galiot, who flourished in the second half of the fourteenth century. His style is close to that of Matheus de Sancto Johanne, though he has left only three compositions, two *ballades* and an isorhythmic *rondeau*. It has to be admitted that he is too preoccupied with syncopation and cross-rhythms to produce music that is moving as well as technically proficient. Guido, another late fourteenth-century composer of the French school, discusses his musical procedures in the texts of his three songs. In *Dieux gart*, a three-part *rondeau* abounding with syncopation, he says, 'God save the man who can sing this.' Syncopation does at least lead to longer melodic phrases, and in addition this piece has a lively melody which springs along in very cheerful fashion. The less syncopated *ballade Or voit tout en aventure* has the same attractive melody.

The Cyprus composers often used Machaut as the model for their texts, but their music resembles most closely that of the court at Barcelona. Baude Cordier, who says himself that he was famous from Rheims to Rome, is an interesting composer who could not only write in the most complicated late Ars Nova style but undoubtedly led the way to the new, simple style of *rondeau* which completely displaced the *ballade* in the repertoire of the Dufay period. Cordier, like Cesaris, is a melodist of the first order, as we can see from simple accompanied *rondeaux* like *Je suy celuy* and *Tant ay de plaisir*, or the particularly mature *Belle, bonne, sage* which is so tender in its offer of a New Year gift to the poet's beloved. It is this melody that makes the rhythmically complex *rondeau Amans, amés* and the typical late-fourteenth-century *Gloria* stand out among contemporary compositions. If, however, late Ars Nova works appear on the surface to be exaggerated and excessively difficult, performance proves that they can be extremely beautiful and deeply satisfying.

OTHER TYPES OF SECULAR MUSIC

Since canon in quite developed forms is employed by primitive peoples, it is not surprising that it should be employed in late medieval music. In fourteenth-century France it took the form of the *chace*, a canon at the unison for three voices with texts reminiscent of the realistic *virelais*. Only four complete works are extant, but these are remarkably mature, particularly one depicting a hunt down to such details as the barking of the dogs and the kill (*Se je chant main que ne suel*). Guillaume de Machaut employed *chace* technique in a *ballade* and two *lais*, though the texts were concerned as usual with courtly love. Few manuscripts indicate that the single voice-part given is to be performed as a *chace*, but it would in any case have been a waste of valuable parchment to write out more than one part.

The *lai* was cultivated in its lyric form long before the fourteenth century and it is likely that it would have been abandoned earlier but for the presence of four fine works in the *Roman de Fauvel*. Whether these compositions were new or old, they were probably instrumental in inspiring Machaut's own collection of nineteen *lais*. They seem extremely long to the modern reader or listener, since they consist of no less than twenty-four stanzas of text, and the music is for a single voice without accompaniment. Still, the music is more accessible to modern ears than that of the *ballades*, since it is primarily melodic and the rhythm follows the text closely. The extreme length of these compositions means that variety is needed, and Machaut often provides it by making the voice move into different octaves. In fact he modulates from what we may call one key to another, and this seems to have been an innovation. Even the time could be changed if necessary, and in the poetry every possible type of line could be used in the course of a single stanza, though short lines were preferred.

LITURGICAL MUSIC

Although music for the Mass was written by most of the great composers of the classical period, in the Middle Ages polyphonic writing of the familiar *Kyrie*, *Gloria*, *Credo*, *Sanctus*, and *Agnus Dei* texts was not established until the fourteenth century. Machaut himself wrote one complete Mass, though this may be later than the Mass preserved in a Tournai manuscript. The Tournai Mass appears to be a composite work, like the later Masses from Toulouse and Barcelona, but Machaut's work has the honour of being a complete unity, though admittedly it is not unified by musical means as a whole. It is possible that Machaut knew the Tournai Mass, for, not only do his *Gloria* and *Credo* closely resemble those of the Tournai work, but also the *Kyrie*, *Sanctus*, and *Agnus Dei* form a unit in both works and both have a concluding *Ite missa est*. The texture of the Tournai Mass is very straightforward and must have pointed the way to fourteenth-century Mass composers, whereas Machaut's far more complex work in four rather than three parts employed the paraphernalia of the isorhythmic motet and other rhythmic ingenuities. An *Ite Missa Est* also appeared in the Toulouse Mass, but this type of movement soon ceased to be set polyphonically. The presence of a secular text in one voice of the Tournai *Ite* is clear proof that Pope John XXII's criticisms were justified and that these texts were actually performed in church. A note-against-note conductus style prevailed in the early Mass movements, but soon a simple three-part song style was predominant. Duple rhythms and simple accompanying parts doubtless helped to make the words clear in performance. Complete Masses were exceptional in the fourteenth century and the rule was to write single movements or occasionally pairs such as *Gloria* and *Credo*, *Sanctus* and *Agnus*. The *Kyrie* was rarely composed. As in the secular field, we meet a varied collection of composers with a small output in the second half of the century, and these were mostly connected with the Papal court at Avignon. They include Depansis, Chipre, Orles, Sert, Loys, Perrinet, Suzoy, Tailhandier, and, around 1400, Tapissier, Cordier, Bosquet, Gilet Velut, and Cameraco.

Velut, a French composer who flourished in the early years of the fifteenth century, has left examples of most of the forms of composition cultivated at this time. His three *ballades* are complicated rhythmically but attractive. *Jusqu'au jour d'uy* has the most varied cross-rhythms and syncopations, but also some very pleasant sequences in $\frac{3}{4}$ time compared with the prevailing common time. The *rondeau*, *Je voel servir*, is more modern and reminiscent of the simpler style of Cordier, for instance. The *Gloria* and *Credo* follow the style of Cordier and Tapissier while the two motets represent conservative and modern trends respectively. The non-isorhythmic *Summe summy | Summa summy* in triple time has an introduction in echo imitation like Ciconia's *O felix templum jubila*, and is equally effective. The recent discovery that Velut arrived in Cyprus in 1411 may be crucial for a true estimate of the musical repertory of the Cyprus court.

Styles changed little before the early works of Dufay, though Guillaume Legrant introduced the alternating pattern of solo duet and three-part chorus in his harmonically conceived *Gloria* and *Credo*. Like Bosquet and Cameraco, he is traceable as a member of the Papal Choir immediately after the end of the schism. The tendency to write one note per syllable is very evident in the composers of this generation and stems from the constant search for clear pronunciation of the sacred texts. Even more straightforward than Mass composition is polyphonic hymn writing which first comes to light in the Apt codex. While it was the later practice to paraphrase the plain-song in the top voice, these works scarcely do more than give the chant in measured values accompanied by simple tenor and contratenor parts.

The *Hoquetus David* by Machaut is an isolated example of a form that was out-of-date by 1300. One can only assume that it was written for some special occasion, and certainly it is a masterly piece of writing. Whether it was intended for performing in church is uncertain, but it is in any case based on the plainsong *David* from the *Alleluia Nativitas*. The by no means unreasonable suggestion has been put forward that it was written as a brilliant conclusion to Pérotin's three-part organum *Alleluia Nativitas*. This suggests a performance by voices in spite of the absence of text, though it is customary to employ wind instruments only.

MUSICAL PRACTICE

The performance of late medieval music is very much a closed book today, since contemporary sources practically never mention it in detail. The manuscripts never say that certain instruments are to be used or even certain voices. Indeed, the wide variety of instruments employed suggests that these were often interchangeable. We have to judge from the groups of musicians which are so often represented in manuscripts, sculpture, ivories, etc. Only the singers usually have manuscripts, but it is quite possible that instrumentalists learned their parts by heart. Women seem to have played a small part as performers, and, if they did sing, it would be in secular songs. Boys sang the upper parts in Church music and doubtless in motets, while the lower parts seem to have often been performed on instruments. The absence of text in under parts forces this interpretation on us, though it is possible that voices sang the textless parts of motets as they would have known the texts of the plainsong employed in them. The profusion of instruments is a little disconcerting, but some enjoyed great popularity and others would only be used in very large ensembles. In any case, few princes could afford or obtain more than half a dozen performers, and the best men were constantly in demand so that they were often absent from the court to which they belonged. One of each kind of instrument was desirable, and in any case there was no question of employing large ensembles of instruments belonging to one family. The nearest approach to a family group was the popular dance trio consisting of shawm or bagpipe, bombard (large oboe), and slide trumpet. Other popular instruments were the small harp with only a few strings, the portable organ, and the viol. Natural trumpets were popular with the nobility because of their warlike sound, and the more of them a prince could afford, the more highly he was esteemed. If these were not much use in art-music, a good many other instruments were, such as the cornett, recorder, flute, citole, rote, psaltery, guitar, and stringed keyboard instruments as well as the instruments already mentioned. Many of these instruments were treble ones, and so they must have doubled the voices when they played. Only the viols were ideally suited to lower parts though the bombard and slide trumpet could play them. Still, these were relatively new instruments at the end of the century.

Secular pieces performed at princely courts were usually played and sung after meals. The tables would be cleared for dancing and someone would sing, apparently unaccompanied in many cases. A gentleman might be followed by a lady singing, and she by an instrumental group. The ability to compose verse in company was considered an elegant accomplishment, though the music might be some stock tune of the time. Under these circumstances it seems likely that polyphonic songs were purely art-music unconnected with the dance and suitable for recitals. The virtuoso nature of many late-fourteenth-century songs is explained by the interest of princes in the spectacular and their pride in possessing the best performers. This applied, for instance, to the new keyboard instruments with strings, which could play independent *estampies* as well as arrangements of secular songs. The *estampie* was a dance piece suited to the popular dance called the *carole* and could be monodic or polyphonic. It was generally improvised, and this fact accounts for its rare occurrence in manuscript sources. Many percussion instruments were used in dance music, but probably they were more popular in outdoor music with a single viol or bagpipe than in the refined atmosphere of the princely dining-hall with its minstrels' gallery. However this may be, it is obvious that music was cultivated by noble patrons at a very high cultural level in the fourteenth century and the key figures in this development were Philippe de Vitry and Guillaume de Machaut, who were called respectively by their contemporaries 'flower and jewel of musicians' and 'earthly god of harmony'.

4. Ars Nova in Italy

THE sudden appearance of an apparently fully-developed Italian Ars Nova simultaneously with the French is not easy to explain, though it is clear that the musical sources do not give a full picture of the situation. Only one manuscript dates from the first half of the century and even that is quite short. Processional works intended to be performed by the young cathedral clerks on Holy Days when they took part in sacred plays have little in common with *trecento* secular music and date from around 1300. The polyphony is of the simplest, though in its note-against-note style it may have influenced the early Italian madrigal. At all events, it is evident that the Italian method of notation was fully developed quite as soon as the French owing to the description of both methods by Marchettus of Padua. It seems admissible that Philippe de Vitry played the role of an innovator to some extent in his *Ars Nova*, but Marchettus is obviously describing a traditional system of notation in the Italian one. Indeed, he prefers certain aspects of the French system, as for instance the placing of the long note first in ⁶₈ time. On the other hand, the Italians employed more different kinds of measure than the French and would often change time more than once in the course of a piece. Their notation was also very suitable for the display of strings of short notes in *coloratura* style, as against the French way of writing in jerky dance rhythms which were frequently interrupted by rests or disturbed by syncopation. But it was limited by the fact that it was normally impossible to cross the equivalent of our barline. From judging after the event it appears that the Italians developed the notational system of Petrus de Cruce, who limited groups of semibreves forming breve groups by dots at each end of the group. All that was necessary was to systematize the procedure and have groups of six semibreves for a ⁶₈ bar, nine for a ⁹₈ bar, eight for a ⁴₄ bar, and so on. The addition of tails below and above certain notes to define their values may well have been borrowed from the French, in which case the influence of the French Ars Nova would be clearly marked but not fundamental.

THE MADRIGAL AND CACCIA

These two forms thrived above all in the earliest *trecento* compositions, and indeed the *caccia* is considered to be based on the madrigal form. Practically, there is no connexion between the fourteenth- and sixteenth-century madrigal. The earlier form is usually for two voices and has a relatively fixed poetic structure (cf. *Fenice fu* by Jacopo da Bologna). This consists of a number of short stanzas, usually two or three-line strophes, followed by a concluding line or two lines known as the *ritornello*. The *ritornello* is usually clearly set off from the rest of the piece by a double bar and often by a change of time. In the work of a composer like Giovanni da Cascia (cf. *Nascoso el viso* and *Nel mezo a sei paon*) each line has its opening and concluding coloratura passage, so that a three-line stanza can be quite long. For this reason it is customary to sing the same music to each strophe, though in his three-part madrigals Landini has the vocalized coloratura passages at the beginning and end of each stanza only, making the whole piece through-composed with new music for each stanza. The three-part madrigals are, however, exceptional in some way, whereas the two-part form is standard with text in both voices like the conductus. This means that, although single voices of madrigals were sometimes performed on their own in fourteenth-century Italy, such pieces were considered incomplete unless there were at least two distinct parts. Jacopo da Bologna actually has a two-part and a three-part version of the same text (*Uselletto selvaggio*), which is one of the frequent attacks on amateur composers and musical theorists such as appear in both French and Italian Ars Nova music. He says the world is full of little masters who write a few madrigals or motets and consider themselves Philippe de Vitrys or Marchettus de Paduas. The first piece is a typical two-voice madrigal, but the second has the two top voices in canon and the lower part accompanying independently. At least, this is true till shortly before the *ritornello*, where the two top voices become independent themselves. This piece is usually called a canonic madrigal, but it is essentially a *caccia*. Of Jacopo's twenty-nine madrigals, some of the two-part ones like *Quando veggio* seem rather immature, but the best of them, like *Non al suo amante* and *Fenice fu*, are more effective than anything by Giovanni or Piero. There is a sureness about the melodies, which do not fall into short groups of conventional motifs, but have a unity which is almost modern. Three-part works in *caccia* style are successful, e.g. *Sotto l'imperio*, but this is not always the case with the other three more dissonant three-part works. The motet *Lux purpurata / Diligite justitiam* is a half-way house between the developed madrigal and the three-part French motet. It is not isorhythmic and does not borrow its slow-moving tenor from plainsong, but has quick upper parts, individual texts, and a simple but effective hocket at the end.

The *caccia* (e.g. Gherardello's *Tosto che l'alba*), like the French *chace*, is canonic throughout, but differs from the French form in having only the two top voices in canon instead of all three. Its texts are similar too, describing any exciting scenes in absolute realism, and these range from hunting to fires, battles, and even crab-fishing. Short lines of verse often alternate with longer ones and all the sounds are imitated, the barking of dogs in hunting, the ringing of bells, sounding of horns and the shouting in a fire, the fanfares of trumpets in a battle. Most composers wrote only one *caccia*, though Piero is an exception with five canonic works out of nine known compositions, and Niccolo da Perugia wrote three.

The *caccia* still has much in common with the madrigal: for instance it retains the coloratura passages and the *ritornello*, and quite often the canon is not continued throughout. When it is, there is a fresh start at the *ritornello*, which may well be in a different type of measure, as in the madrigal. The verse form is usually free, in contrast to the strictness of the madrigal, which sticks to its three-line stanzas and eleven-syllable lines. The music still has the same breadth generally, though the descriptive passages often bring in short, sharp exclamations and imitations of fanfares. It is typical of the madrigal style that almost staccato passages with one syllable to a note contrast vividly with coloraturas, and, unlike early Ars Nova French music, triplets occur frequently in passages which are essentially in duple rhythms.

The sudden appearance of a fully developed tradition of madrigal writing may well be connected with certain local courts and princes of northern Italy, and Padua, the home of Marchettus, was important musically throughout the fourteenth century. In 1328 it was taken over by the Scaligeri of Verona and shortly after this, in 1332, Antonio da Tempo wrote one of the three important treatises on the lyric poetry of his time, dedicating it to Alberto della Scala. Alberto, who was a great patron of the arts, and his brother Mastino II ruled the two cities from 1328 to 1337. It has been suggested that the oldest *trecento* manuscript contains music performed in Padua during this period, and certain references confirm this, particularly since the *iguane* or nymphs inhabiting the hills near Padua are often mentioned in the texts. All the pieces are anonymous in the manuscript, but some of the later ones are attributed elsewhere to Giovanni da Cascia and Piero. Doubtless these composers started their careers in Padua and then moved to Verona, for most of their music dates from the 1340s, like that of Jacopo da Bologna. We know that all three competed together at the court of Mastino II, and indeed the use of the same or similar texts is proof of this activity. As at the French courts, love was often the subject and a certain set of madrigals set by these composers is concerned with a lady called Anna who lives in a lovely garden near a river and close by a tree called a *perlaro*.

Giovanni da Cascia, who is also known as Johannes de Florentia, has left us sixteen madrigals, all two-part works, and three *caccie*. The madrigals are models of clear harmony and flowing melody. There is none of the jerkiness to be found in, for instance, the *ballades* of Machaut. Instead the upper voice, e.g. in *Appress' un fiume*, which is more elaborate than the lower one, sustains lyrical coloraturas of great charm over the supporting tenor, which harmonizes in simple octaves, fifths, and unisons. These long lines are made to live by the varied rhythms they employ, first slower notes, then semiquavers, then triplet quavers, while the text is often pronounced in clearly contrasting staccato quavers. In the *caccie*, which employ three voices, there are more rests between voices, often for the purpose of contrast or, when they alternate between voices in quick succession, to create a feeling of excitement, as in *Con brachi assai*.

Jacopo also worked for the Visconti of Milan, for four of his works are dedicated to Luchino Visconti. One is dated 1346, and he probably entered the service of this prince about that year, though Luchino died in 1349. Mastino and Alberto died in 1351 and 1352 respectively, and it seems as though this first generation of composers died with them.

The scene changed to Florence in the second half of the century and interest focuses on the work of Francesco Landini (d. 1397), partly because his biography is well defined, but most of all because of his 154 extant works, which have all been published. The other composers who could hardly have lived later than 1400 are shadowy figures because so little is known about them and their considerable output has only recently been published. They include Bartolino da Padua (a Benedictine monk), Lorenzo Masini, Gherardello da Firenze, Abbot Vincenzo da Rimini, Donato da Cascia (another Benedictine), and Niccolo da Perugia. Niccolo, with twenty-one *ballate* out of forty-one compositions, seems to have spent some time in Florence, perhaps 1360–65, since several of his compositions have texts by Franco Sacchetti, but he also wrote a piece in honour of the Visconti of Milan. A frequent tendency to a more popular tone makes his works particularly satisfying to present-day listeners. Such is the case in an amusing dialogue *Donna, posso io sperare*, in which the upper voice is the suitor and the lower the unyielding lady. Often there is here only one voice singing at a time. *Ciascun faccia per se* is equally short, but more reminiscent of the continuous madrigal style.

Landini was a master of numerous instruments, in spite of his blindness, and seems to have studied the seven liberal arts, philosophy, and astrology. His madrigals amount to no more than twelve, and of these the two-part ones are evidently the earliest and follow the pattern of the earlier generation, under whom Francesco seems to have studied. The three three-part madrigals are all mature works and individual studies in special techniques, namely three-part canon, the simultaneous combination of different texts in motet style, and isorhythm. The one *caccia* (*Così pensoso*) is concerned with fishing and proceeds in $\frac{6}{8}$ time till the *ritornello*, like many another work of this kind. After the stir and flurry conjured up by the triplets of this 'French' rhythm, the *ritornello* proceeds in duple rhythms with calm thoughts about a group of lovers and their welcome to the composer.

Although it was so popular in the first half of the century, the madrigal lost favour later on. The influence of French music became more and more powerful as the century wore on, and undoubtedly Florence was a centre of this influence. A recently published treatise written in Italian for the use of girls at a Florentine convent is entirely concerned with French methods of notation and rhythm and the pieces quoted are from French sources. The Chantilly codex itself with a repertory of French music was written in Italy and probably at Florence, since a mid-fifteenth-century note on the front page refers to an Italian owner with the name of a famous Florentine family. Moreover, pieces were obviously copied direct from the manuscript into one of the most important Florentine *trecento* manuscripts. Certain Florentine composers like Gherardello and Donato seem to have continued writing madrigals, but it is possible they belong to the decade or two immediately after 1350. Gherardello anyhow died about 1364 and his death was mourned by Franco Sacchetti and Francesco di Simone Peruzzi, the former an important source for poetry set to music by *trecento* composers. Indeed, there are many such cases where musicians did not write their own poems, though such names as Petrarch and Boccaccio do not often occur in Italian music of this period. There are madrigal settings of Boccaccio by Lorenzo and Niccolo and of Petrarch by Jacopo (*Non al suo amante*), Niccolo, and Bartolino, but Sacchetti's poems form the basis for at least twelve known compositions. Lorenzo must be coupled with Gherardello and Donato, since he left ten madrigals out of some seventeen compositions. Bartolino da Padua also wrote ten madrigals, but three-quarters of his output consists of *ballate* and apparently he was active even after 1400. If he is a slightly younger contemporary of Landini, Niccolo da Perugia may be a slightly older one, since out of forty-one compositions sixteen are two-part madrigals and four *caccie*. The position of Johannes Ciconia (*c.* 1335–1411) has only recently been clarified. Long known as the composer of motets dating from around 1400, addressed to Paduan nobilities, he is now known to have made a much earlier Italian journey between 1358 and 1367 and to have been active at Liège. His madrigals must have been written about 1360 as must his compositions on *caccia*-like texts. He is one of the earliest northerners to make the trip to Italy which was to become normal after the return of the Papal Choir from Avignon to Rome. In Ciconia's case, however, an early success at Lucca must have been followed near the end of the century by close connexions with the Carrara family of Padua, where he was a canon, and finally by commissions from Venice, which conquered Padua in 1406. His extant madrigals comprise three two-part works and one three-part piece, which is addressed to the lord of Lucca (*Una panthera in Marte*). The use of imitative technique is striking, and Ciconia led in the development of this procedure which was to be of the greatest importance in Renaissance music. Two of these works show frequent changes of time signature, an indication of early date, though the style is not wholly Italian.

Some of his madrigals and *ballate* are, however, hard to distinguish from works by Italian composers. For instance, the two-part madrigal *Cacciando un giorno* with a *caccia* text has a long textless introduction, staccato crotchets for the text, brief imitations and repetitions of short snatches of melody. It is a clean-lined, pleasing work to modern ears, as is the more poignant *ballata*, *Merce, merce, o morte*, which is anonymous but very like other works of Ciconia and in any case a small masterpiece. Although Ciconia wrote several fine isorhythmic motets, the new non-isorhythmic motets like the brilliant *O felix templum jubila*, which is full of novel features, are of most interest. Here the trumpet-like tenor supports an opening in imitation which is so arranged that the second voice does not come in till the first has finished, giving an echo effect. This technique is particularly developed at the Amen where, over fanfares in the tenor, short phrases are triumphantly echoed through the upper voices till the final cadence.

Paolo da Firenze, also called *tenorista*, wrote eleven madrigals out of a total of some thirty-three works. These are probably earlier works than his *ballate*, which are full of complex rhythms indicating early fifteenth-century French influence. The fact that he was abbot of Pozzoveri near Lucca doubtless accounts for the presence of one of his compositions in the Lucca codex, but he seems to have been a member of the suite of Cardinal Angelo Acciaiuoli, with whom he must have travelled about.

THE BALLATA

After Paolo the madrigal was abandoned altogether, and the same may be said of the *caccia*, though Zacharias wrote a piece with an independent text in the tenor, portraying the hustle and bustle of the market-place. The *caccia* type of text continued to be used throughout the fifteenth century, but was divorced from canonic technique. In this form it is reminiscent of the programme *chansons* of Clément Jannequin in the sixteenth century. The *ballata* was a smaller form than the madrigal or *caccia*, though it could attain considerable length, and was usually in three parts. Its origins stretch back into the thirteenth century, but, although it was never altogether neglected by *trecento* composers, it only achieved distinct popularity in the second half of the fourteenth century and then to such an extent that it became the only Italian secular musical form. Unlike the madrigal, which was essentially polyphonic, the *ballata* was originally for a single voice and in the first half of the century the oldest *trecento* manuscript contains five pieces of this kind out of twenty-nine compositions. Gherardello has left five monodic *ballate* too and so has Lorenzo Masini, but the madrigal had made polyphony too general in the fourteenth century for this state of affairs to last, just as in

France the essentially monodic *virelais* acquired first one more part and then another. The *virelai* and the *ballata* have much in common, since both begin and end with the music of the refrain, both have a middle section consisting of two identical parts, and both follow this middle section with a concluding passage before the refrain based on the metre and the actual music of the refrain. It is strange that the *virelai* was practically abandoned in France while the *ballata* attained such popularity. The two-part *ballate* tend to be like the madrigals and have text in both parts, but with the three-part form there is a much smaller proportion of works with text in two parts out of three (as in *Gran piant' agli ochi*) than with text in only the top part like the French *ballade* and *rondeau*. This is but one sign that from the 1360s onwards French and Italian traditions were equally powerful. The notation too shows French influence, for the dots conveniently marking off measures in Italian notation begin to disappear, doubtless owing to increasing rhythmic complication and particularly syncopation. Frequent changes of time signature become rare and the use of different coloured notes and different note-shapes more usual. The Italian time signatures themselves disappear eventually in favour of the French. But before French and Italian notations become indistinguishable, there is a period of balance best typified by the *ballate* of Francesco Landini.

Out of his 155 compositions, 141 are *ballate*. The fact that 92 of these are for two voices only is indicative of the transition period when Landini flourished, for even in Italy the two-part works had diminished in size and popularity by the end of the century. Not only did three-part writing come into fashion, but, where French influence was most prevalent, four-part writing too was cultivated. However, three-part work remained the norm, and even two-part compositions continued in popularity till the end of the *trecento*. Indeed, if the early two-part madrigal can be considered as a product of both organum and conductus traditions, the late *trecento* two-part *ballate* represented in the works of men like the Provost of Brescia (Prepositus Brixiensis) and Petrus Rubeus show so little independent part-writing that they can be called simply conductus, like the early fourteenth-century Paduan processional works. The Provost of Brescia has left four *ballate* of which two have the typically Italian two-voice form with text in both parts and two the French three-part form with text in the top part only. The Italian tendency to simplify the lower parts results in a greater impact by the flowing upper voice, as in *I ochi d'una ancolleta*. In a two-part work like *O spirito gentil* on the other hand the parts move together more, though it is difficult to resist the charm of repeated motifs in dialogue, for instance, at the words '*tu m'ay percosso*'.

In Landini, however, the French influence is at its most fruitful stage (as in *Amar si li alti tuo gentil costumi*). Native talent is not Frenchified, but the Italian style incorporates French features into the music if it so desires. Thus $\frac{6}{8}$ and $\frac{9}{8}$ time are by no means as common as one might expect, and in fact $\frac{4}{4}$ time is most usual. The use of French texts and forms is extremely rare, for only one piece has such a text and one a form incorporating the *ballade*-like repeat of the first half of the composition. It has to be admitted, nevertheless, that the French habit of breaking up the melodic line with rests is becoming noticeable in Landini, as also a loss in breadth. Still, his works reveal a pure melody which may be called classic, together with simple accompanying parts which enhance and bring out its charm. The texts are very much the same as in a writer like Machaut, in other words they are concerned with courtly love. It is not unusual for all three voices of a three-voice *ballata* to have the text, as in *Nessun ponga sperança*, though this procedure is most exceptional in French music. Still, there must have been considerable flexibility about the matter of which voices were sung, since one, two, or all three voices could have text and we know instruments were in frequent use.

Niccolo da Perugia wrote twenty-one *ballate* out of forty-one compositions, and it is striking that all except one monody are two-part works. Some of them are relatively short and simple, while others follow Florentine examples. Bartolino da Padua also wrote mainly two-part *ballate* but he has also left five three-part examples. The French influence is clearly marked in the chopped-up melodic lines, syncopations, and varied rhythms. Andrea dei Servi, who is mentioned in the accounts of Pistoia Cathedral in 1366 and 1380–89, is known by thirty *ballate* and perhaps a single French *ballade*. If Andrea has left practically nothing but *ballate*, Paolo is exceptional in writing so many three-part works, in fact, three times as many as his two-part *ballate*. Johannes Ciconia's dozen *ballate* include a work addressed to Francesco Carrara of Padua who died in 1393 as well as masterpieces like *Lisadra donna* and *O rosa bella*. It is not excessive to describe Ciconia in these pieces as the originator of modern methods of motivic development. Not only do we find the repetition of a motif at a different pitch in one part, but the snatch of melody may well be passed between two parts in dialogue, thus breaking down the barriers that had existed between individual voices in medieval music. Admittedly, the organa of the Notre Dame school had shown a similar relationship, described under the general term *color* by contemporary writers, but this was largely disguised by crossing parts, while Ciconia stresses it by placing rests before and after the motif.

It is necessary to distinguish between Zacharias, Nicolaus Zacharie, and Antonius Zacara da Teramo, though doubtless there is some confusion in the manuscripts between these names. Zacharias is particularly attractive in his simple two-part *ballate* like *Benche lontan mi trovo* and *Gia per gran nobelta*. He is nevertheless capable of much more elaborate writing, as in his motet *Letetur plebs | Pastor*, which is in the new imitative style without isorhythm. In his famous *Gloria* with the trope '*Gloria, laus et honor*' in the middle voice, he shows more independent part-writing than do many French works and at the same time is a match for any French writer in his capable but unobtrusive handling of rhythm.

Nicolaus seems slightly younger than Zacharias, who is described as a papal singer in one source, but Nicolaus himself wrote a *ballata* addressed to Martin V and these two names may apply to one and the same man. In any case all these men must have been writing around 1400, and here the simple two-part *ballata* style of Zacharias is particularly significant. The

handful of secular compositions by Antonius Zacara are not so
easy to place, but it is likely that his Mass movements based
on these songs were written after 1400. One very modern feature to be found in his works is the frequent repetition of words
or short phrases. Usual as this may be today in vocal music, in
the Middle Ages such repetitions were generally avoided and
their introduction must be considered a novelty. In spite of
frequent use of the lively French $\frac{6}{8}$ time, his Italian origin is
evident in the more human melodic line. The harmonies too
are more modern in sound than those of writers like Jacopo da
Bologna and Giovanni da Cascia. Antonello da Caserta too
wrote half a dozen *ballate* of which all except one are for two
voices, but, like Philip of Caserta, he is best known today for
his three-part compositions on French texts. These are as
complicated rhythmically as any produced by native Frenchmen and show extended syncopations, the combination of
different measures in all three voices, in fact, all the paraphernalia of late Ars Nova French music in its most extreme forms.
Sometimes it was even necessary to give written instructions
under the music as to how the notes were to be read. Antonio
da Civitate was also fond of French texts and seems to have
copied Machaut's poetic style. Nevertheless, in a *virelai* by
him the technique is that of the *caccia* and the characteristic
Italian line of eleven syllables tends to intrude into French
decasyllables. Bartholomeus de Bologna, a prior, wrote secular
compositions in both the French and the Italian manner, but
none have been preserved with French texts. One of his
Italian *ballate* opens just like a *rondeau* by Binchois, and
this and another form the basis of two of his own Mass pieces,
a *Gloria* and a *Credo*. Matteo da Perugia, a singer at Milan Cathedral in the early years of the fifteenth century, left a large collection of music compared with other composers of the period,
though again twenty-two out of thirty pieces are French songs.

He is complete master of the flexible rhythms and syncopations of the late Ars Nova, as in the *ballade*, *Le greygnour bien*,
but many simpler pieces have great melodic charm, like the
virelais, *Dame souvrayne* and *Belle sans per*. Even the canon
Andray soulet is cheerful and harmonically satisfying to

modern ears. The same cannot be said of the two Italian *ballate*, which seem experimental, move in low registers, and have little melodic appeal. It is in his Glorias that the distinctive melodic character of this composer's work is most apparent, particularly where one part imitates another. His vocal duets with accompaniment are his best work, and unite all that is good in late Ars Nova techniques with Italian melody and craftsmanship. In quite a number of cases he composed contratenors to two-part compositions, and this happened with works by Machaut, Ciconia, and Grenon.

MASS AND MOTET

Compared with the large number of secular pieces which have been preserved, sacred music is but poorly represented in Italian *trecento* manuscripts. Gratiosus de Padua is known by only two Mass settings and a *lauda*, the religious counterpart of the *ballata*. These pieces may date from around 1400, while actual *trecento* Mass settings are only preserved in a *Gloria* by Gherardello, a *Credo* by Bartholus, a *Sanctus* by Lorenzo, and an *Agnus* by Gherardello. These compositions were put together as a whole in the manuscript, but, as with complete French settings of a similar character, they may not have been written as a cycle. This is suggested by a concluding *Benedicamus domino* in three parts written by Paolo. Nevertheless, the other four pieces are all in what we would call D minor, and in two-part madrigal style with several changes of time signature; and it seems possible that Paolo wrote his piece specially to complete the cycle. One specialist thinks Bartholus is not Bartolino da Padua but Bartholus de Florentia, a composer otherwise unknown but who is actually reported by the historian Villani to have written a *Credo*. Gherardello too apparently wrote a *Credo* and a *Hosanna* which have not been preserved.

By the end of the century three-part works are normal in sacred as in secular music but, although French influence is strong enough to impose the style of the solo song with textless lower parts on the Mass, such men as Engardus and Zacharias

continue to put the text in all three parts. The influence of the
caccia is noticeable in a *Gloria* by Matteo da Perugia, whose
late Ars Nova complexities are expressive and exciting. He
also borrows the motet style for two works in four parts. In
spite of the appearance of many lesser-known names like
Barbitonsoris and Mediolani, Ciconia is probably the most important Mass and motet composer in early fifteenth-century
Italy. It is not altogether clear which are his innovations and
which belong to other composers. The alternation of solo duet
sections with three-part chorus occurs in his Glorias and
Credos as in those of Guillaume Legrant. This practice could
have an English origin, while the use of a full text in all three
parts of the chorus sections, which occurs in certain Mass
movements, may stem from Ciconia himself or the group of
composers which includes Engardus and Zacharias. Certainly
it is evident that he had a predilection for thematic relationships between parts, often by imitation, but even this trait
occurs, for instance, in Matteo da Perugia.

There is ample evidence to show that the motet was cultivated in fourteenth-century Italy to a degree which is not even
remotely indicated by the manuscripts. Jacopo da Bologna was
at one time the only Italian composer before Ciconia with a
motet to his credit (*Lux purpurata radiis | Diligite iustitiam*).
Like other compositions he wrote, it is in honour of Luchino
Visconti, and so it must be dated before 1349. Isorhythm is
absent and, in fact, the Italians were not keen about this technique, but there are different texts in both upper voices as in
French works of this kind. Recently one voice of another
motet with an acrostic giving the name Luchinus was discovered, and it seems likely that it is a further work by Jacopo.
In the same manuscript another single voice was discovered
whose text apostrophizes a great Venetian doge, Andrea Con-
tarini. The work must, therefore, have been written between
1368 and 1382. Moreover, the composer names himself in the
text as Franciscus, and it is unlikely that this could be any
other than Francesco Landini, who is known to have been
paid for writing five motets in 1379. If the story is true, he was
publicly crowned with a laurel wreath by King Peter II of

Cyprus in Venice in 1364 as a testimony to his achievements in both music and literature. Out of three motets to be found in the Modena codex Engardus is the composer of one and the other two are anonymous. The isorhythmic motet style is cultivated with such complexities as tenor melodies repeated backwards or with diminished values.

The valuable fragments already mentioned contain a motet in honour of John the Baptist in two-part madrigal style, even down to an Amen which takes the place of the *ritornello*. Ciconia seems to have taken an interest in such works, for he is represented by two two-part motets, one of which has been dated 1363. The tenor of this work is an early example of the fanfare-like tenors which gradually become more prevalent in Mass and motet and suggest the use of a slide trumpet. Together with a second similar part as contratenor, a very strong harmonic basis can be formed, as in Ciconia's motets in honour of the Paduan bishop Albano Michiel (1406) and St Nicholas. Although he often retains an isorhythmic framework, Ciconia was sufficiently influenced by Italian usage to write two motets with identical texts in both upper parts, which are unified by thematic relationships, while the tenor is free. None of these factors escaped the assimilative brain of Guillaume Dufay, who was to follow in the steps of Ciconia with a motet on St Anthony of Padua.

Antonio da Civitate was one of the few composers of the late *trecento* who wrote in isorhythmic motet style, for instance in a piece in honour of Giorgio Ordelaffi, lord of Forlì, and his wife. Antonius Romanus wrote motets for two doges and Giovanni Francesco Gonzaga of Mantua. All are four-part works and one is isorhythmic. Composers under French influence like Bartholomeus de Bologna, Corrado da Pistoia, and Zacharias wrote not only in *ballade* style but also in Latin, rather than turn to the dignity of the motet. However, this preference may have been caused by the greater capacity of the late-fourteenth-century *ballade* to express rhythmic nuance and virtuosity, since these works were expressly written for one of the schismatic popes. It seems as though in the long run Italian composers could not keep pace with the northerners, of whom they became mere imitators, and, while isorhythmic motets continued to be written for Italy by men like Guillaume Dufay, Dunstable and the English popularized the free liturgical motet with its melodic and harmonic novelty.

INSTRUMENTAL MUSIC

While France had left nothing in the way of instrumental music, and England only a few arrangements of motets and one or two *estampies* for keyboard, *trecento* Italy preserved for posterity a number of dances for a single instrument of the string or wind family together with a large collection of keyboard music, mainly arrangements of vocal music. The monodic pieces consist of eight *estampies*, four *saltarelli*, a *trotto* and two compositions called *Lamento di Tristano* and *La Manfredina*. The *estampies* are longer than the *saltarelli* and *trotto*, though they are constructed in the same way. The *saltarelli* must have been played very quickly in some cases and the frequent use of fanfare-like motifs suggests the use of a stringed instrument like the viol.

The keyboard manuscript contains no less than forty pieces, though an accurate total can only be given when the whole collection is published. This is due to the absence of titles for many compositions, though twenty-nine have them. The general appearance of these works on the page corresponds to the modern piano score, with fairly long notes in the lower part and rushing semiquavers in the top one. The manuscript probably dates from about 1400 and the majority of works in it seem to be arrangements of vocal pieces taken from the French and Italian repertoire of polyphonic song. Composers represented are Guillaume de Machaut, P. des Molins, Jacopo da Bologna, Bartolino da Padua, Francesco Landini, and Antonio Zacara da Teramo. These settings are usually highly ornamented in the top part as compared with the vocal originals, but they are never written for more than two parts, no matter how many parts the original had. An important discovery was that there were five arrangements of Mass pieces for keyboard, probably organ, in the manuscript, and these were written to alternate with each distinct section of sung plainsong, like the later organ Masses of the fifteenth and sixteenth centuries. Interestingly enough, all five pieces, three *Kyries* and two *Glorias*, are based on the music of Vatican Mass VII. In other words, the notes of the plainsong are set out in the tenor, usually one note to a bar with slight variants and repetitions.

There is probably more information available about the performance of music in fourteenth-century Italy than about that in France, but even here it is restricted. The reports of payments to minstrels are interesting, but do not lead to a better knowledge of actual music. One thing, however, is clear, namely that wind instruments were extremely popular, whether in the form of trumpets, pipes, or shawms. It is also evident that large bodies of singers or instrumentalists were most exceptional. In fact, there is rarely mention of more than two or three men. At Milan in 1407 the cathedral was reduced to the services of one singer, Matteo da Perugia, though later we find three men serving as soprano, tenor, and contratenor, clear indication of the vocal performance of three-part compositions.

Three literary works give detailed descriptions of the way music was executed in *trecento* Italy. These are Boccaccio's *Decameron*, Giovanni da Prato's *Il Paradiso degli Alberti*, and Simone Prodenzani's *Il Saporetto*, dated respectively 1353, 1389, and *c.* 1400. Although music usually begins and ends each day in the *Decameron*, the other two works are more interesting for what they actually say about musical performance. Giovanni da Prato discusses the meetings of a group of Florentine intellectuals at the villa Paradiso owned by the Alberti family, and they talk about philosophical matters and tell stories. This ideal circle of contemporary notabilities includes Francesco Landini, who tells a story about a musician whose serenade so enthralls a local despot that he is taken into his service. On one occasion two girls sang one of his *ballate* and everyone was much affected; even the birds were moved to be

silent, then to sing with redoubled energy, and finally a nightingale came and perched on a branch right above Francesco. In
Il Saporetto the hero is a virtuoso called Sollazzo who sings and
plays on any instrument, and the works performed are often
named. They come from the French, Italian, German, and
Spanish repertory and include sacred as well as secular music.
It is interesting to find that madrigals can be played as harp
solos, for this surely necessitates some form of arrangement or
adaptation to the possibilities of the instrument. Singing to the
accompaniment of lute or viol is also mentioned in *trecento*
literature, and an Italian picturebook of the period shows a
singer together with a portable organ and viol.

It is easy to describe in general how music was performed in
Italy at this time, but nothing like so simple in detail. Two-
part madrigals might have been performed by voices alone, or
discreetly accompanied by instruments, or even on instruments alone. Obviously voices and instruments were almost
interchangeable. But it is clear that performance by voices
was normal for the two-part madrigal and Mass music. For
three-part works with textless lower parts instruments like the
viol appear more desirable, though the possibility always exists
that textless lower parts were sung and simply followed the
text of the upper part. This is suggested in Italian works where
a part may have a text in one manuscript but not in another.
Still, it is the present custom to perform any part without text
on instruments. As in France most dance music was improvised and must have often been in three parts, considering the
popularity of wind ensembles such as shawm, bagpipe, and
trumpet. Italians seem to have been more interested in solo
performance than the French and therefore it is likely that they
were more prone to use a single instrument like the harp, the
lute, or the small organ for independent performances of polyphonic songs. It is more difficult to assess the role of such instruments in the accompaniment of the top part of a three-part
song. They may have been highly ornamented, like the existing keyboard arrangements, or they may simply have doubled
the voice and sometimes replaced it. Future research may provide answers to some of these problems.

5. *Ars Nova in England*

IN the thirteenth and fourteenth centuries much English music appears conservative beside contemporary French compositions, though this is not altogether a correct impression. In the Middle Ages French influence was almost overpowering in music as in other artistic fields, but insular England had its sturdy and sonorous Church music and an unspoiled vein of lyric song. French influence was most evident in the eastern counties and the abbey of Bury St Edmunds a most important centre for it. In the fourteenth century Ars Nova music was soon cultivated there in the form of the motet, as an Oxford manuscript from Bury containing at least two French motets proves. The French language itself was usually replaced by Latin, which may account for the complete absence of French polyphonic songs in fourteenth-century England, even though Chaucer translated two of Machaut's lyric poems into English and obviously knew the Frenchman's work well. In any case, although Ars Nova notation gradually became general in England, it cannot be said that its use was widespread before the second half of the century. At Bury, however, not only the Paris-inspired *Four Principles of Music* was well known at this time but also Egidius de Murino's brief guide to the complex notation of the late Ars Nova.

The situation is complicated by the very varied collection of fragments that exist from this period. Often these are odd pages or parts of pages which may come from almost anywhere in England. Mere chance has preserved an important batch of separated pages from Worcester, which was a conservative if active centre of musical composition in the fourteenth century. These pieces date generally from the early part of the century and consist mainly of motets (e.g. *Alleluia psallat / Alleluia concinet*). Mass pieces tend to have the interpolated words of tropes. At Fountains Abbey, equally distant from Bury St Edmunds, manuscripts dating from the second half of the fourteenth century contain polyphonic sequences, antiphons, and motets in a more advanced English style, employing developed Ars Nova notation. Mass pieces gradually become more popular, and a British Museum manuscript, probably from Tattershall in Lincolnshire, as well as one from Durham Cathedral, are evidence of this. The *Kyrie* even enjoyed considerable favour, though later, in the fifteenth and sixteenth centuries, this was not the case. The repertory of the Chapel Royal, which followed the king on his journeys and was not stationary in London, seems to have consisted of little else but Mass sections in conductus and motet style about 1400, though here, if nowhere else, the French polyphonic song style was gradually introduced. French influence is particularly obvious in the repertory in question, for isorhythm occurs in it in both Mass and motet and the complex rhythmic manipulations of the late Ars Nova are one of its most noticeable features.

Secular song was not altogether as inconsequential as the manuscripts suggest. But after all the French language was as welcome as English at court, as we may judge from the presence there of French poets like Jehan de le Mote and Oton de Granson. Hence the lack of English songs in manuscripts is not surprising, though from a large number of lyrics no music has been preserved. The pieces of music that do remain show a remarkable freshness and simplicity which contrast strikingly with the art for art's sake that is contemporary French music. Records at Durham prove that secular music was welcome in monasteries on special occasions, for on St Cuthbert's Day, for which a three-part *Kyrie* is preserved, minstrels were invited to perform. Even secular songs tended to be polyphonic, and one early-fourteenth-century example with the second part missing (*Bryd one brere*) is another example of ecclesiastical destination, for it is written on the back of a twelfth-century Papal bull. From about the same period comes a short lullaby (*Dou way, Robin*) which has been used as the tenor of a motet.

In the fourteenth century the non-liturgical but religious or moralizing song gained ground at the expense of the simple, descriptive nature lyric. *Angelus ad virginem* was a very well-known example which Chaucer mentions in his *Canterbury Tales*. It dates as a melody from the thirteenth century, but is set polyphonically in the common fourteenth-century style with the original melody in the middle of a three-voice setting. An English translation of the Latin is known, and this is but one example of the interchange between the two languages that continued till well into the fifteenth century. The carol, which developed from this type of song, could be written in either language, and was not merely a Christmas piece like the modern carol. There are few remains from the fourteenth century, and all the music occurs in fifteenth-century manuscripts. Originally it must have been a dance-song with a single voice part and a form rather like the French *virelai*. Most known pieces are, however, polyphonic, and there is a widespread tendency to contrast two-part solo verses with three-part chorus for the refrain or 'burden'. One of the best-known carols is the so-called Agincourt song (*Deo gratias Anglia*), a proud expression of thanksgiving for the success of king and country in France, but most carols were simple songs of praise to God or the Virgin Mary.

It cannot be said that Ars Nova influence affected the carol or secular song much before 1400, but odd pieces in English exist after that date in continental song-style. On the other hand, like the carol, other secular pieces are reminiscent of the conductus with note-against-note writing, sometimes very primitive harmony and textless passages separating those with text. A drinking-song from the *Carmina Burana* occurs in one collection of carols set as a three-part isorhythmic motet, but it is curiously simple for this type of composition. A factor which affected both carols and much fifteenth-century continental music was the peculiarly English form of harmony consisting principally of chains of thirds and sixths. Based on the extension of a primitive type of improvised harmony in two parts, this English discant, as it is generally called, first appears in the manuscripts in three parts at the end of the thirteenth century. In the fourteenth century it was extremely common and can generally be recognized immediately by the setting of all three voices in score, as in the old conductus. At Fountains Abbey the plainsong, which was usually in the middle voice, was distinguished from the rest by red notation, a feature mentioned by Philippe de Vitry in his *Ars Nova* but not otherwise known in French fourteenth-century music. All through the fourteenth century the improvisatory nature of this English harmony remained clear, and it could not develop till Dunstable and his contemporaries incorporated the sweet consonances of this style into the accepted traditional harmonic system of the Middle Ages. That is why, by the side of Mass settings, antiphons, and sequences in English discant style, the motet style was retained for more elaborate pieces.

Although isorhythm was eventually adopted by English composers, the English motet tended to preserve certain characteristics generally which have made it appear conservative. The use of similar or identical texts for both upper voices of a three-part motet is very common, while in France differentiation of these texts was considered desirable. The first few words or the first line of text might well be identical in the upper voices of English motets, even where the continuation was quite different. Before isorhythm became popular, the principle of voice exchange was often used to hold the musical structure together. Essentially this was a matter of one part taking over the music of the other and vice versa every few measures, but the technique was worked out with great subtlety. Canon was frequently employed by composers writing at the end of this period, and one cannot help seeing in this the influence of semi-learned compositions like *Sumer is icumen in* and the so-called *rotundelli* or rounds. If *Sumer is icumen in* could be sung in up to six parts, full sonorities were always pleasing to Englishmen and many fourteenth-century compositions are in four parts, while even five-part writing occurs in the Old Hall manuscript, though in France no five-part compositions are extant before Dufay. Pycard achieves this by employing two canons simultaneously in a Gloria, though Mayshuet's motet is in five distinct parts.

It was only in the fifteenth century that composers began to enter their names in manuscripts of English provenance, and the Old Hall manuscript contains such names as Aleyn, Cooke, Burell, Damett, King Henry, Byttering, Tyes, Excetre, Leone, Power, Pycard, Rowland, Queldryk, Jervays, Oliver, Chyrbury,

Typp, Swynford, Pennard, Lambe, and the Frenchman May-shuet (Matheus de Sancto Johanne).

Matheus de Sancto Johanne (Mayshuet de Joan), composer of three *ballades*, two *rondeaux*, and a five-part motet, was chaplain and clerk to Louis, duke of Anjou, in 1378. Connexions with the Papal court at Avignon are revealed by a Latin *ballade* in honour of Clement VII. His secular compositions tend towards the more complex style of the late fourteenth century, in which lengthy syncopations and cross-rhythms sometimes become the be-all and end-all of the writing (cf. *Fortune fuusse*). Nevertheless, Matheus usually avoids the extremes of this style and, if his melodies are usually less interesting than those of Trebor or Senleches, he is one of the first to use the melodic sequences which give a more modern flavour to many late fourteenth-century songs, as in *Inclite flos*. Byttering, an early-fifteenth-century English composer, is capable of writing complex isorhythmic motets and canonic Glorias, which, nevertheless, retain their appeal and do not deteriorate into mere form-play. On the other hand nothing could be simpler and more pleasing than the *Nesciens mater*, with its modern triple time and up-to-date English harmonies. And yet this innocuous movement too is bound together by the plainsong which infiltrates all three voices.

King Henry's *Gloria* and *Sanctus* are in two quite different styles. The archaic style of the *Sanctus* suggests Henry IV, who is known to have played the recorder. It is also reminiscent of Aleyn's *Gloria*, though it does briefly change time from $\frac{6}{8}$ to $\frac{3}{4}$ at the *Benedictus*. Still, the chordal style predominates, and, in spite of rather clumsy melodic leaps, is musically acceptable. The *Gloria*, again in three parts but this time with the text in the top part only, like the French secular song, is more interesting. The second half of the piece changes from $\frac{6}{8}$ to common time and attains a climax with triplets, syncopations, and an Amen that twice reaches top F. Burell, Cooke, Damett, Sturgeon, Chyrbury, and Excetre are all mentioned in documents from the reign of Henry V as clerks of the Chapel Royal. Excetre was there in the reigns of Henry IV and Richard II, while John Aleyn died in Edward III's time in 1373. Various events of Henry's reign are mentioned or hinted at in motets and Mass pieces of the period, such as Agincourt, Henry's marriage to Catherine of Valois, and the Peace of Troyes. At Henry's wedding there were no fewer than thirty-eight clerks and chaplains and sixteen singers.

6. Ars Nova in Other Countries

GERMANY forms a complete contrast to England in the four-teenth century, for not only did the *Minnesinger* continue to flourish but, where polyphony was cultivated, it was of the most primitive and restricted kind. Two parts were often suf-ficient and the writing was mainly in fifths and octaves, except where French influence crept in. Even in these cases it is the thirteenth-century style and thirteenth-century French works that are copied. Two songs by the Monk of Salzburg are not untypical of the backwardness of German polyphony at this time. They are both in two parts and the lowest parts represent either instrumental lines or imitations of instrumental writing. One represents the trumpet and the other the bombard. Both are very simple fanfares. While there may be only odd pieces of polyphony in German manuscripts, this is not necessarily because they are fragments. Often a very large manuscript may contain but a handful of polyphonic works simply because polyphony was neglected. This is the case with the Mosburger Gradual, which is an immense collection of monodic chants of all kinds written down in the year 1360. A three-part canon for St Martin exists in Vienna, but this is also relatively simple compared with the French *chaces*, and in any case canonic pieces are not part-music in the same sense as polyphonic songs and motets since they are essentially repetitions of the same music.

Count Hugo of Montfort (1357–1423) is an example of the troubadour tradition according to which the poetry of songs might be written by the nobility while the actual music was composed by minstrels, in this case Burk Mangolt. None of his ten pieces is polyphonic, but this is not surprising, considering how the Mastersingers carried on single-line writing into the sixteenth century. Oswald von Wolkenstein (1377–1445) is more important. With some 125 compositions, of which about a quarter are polyphonic, his work does show some Ars Nova influences. The two manuscripts which contain his complete works were written between 1425 and 1432, and it would appear that his earliest pieces date from around 1400. He travelled a good deal as a member of King Sigismund's suite between 1415 and 1437, and he must have been particularly influenced by French music at the Council of Constance in 1417 and by Italian in 1432. France and Spain were only a few of the many countries he visited, but nevertheless all his music is composed to German words. His polyphonic compositions are extremely varied and range from the primitive type of harmony already mentioned to complex arrangements of original French pieces. Six of these borrowings have already been traced and it is in them that the more complex rhythms appear.

The most archaic in style are *Des himels trone* and *Mein herz jüngt sich*, which already existed as monodies. Thus, Wolkenstein's difficulty may be likened to that of the writer of a folksong accompaniment. The result may be described as an organum. As in pieces by the Monk of Salzburg, Wolkenstein also imitates the horncall of the watchman in two *Tageliedern*. Observation of French methods did not necessarily produce good results. Still, the canon *Gar wunnikleich* is agreeable, and *Wach auff, mein hort* with its folk-like flavour is strangely moving. In many respects Wolkenstein follows directly in the path of the *Minnesinger* with his four-square melodies and frequent leaps, and undoubtedly this is at the same time a limitation and a source of power.

Ten of Wolkenstein's compositions are for three voices and of these one is a canon and four arrangements of French or Italian compositions (e.g. *Der may* is essentially the same piece as Vaillant's *Par maintes fois*). It is clear that even in the other five compositions, one of which may not be his, Wolkenstein is not at home with three-part writing. However, it must be said that his songs are very varied examples of most types of contemporary German song and show besides an enviable knowledge of many kinds of foreign music, even if the French compositions are fifty years old.

It would be pleasing to think that Wolkenstein helped to make Italian music known in Poland, and in fact one piece which he seems to have brought back from Italy appears in a Polish manuscript of the early fifteenth century. Other pieces arrived there by way of the Benedictine monastery of St Emmeram in Regensburg, to judge from the appearance of identical pieces in a Regensburg and a Polish source. A piece in praise of Cracow is nevertheless very Italian in style and Nicholas of Radom may have learned how to write in imitative counterpoint from the Italians. The humanist Gregory of Sanok has been considered as the man who first made Italian influence felt in Poland when he returned there in 1439, but the pieces in honour of King Ladislas Jagiello in the manuscript already mentioned point to a date around 1425, and the manuscript itself may have been written about 1430. A parallel source now at Poznan contains seven of the compositions in the Warsaw manuscript, and all told a total of some fifty compositions in all sources of this period testifies to an important late Italian Ars Nova influence in early-fifteenth-century Poland. The compositions are Latin Mass pieces and motets which avoid the rhythmic excesses of the late Ars Nova but frequently employ the polyphonic solo song style.

Strassburg seems to have been a meeting-point for French, Italian, German, and Dutch music about 1400. Here Ars Nova influence met the conservative German polyphonic style and a curious interchange may be observed in the Mass pieces of Zeltenpferd and other local composers like Heinrich Hessmann and Heinrich Louffenberg. Dutch pieces were rarely for more than two voices and French and Italian works were often given new texts and used as sacred compositions. Louffenberg is responsible for a piece with two trumpet parts, and an original French piece by the composer P. des Molins becomes at Strassburg a descriptive composition with the title *The Mill in Paris* when it has its top part gracefully ornamented.

Spain was clearly under French influence in the northern kingdoms of Aragon and Navarre, though apparently Castile was less progressive for King John I of Aragon says that the court there was out of date musically. King John himself is known as a composer and he constantly sent his minstrels to northern France to learn new music at the schools there. Evidently they were skilled in the complex *ballades*, *rondeaux*, and *virelais* of the late Ars Nova, for those were what he liked. Native composers like Trebol and Rodericus studied the French style and, although Rodericus has left only one composition, it is one of the most complex *ballades* in existence. This composer may be Rodriguet de la Guitarra who was in the service of Alphonso the Magnanimous of Aragon (1401– 1458). Trebor may be an inversion of the name Robert or else an erroneous copy of the name Trebol. Trebol was a member of the chapel of the court of Barcelona as late as 1409, though the six *ballades* attributed to Trebor date from the 1380s. However, Borlet (an anagram of Trebol) is represented in the same MS. as Trebor's six compositions by a *virelai* on the nightingale, which can hardly date from later than the 1380s. It is a charming work with the three upper parts all imitating the song of the nightingale at various times while the tenor sings a folk-song in long notes. Trebor worked for the Aragon princes, for two of his *ballades* are dedicated to Gaston Phébus, count of Foix, and two to John I, king of Aragon. He is fond of syncopation and rests often break up the melodic line. Nevertheless, the effect is usually exciting and intense.

The brilliance of the Cyprus school of Ars Nova composition is represented to the full by the one codex which escaped the destruction of Nicosia and was apparently brought to Italy by Anne of Lusignan as a dowry for Louis of Savoy, whom she married in 1434. A contemporary chronicler states that Louis was far too interested in frivolous songs and *ballades*, and the duke's musical predilections are confirmed by his connexions with Guillaume Dufay, who was in charge of the music at Louis' wedding. The manuscript must have been written for King Janus of Lusignan, for some motets in it are addressed to him and an office for St Hilarion initiated by him in 1413 occurs there complete with accompanying Mass. An office for St Anne in the same manuscript was doubtless written with Janus' daughter in mind. Although most of the music is unpublished, it is clearly very closely modelled on French compositions by Machaut, Vitry, and their successors. This is evident from the texts alone, and the few *ballades* published or recorded (*Le point agu poignant a desmesure*) show that the late

Ars Nova style cultivated by the composers of the Chantilly codex was popular in Cyprus too.

The final impression left by the music of the fourteenth century is inevitably one of French hegemony. The very youth of the flourishing new Italian art proved a disadvantage at the side of the tried craftsmanship of the French Ars Nova, which rested on a century of motet composition in the Ars Antiqua style. Moreover, the technical finish of French music was matched by the mathematical correctness of Ars Nova theory. The wedding of music and mathematics found its perfect offspring in the isorhythmic motet, which in its turn led to the application of mathematically inspired subdivisions and proportions to the rhythm of polyphonic song. Such an esoteric art was eminently suited to the art-loving princes of the late Middle Ages, but, like the courts of these aristocrats, it represented the end of a period. The sheer technical achievement of the French school was so much in advance of most others that its success was a foregone conclusion. Only in Germanic countries where polyphony was still in its infancy was the influence of the Ars Nova less pronounced.

BOOKS FOR FURTHER READING

DISCOGRAPHY

INDEX

Books for Further Reading

I · NON-WESTERN MUSIC

I. ANCIENT MESOPOTAMIA

Galpin, F. W. *The Music of the Sumerians and Their Immediate Successors, the Babylonians and Assyrians.* Cambridge, 1937.

2. ANCIENT EGYPT

Hickmann, H. 'Ägyptische Musik.' *Die Musik in Geschichte und Gegenwart* (Kassel, 1949–51), i, cols. 92–106.

3. INDIA

Daniélou, Alain. *Northern Indian Music.* London, 2 vols., 1949.
Fox-Strangways, A. H. *The Music of Hindoostan.* Oxford, 1914.
Fyzee-Rahamin, A. B. *The Music of India.* London, 1925.
Gosvami, O. *The Story of Indian Music.* Bombay, 1957.
Marcel-Dubois, Claudie. *Les Instruments de musique de l'Inde ancienne.* Paris, 1941.
Sambamoorthy, P. *South Indian Music.* Madras, 4 vols., 3rd ed., 1941.

4. CHINA

Courant, Maurice. 'Essai sur la musique classique des Chinois.' *Encyclopédie de la musique* (Paris, Lavignac), i, i (1913), pp. 77–241.
Crossley-Holland, Peter. 'Chinese Music.' *Grove's Dictionary of Music and Musicians* (London), 5th ed., ii (1954), pp. 219–48.
Gulik, R. H. van. *The Lore of the Chinese Lute.* Tokyo, 1940.
Ma Hiao-ts'iun. 'La Musique chinoise.' *La Musique des origines à nos jours* (Paris, Dufourque, 1946), pp. 438–46.
Picken, Laurence. 'Music of Far Eastern Asia – 1: China.' *New Oxford History of Music* (London), vol. 1 (1957), pp. 83–134.
Scott, A. C. *The Classical Theatre of China.* London, 1957.

5. JAPAN

Courant, Maurice. 'Japon: notice historique.' *Encyclopédie de la musique* (Paris), 1 (1913), pp. 242–56.

Harich-Schneider, Eta. 'The Present Condition of Japanese Court Music.' *The Musical Quarterly* (New York), XXXIX (1953), pp. 49–74.

Piggott, F. T. *The Music and Musical Instruments of Japan*. London, 1893.

Scott, A. C. *The Kabuki Theatre of Japan*. London, 1955.

Tanabe, Hsiao. *Japanese Music* (trans. Shigeyoshi Sakabe). Tokyo, 1936.

Waley, Arthur. *The No Plays of Japan*. London, 1921.

6. TIBET

Crossley-Holland, Peter. 'Tibetan Music.' *Grove's Dictionary of Music and Musicians* (London), 5th ed. (1954), pp. 456–64.

Francke, A.-H. 'La Musique au Thibet.' *Encyclopédie de la musique* (Paris, Lavignac), V (1922), pp. 3084–93. (Mostly concerns music in Ladak.)

7. SOUTH-EAST ASIA

Daniélou, Alain. *La Musique de Cambodge et du Laos*. Pondicherry, 1957.

Duriyanga, Phra Chen. *Siamese Music*. Bangkok, c. 1948.

Knosp, Gaston. 'Histoire de la musique dans l'Indo-Chine.' *Encyclopédie de la Musique* (Paris), I (1922), pp. 3100–46.

Kunst, Jaap. *Music in Java*. The Hague, 2 vols., 1949.

Zaw, Khin. *Burmese Music*. Burma Research Society, 1941.

Zoete, Beryl de, and Spies, W. *Dance and Drama in Bali*. London, 1938.

8. ANCIENT GREECE

Bowra, C. M. *Greek Lyric Poetry from Alcman to Simonides*. Oxford, 1936.

Macran, H. *Aristoxenus*. Oxford, 1902.

9. THE JEWS

Gradenwitz, P. *The Music of Israel*. New York, 1949.

Idelsohn, A. Z. *Jewish Music in its Historical Development*. New York, 1944. (First published in 1929.)

Stainer, John (ed. F. W. Galpin). *The Music of the Bible*. London, 1914.

Werner, Eric. *The Sacred Bridge*. London, 1959.

10. THE ARABIC WORLD

D'Erlanger, R. *La Musique arabe*. Paris, 6 vols., 1930 onwards.

Farmer, H. G. *A History of Arabian Music to the XIIIth Century*. London, 1929.
The Sources of Arabian Music. Bearsden, 1940.

Ribera, Julian. *Music in Ancient Arabia and Spain* (trans.). Stanford University Press, 1929.

Yekta Bey, Ra'uf. 'La Musique turque.' *Encyclopédie de la musique* (Paris, Lavignac), 1 (1922), pp. 2945–3064.

11 · PLAINSONG

Apel, Willi. *Gregorian Chant*. Burns & Oates, 1958.

Dean, Dom Aldhelm. *Practical Plainsong*. Burns & Oates, 1957.

Hughes, Dom Anselm, ed. 'Early Medieval Music up to 1300.' (*The History of Music in Sound*, vol. 2, O.U.P., 1953.)
New Oxford History of Music, vol. 2, O.U.P., 1954.

Reese, Gustave. *Music in the Middle Ages*. Dent, 1941.

Robertson, Alec. *The Interpretation of Plainchant*. O.U.P., 1937.

Steuart, Dom Benedict. *The Development of Christian Worship*. Longmans Green, 1953.

van Waesberghe, J. S. *Gregorian Chant*. Sidgwick & Jackson, 1949.

SERVICE BOOKS

Roman

Liber Usualis (a comprehensive collection of the chants of the Mass and the Office); *Graduale* (chants of the Proper and Ordinary of the Mass); *Antiphonale* (chants of the Office – excluding Matins); also two small volumes in the series *Plainsong for Schools*. All these books have plainsong notation with the Solesmes rhythmic signs, and Latin texts only. They are published by Desclée & Co., but can be obtained from Messrs Chester & Co. of London or Messrs Rushworth & Dreaper of Liverpool.

Ambrosian

Antiphonale Missarum (the chants of the Mass). Desclée.

Byzantine

Wellesz, Egon, ed. *The Music of the Byzantine Church.* O.U.P., 1959. A selection of chants, odes, and hymns in modern notation.

III · ARS ANTIQUA

Apel, Willi. *The Notation of Polyphonic Music.* Mediaeval Academy of America.

Grout, Donald J. *A History of Western Music.* Norton, 1960.

Harman, Alec. *Early and Mediaeval Music.* Rockcliff, 1958.

Harrison, Frank. *Music in Medieval Britain.* Routledge & Kegan Paul, 1958.

Hughes, Dom Anselm, ed. *New Oxford History of Music,* vol. 2. O.U.P., 1954.

Lang, Paul Henry. *Music in Western Civilization.* Dent, 1942.

Parrish, Carl. *The Notation of Mediaeval Music.* Faber & Faber, 1958.

Reese, Gustave. *Music in the Middle Ages.* Dent, 1941.

Strunk, Oliver. *Source Readings in Music History.* Faber & Faber, 1952.

IV · ARS NOVA

Apel, Willi. *The Notation of Polyphonic Music.* Mediaeval Academy of America.

Grout, Donald J. *A History of Western Music.* Norton, 1960.

Harman, Alec. *Early and Mediaeval Music.* Rockcliff, 1958.

Harrison, Frank. *Music in Medieval Britain.* Routledge & Kegan Paul, 1958.

Lang, Paul Henry. *Music in Western Civilization.* Dent; 1942.

Reese, Gustave. *Music in the Middle Ages.* Dent, 1941. *Music in the Renaissance.* Dent, 1954.

Stevens, Denis, ed. *A History of Song.* Hutchinson, 1960.

Strunk, Oliver. *Source Readings in Music History.* Faber & Faber, 1952.

Discography

I · NON-WESTERN MUSIC

For an extensive analysis and review of recordings (including some 50 LPs), readers are referred to 'Oriental Music on the Gramophone', by Peter Crosslcy-Holland, in *Music & Letters*, Vol. 40, no. 1 (Jan. 1959).

The following abbreviations are used in referring to the names of gramophone companies below:

ARGO: Argo Record Company (England)
BAM: Boite à Musique (France)
CDM: Chant du Monde (France)
CND: Club National du Disque (France)
COL.: Columbia (England)
COL. FR.: Columbia (France)
COL. (USA): Columbia (U.S.A.)
CONT.: Contrepoint (France)
COOK: Cook Laboratories, Inc. (U.S.A.)
DECCA: Decca Record Company (England)
DTL: Ducretet Thomson (England)
EFL: Ethnic Folkways Library (Folkways Record & Service Corporation) (U.S.A.)
HMV: His Master's Voice (England)
LYR.: Lyrichord (U.S.A.)
PARL.: Parlophone (England)
PHIL.: Philips (France)
RCA: Radio Corporation of America (England & France)
REC. SOC.: The Record Society (England)
RR: Ryugaisha Records (Japan)
SUPR.: Supraphon (Czechoslovakia)
WESTM.: Westminster (U.S.A.)

To the following records should be added the indispensable Parlophone series *Music of the Orient* (M.O. 100–111, ten-inch, 78 rpm); though now virtually unobtainable, some copies exist in libraries.

3. INDIA

ARGO:RG 61; RG 62
BAM: LD 014; LD 015; LD 310

CDM: LDY 4050; LDY 4092
COL.: GE 6875; 33 SK 115
COL. (USA): KL 215
CONT.: MC. 20.110
DTL: 93111–3
EFL: P. 409; P. 425; P. 431; FE 4447
HMV: ALPC 2; ALPC 7; ALP 1665; 7 EPE 57–60
HMV: HLP 2
REC. SOC.: RSX 7
WESTM.: WF 12016–7

4. CHINA

CDM: 4039 (Mongolia and Sin-Kiang); 4040; 4041; LDY-M-8099
COL.: 33. CCX3
COL. FR.: ESBF 125A
EFL: FP 12, FP 804
HMV: HLP 1, side 1
LYR.: LL 172
PHIL.: 427 011 NE
SUPR.: LP M188

5. JAPAN

COL. (USA): ML 4925
COOK: LP 1132
EFL: P. 429; P. 449
HMV: HLP 2
RCA: F 130.032
RR: 5 LPs of music performed by the Music Department of the Japanese Imperial Household

6. TIBET

HMV: HLP 1, side 2
CONT.: MC. 20. 119 (Tibetan music from Sikkim)

7. SOUTH-EAST ASIA
Burma

EFL: P. 423; P. 436

Indo-China

BAM: LD 326
CDM: LDY 4246

EFL: P. 406; P. 423; P. 460
HMV: HLP I

Indonesia

ARGO: RG 1; RG 2
CONT.: MC. 20.112; MC. 20.113
EFL: P. 406
HMV: HLP I
PHIL.: N. 00165 L

Siam

EFL: P. 423

8. ANCIENT GREECE

HMV: HLP 2, side 4
PARL.: R 1016

9. THE JEWS

BAM: LD 356
EFL: P. 408; FP 841
HMV: HLP 2
PARL.: R 1016

10. ARABIC, TURKISH, AND PERSIAN

CND.: 92. v (Turkey)
CONT.: EXTP 1033–4 (Persia)
EFL:FE 4480 (Arab and Druse); P. 404 (Turkey); P. 421
    (S. Arabia); P. 469 (Kurdistan); FP 80/1 (Turkey)
HMV: HLP 2, side 4 (Near East), 7–8 (Iraq), 9–11 (Maghrib)
PHIL.: N. 76.048 R.
WESTM.: WL 5332–4

II · PLAINSONG

Four of the 78 rpm discs in the second volume of *The History
of Music in Sound*, edited by Dom Anselm Hughes, contain examples of Byzantine, Ambrosian, Mozarabic, pre-Gregorian, and
Gregorian chants and Liturgical Drama (HMV). These can
be had also on one LP disc (HLP 3).

There are four collections of chants, one for Lent and Easter, the other for Christmas, sung by the men of the Hofburgkapelle Choir on Turnabout TV 34070 S.: TV 4070 M. and TV 34181 S.: TV 4181 M., and a wide range of chants from the *Graduale* and the *Antiphonale*, responsories of Holy Week, antiphons and hymns of the Office, graduals and alleluias and Communions of the Mass, and the four Marian antiphons (in the short form) sung by the Carmelite Priory Choir (mixed voices) on Oiseau Lyre SOL 60040 and OL 50209, and directed by John McCarthy. The fourth of these collections contains a lot of material no longer in liturgical use; tropes, sequences, an Epistle with polyphonic sections, hymns sung in unequal notes. These are sung by a male octet of the Munich Kapella Antiqua, directed by Konrad Ruhland on Telefunken SAWT 9493–A and AWT 9493–A.

MASSES

Christmas Day No. 1
    St Martin's Abbey, Beuron: SAPM 198153

Christmas Day No. 2
    St Martin's Abbey, Beuron: SAPM 198036

Midnight Mass; Mass of the Day
    Saint Pierre de Solesmes: LXT 5251

Easter Sunday Mass: Saint Pierre de Solesmes: LXT 5171

Mass of the Ascension; Mass of the Assumption: Saint Pierre de Solesmes: LXT 5227; Mass of the Assumption: Varensell Nuns: SAPM 198046

Mass of Pentecost; Mass of Corpus Christi: Saint Pierre de Solesmes: LXT 5226; Mass of Pentecost: Varensell Nuns: SAPM 198303

Requiem Mass (Proprium)
    St Martin's Abbey, Beuron: epa 37042

III · ARS ANTIQUA

Music of the Middle Ages (Brussels Pro Musica Antiqua): APM 14018

Mediaeval Secular Music and Organa (Brussels Pro Musica Antiqua): APM 14068

Early Mediaeval Music up to 1300 (various ensembles): HLP 3 and 4

Music of the Middle Ages, Vols. I–V; VII (Various Ensembles): EA 0012, 0021, 0023, 0024, 0029, 0035. (Available only from America, Lyrichord Discs, 141 Perry Street, New York 14, U.S.A.)

Treasury of English Church Music (I) (Ambrosian Singers and Instrumental Ensemble) CLP (CSD) 3504

Missa Salve and Missa de Sancta Maria (Ambrosian Singers) DOVER HCR 5263

13th Century German Music (Studio der frühen Musik) (s) AWT 9387

Carmina Burana (Studio der frühen Musik) (s) AWT 9455

Medieval Dances (Krainis Recorder Consort) ACL–R 271

Medieval Dances (Zürich Ricecare Ensemble) ORYX 709

The Play of Daniel (New York Pro Musica) AXTL 1086 (SXA 4001)

Cantigas of Alphonso the Wise; Liturgy of Santiago da Compostela (New York Pro Musica) AXA 4513 (SXA 4513)

IV · ARS NOVA

Music of the Renaissance (Brussels Pro Musica Antiqua): APM 14019

French Ars Nova (Brussels Pro Musica Antiqua): APM 14063

Ars Nova and the Renaissance (various ensembles): HLP 5, 6 and 7

XIVth and Early XVth Century English Polyphony (Oberlin, Bressler, Myers, Wolfe): EA 0031. (Available only from America, Lyrichord Discs, 141 Perry Street, New York 14, U.S.A.)

Treasury of English Church Music (I) (Ambrosian Singers and Instrumental Ensemble CLP) (CSD) 3504

Oswald von Wolkenstein: Songs (Wolf-Matthaeus, Michaelis, and Instruments) APM 14512

Italian Dances (New York Pro Musica) AXA 4517 (SXA 4517)

Index

MORE ABOUT PENGUINS
AND PELICANS

Penguinews, which appears every month, contains details of all the new books issued by Penguins as they are published. From time to time it is supplemented by *Penguins in Print*, which is a complete list of all titles available. (There are some five thousand of these.)

A specimen copy of *Penguinews* will be sent to you free on request. For a year's issues (including the complete lists) please send 50p if you live in the British Isles, or 75p if you live elsewhere. Just write to Dept EP, Penguin Books Ltd, Harmondsworth, Middlesex, enclosing a cheque or postal order, and your name will be added to the mailing list.

In the U.S.A.: For a complete list of books available from Penguin in the United States write to Dept CS, Penguin Books Inc., 7110 Ambassador Road, Baltimore, Maryland 21207.

In Canada: For a complete list of books available from Penguin in Canada write to Penguin Books Canada Ltd, 41 Steelcase Road West, Markham, Ontario L3R 1B4.

A SHORT HISTORY OF WESTERN MUSIC

Arthur Jacobs

Written by the author of *A New Dictionary of Music*, this popular history traces the development of music in the western world from the medieval troubadours and the *Ars nova musicae* of the fourteenth century down to the jazz invasion of this century and the music of Stravinsky, Britten and Stockhausen. It is designed specifically for the listener in this prolific age of records and radio.

As Arthur Jacobs notes in his preface a history of music must be more than a history of composers. Sheer genius allowed Beethoven or Wagner to give unpredictable twists to the course of music: but at all times there has been the continuing influence of patrons (from the Catholic Church to the concert-hall box-office); of performers, of the evolution of instruments, of occasions (whether opera or wedding service); and even of words.

All these factors find due emphasis in a history which also gives meaning to such stylistic labels as baroque, classic or romantic, and which takes the listener into the new fields of electronic and computer-composed music.

KEYBOARD MUSIC

Denis Matthews

The versatility and popularity of the piano and the wealth of its repertoire have given it a unique place among solo instruments. This book provides a player's and listener's guide to the solo repertoire of the piano and its precursors, from the earliest known pieces of the fourteenth century up to those of the present day. The middle chapters deal with Bach and Handel, Haynd and Mozart, Beethoven, Schubert and Brahms, the romantics, and the national schools. For reasons of space, duets and organ music have had to be excluded.

The whole has been planned and edited by one distinguished pianist and includes chapters written by others, such as John Ogdon and Charles Rosen. The great range of works they discuss with practised insight will recommend *Keyboard Music* to both professional and amateur musicians: but this companion to *Chamber Music*, *Choral Music*, *The Concerto*, and *The Symphony is* 'also, in the main, addressed to the wider public of music lovers'.

THE SYMPHONY
(in two volumes)

Edited by Robert Simpson

This completely new work in two volumes provides a comprehensive introduction to the whole symphonic scene from Haydn to the present day.

Robert Simpson – himself a well-known symphonist – has done more than compile programme notes of the great symphonies: he has, in his two introductions, analysed the essence of symphonic form. By identifying the elements of rhythm, melody, harmony, and – vitally important – tonality as *all* being present in full measure in any successful symphony, he has provided a frame of reference which binds together symphonists from Haydn to Holmboe, from Mozart to Martinu.

His team of distinguished contributors, which includes Deryck Cooke, Hans Keller, and Hugh Ottaway, has thus been able to provide a connected, unified study of all major composers who have 'attempted to achieve in an orchestral work the highest state of organization of which music is capable'.

Volume 1: HAYDN TO DVOŘÁK
Volume 2: ELGAR TO THE PRESENT DAY

THE THIRD PENGUIN GUIDE
TO BARGAIN RECORDS

Edward Greenfield and Ivan March

'You can build up an exciting record collection at about half the normal price with this handy little volume to refer to'

What the *Observer* said of the first guide goes too for this supplementary volume with its reviews of all bargain records issued between the summer of 1970 and the end of 1971.

A NEW DICTIONARY OF MUSIC

Arthur Jacobs

A basic reference book for all who are interested in music, containing entries for composers (with biographies and details of compositions); musical works well known by their titles; orchestras, performers and conductors of importance today; musical instruments; and technical terms.

This new edition incorporates hundreds of changes bringing the dictionary even more up to date – new composers and performers, titles of new works and technical terms in newer use are all to be found.

THE PELICAN HISTORY OF MUSIC

Edited by Alec Robertson and Denis Stevens

VOLUME II: RENAISSANCE TO BAROQUE

This second volume of the Pelican History of Music is particularly concerned with the social and artistic environment during the two centuries associated with Renaissance and Baroque music. By the mid fifteenth century the Church's monopoly of influence was less: alongside its rites a wealth of courtly and civil occasions demanded music and opened the way to every kind of experiment.

Europe knew no musical frontiers and it is possible to trace a whole pattern of influence and counter-influence: the motet, the chanson, and early opera are much alike in their regional forms and adaptations.

By the late seventeenth century the musician, like the artist, has become emancipated. Composers such as Monteverdi, Vivaldi, Purcell, and the Bachs are as individually distinct as the works that make them famous.

VOLUME III: CLASSICAL AND ROMANTIC

The third volume of the Pelican History of Music is mainly concerned with the eighteenth and nineteenth centuries, but works by Mahler, Bloch, Bax and others are discussed in a coda.

Even in the age of enlightenment a patron's 'good taste' was something that composers had to contend with and the so-called *style galant* forms the background to the achievement of C. P. E. Bach, Mozart and Haydn. But Beethoven scorned conventional taste, and the great classical works of later eighteenth-century composers owe their boldness to the *style bourgeois*.

Nineteenth-century romantic composers, such as Wagner and Verdi, were aware of the enormous material expansion and adventure of their age. And unlike previous composers they were conscious of their kinship with writers and painters; some of their greatest musical triumphs are to be found in opera.